KRISS AKABUSI ON TRACK

Kriss Akabusi
on Track

Ted Harrison

A LION BOOK

Copyright © 1991 Ted Harrison

Published by
Lion Publishing plc
Sandy Lane West, Oxford, England
ISBN 0 7459 3378 5
Albatross Books Pty Ltd
PO Box 320, Sutherland, NSW 2232, Australia
ISBN 0 7324 1338 9

First edition 1991
First paperback edition (updated) 1992
Second paperback edition (updated) 1995

Acknowledgements
Photographs:
Page 2: Associated Sports Photography/George
Herringshaw
Page 4 (top): Viewpoint/Paul Carter; (bottom)
Evening Echo, Bournemouth
Page 5: *Daily Express*/Chris Ward
Page 6 (top): Allsport/Gray Mortimore; (bottom)
Billy Graham Association
Page 7: Allsport/Simon Bruty
Page 8: (top) Colorsport; (bottom) Thames Television/
BBC Television
Text:
The extract on pp 234–35 is reprinted with permission
from the December 1993 *Reader's Digest*
copyright © 1993 The Reader's Digest Association

A catalogue record for this book is available
from the British Library

Printed and bound in Great Britain
by Cox & Wyman Ltd, Reading

Contents

Introduction

It is said that the child is father of the man, and it is frequently assumed that a child brought up in deprived circumstances will become an unfulfilled adult. It is also suggested that a person who has no steady source of consistent and undemanding love when young will not be able to give out such love when older. The life and example of Kriss Akabusi is a direct challenge to such thinking.

When Kriss won the 400 metres hurdles final and the gold medal at the Commonwealth Games in 1990, the race commentator described him as 'Mr Popular of English athletics'. It was an apt and accurate description of the man. His fast-talking extrovert personality has won him thousands of fans and admirers. And now that he has retired from the track he has not, like many of his contemporaries, faded from public view. He has taken up a new career as broadcaster and 'personality' and for many young people, who hardly knew him as an athlete, he is the exuberant presenter of the BBC Television 'Record Breakers' series. Yet there is far more to Kriss than just a public image, and the private man is not easy to fathom.

When he was training Kriss talked of how a championship race is made up of building blocks. The race is broken down into its constituent parts and each section is, in turn, carefully rehearsed and practised before being slotted into its allotted place as part of the whole. So it has been with Kriss's life. Each part— his upbringing in a children's home, his army career, the discovery of his royal heritage, his marriage to Monika, the birth of his daughters, his sporting triumphs and the discovery of his

Christian faith, plus all the parallel trials, temptations and tragedies of his 37 years—fit together like building bricks.

Kriss Akabusi stands today as a strong, charismatic person, a role model for many youngsters. Yet he is also a person who would readily admit that the foundations on which he has had to build his life were far from secure. So what is it that has guided and motivated Kriss? How has he managed to arrive at his present position from particularly unfortunate and unpromising beginnings? Does he have, as his traditional Ibo kinsmen might suggest, a guardian spirit, a *Chi*, who has taken him in hand? Is it the strength of his own personality that has won through against the odds? Has it been fate, or destiny? Or has it been, as Kriss would now believe, the benevolent hand of God?

1

Chequered Childhood

What does a police station desk sergeant do when faced with two young boys with no home to go to, no relatives who can look after them, and whose only worldly possessions, apart from the clothes they are wearing, are two large bars of chocolate, which are disappearing fast?

Police officers are trained to deal with the unexpected and often have to take decisions which have a profound influence on the future lives of people they do not know, have only just met and are unlikely to meet again. In all probability the woman police constable on duty that night at King's Cross has by now totally forgotten the two boys she helped. And even if she does remember the older of the two boys, it is highly improbable that she links that memory with the international athlete Kriss Akabusi she sees on television. But unknowingly that police officer had a crucial influence on Kriss's life just by doing her job well and, faced with an unusual challenge, knowing the right thing to do and the right people to contact. But how did the two boys come to be found alone at King's Cross and taken to the police station in the first place?

It is perhaps best to begin the story on the 10th of May, 1955, when the ship, the M.V. *Aureol* set sail from Lagos in West Africa bound for Liverpool. On board was a young Nigerian girl, Clara Adams, travelling to England to enrol as a student nurse. She was the daughter of a successful Nigerian photographer and businessman, Chief Michael Uzoma Adams. She had two brothers but was the only girl in the family. At that time in Nigeria it was not usual for young women to be encouraged to study, but her father, who was a practising Roman Catholic, recognized the potential in Clara and supported her with her education. So it was that in May 1955 she found herself on board ship on her way to take up a place at the Blackburn Royal Infirmary in Lancashire to study nursing.

On route, the *Aureol* stopped at Accra, Ghana, then the British colony of the Gold Coast. There, another student bound for England came aboard to join the many young West Africans on their way to continue their education in Europe. He too was a Nigerian, Kambi Duru Daniel Akabusi, and was on his way to study accountancy and international law at University College, London. He was from Mbano, the same local government area as Clara. Before the ship arrived in Britain, two weeks after leaving Lagos, Daniel and Clara had met and he had declared his love for her.

'I did not take him seriously,' Clara recalls. 'All my thoughts were focused on the nursing studies I was going in for. On arrival I was seen onto the train to Lancashire and I did not know what happened to Daniel.

'Two days later I received his letter from London saying that he hoped I had settled down well and that he was always dreaming about me. I responded and told him all is well. After two years he intensified his approach. He would ring the hospital nurses' home at least twice a week from London. The home sister would send for me saying, "Nurse Adams, hurry up, the lad from Ladbroke 7385 is on, doesn't he ever get tired of ringing?" We would all laugh. He later visited my hospital from London in 1957. One of the Nigerian students studying textiles played host to him. That visit, when he was going, he bought me an engagement ring.'

In January 1958 Clara visited Daniel in London for the first time. Clara Adams took her final nursing exams in June 1958 and she and Daniel were married two months later.

The wedding took place at Westminster Roman Catholic Cathedral. Daniel was then 26 and Clara 23. Clara's address was given on the marriage certificate as the nearby Sisters of

Charity Hostel. On the same document Daniel was described as a student of international affairs and his father, Duru Akabusi, was descibed as an estate dealer.

Clara was given away by her cousin Peter Okereke, and a wedding photograph taken outside the cathedral shows a line-up of around forty friends and relations, including six bridesmaids. The best man and one of the other guests, then law students, were both to go on to become High Court Judges. And to add an extra panache to the occasion, the bride and groom were taken from the cathedral to the reception in a Rolls Royce!

Daniel and Clara's first child was born in Paddington, London, at 1.30 a.m. on Friday 28 November 1958. He arrived by caesarian section after a long labour. He was nineteen inches long and weighed six pounds. He was named Kezie Uche Chukwu Duru Akabusi. Now, over thirty years later, he is best known as Kriss and stands at a height of 6 foot $1^1/_4$ inch and weighs 12 stone 10 pounds, but his mother's first memories of him remain.

'He had long fingers and toes. He thrived fast on breast milk for three months before I introduced him to National Dried Milk. He walked at nine months old.'

With the encouragement of Clara's cousin Peter Okereke, who had a business in London buying and renovating old houses and letting rooms to students from the colonies, Daniel bought two properties. One was in Saltram Crescent in London W9, where he and Clara were living at the time of Kezie's birth, and the other in London W2 near Westbourne Park underground station. This second property was let to students and the income from it (the rate was £3 per room per week and the house had four floors) was used to pay the nannies who looked after Kriss while his parents continued with their studies.

Clara continued nursing and became a qualified midwife, while Daniel completed his degree, graduating in 1960. Clara was in Blackburn and Daniel in London, so, to quote Daniel's recollection of those days, 'When Kezie was born and his mother still wished to complete her nursing education, I took him to a foster mother in London and paid all the costs.' It was at the end of that year that Kriss's younger brother Zeribe, or Riba as he was generally called, was born. Daniel arranged for both boys to be fostered in London and later in Sheerness with a nanny called Norma. 'After some time,' Daniel says, 'I decided to send them to Brighton and Hove for a better care and attention worthy of the money I was sending for their care. I was spending all my weekends with my children in Brighton and Hove in order to keep them company and given them a sense of belonging parentally.'

The story of the early childhood of the two brothers is best told in their own words. Between them they have a collection of memories which, when put together, vividly recall a time of fear, uncertainty and of an absence of love and affection. It was a time when the only constant they had in life was each other. They were moved from one home to another, one adult to another, never quite knowing where they would be staying next. They never starved and were never without something to wear. In due course their itinerant life became quite normal. They could remember no other way of living.

The outgoing Kriss was the senior partner, taking responsibility for his younger, quieter and more cautious brother. Today, as they look back on those early years, some of their memories are hazy. They have problems in dating events; after all when many of the things they recall took place they were barely at an age to have started school. Nevertheless a sad picture emerges of two little boys, caught up in events beyond their control, being denied the loving and secure childhood all children deserve.

Initially, in November 1961, once Daniel and Clara had completed their studies, they took their two young sons home to Nigeria. Kriss has a just a few memories of that time: the smells of cooking, the upstairs room where they lived, the discomfort which followed his circumcision, his father who was very strict and instilled into his young son the responsibilities of being the first born, and eating goat meat, which for a long time he thought was dog. The circumcision is an especially painful memory. It is the Ibo custom to circumcise boys at eight days old, but for some reason the procedure was delayed in Kriss's case until he was of an age to be aware of what was going on. He recalls being petrified by the operation, which was carried out by his mother. He knew something was going to be cut but until it happened he did not know exactly what.

He also recalls a number of people looking after him in Nigeria, where it is accepted that the raising of children is a responsibility shared by the wider family network. Indeed in the village setting it is often the custom for all adults to assume a responsibility for the welfare of all children. He did not see his father very often, but vividly recalls the fear which accompanied each return home.

'I was petrified. I would cower on the stairs as he came past. If I had done something wrong during the week my mother would say my father would beat me when he returned and there were not many weeks when I did not do something to displease her.'

Kriss and Riba stayed in Nigeria for less than two years. It was, and still is, the practice of many West African parents to pay for their children to be fostered in Britain. The private foster parents are seen as part of the extended family and the children, it is believed, get the advantage of a British education. It is a scheme which has its own logic, even though many parents from other parts of the world would be horrified at the idea of abandoning children to the care of strangers thousands of miles from home. So it was that Kriss and Riba came back to the country of their birth to be fostered. They were, according to their father's recollection, nearly five and three respectively, although Kriss believes they were younger, perhaps by two years. The earliest reference to fostering in Kriss's files, held by the social work department responsible for him and Riba from 1967, is one telling how Kriss's father took the two boys to a private foster mother in Brighton in November 1963.

Many years later Clara's brother, the boys' Uncle Tony Adams, justified their mother's decision by telling his older nephew that she had spent her life earnings and fortune to rear him in England, which he said was a rare privilege enjoyed by few Africans. Also, when Kriss was nineteen and he was revisiting Nigeria for the first time since his early childhood, he questioned his mother about why she had left him and Riba in England. She then blamed his father, Kriss recalls, saying that he had tricked her into leaving them behind. As his wife, she told Kriss, she had to obey her husband. She was very reluctant to leave her sons, but was assured it was the best thing to do for their future, that they would be sent to good schools and found the best foster homes.

This is Daniel Akabusi's account: 'In October 1963 my wife was expecting my third child in Nigeria. The doctors in Nigeria advised that she should have her third child where she had had the first and second ones and that is in Paddington in London. Since going to deliver in London is a must to save life, she decided to travel with my two children. My third child, a girl, came in October 1963.' In due course Clara returned to Nigeria leaving her sons with foster parents. The plan was, according to Daniel, to pay for their fostering with the rent from property he had in London, which was collected by his younger brother.

However, finding good private foster parents is something of a lottery. And with only one or two fortunate exceptions, Kriss and Riba were very unlucky.

Kriss remembers the flight back to London. 'We were very smartly dressed. I knew we were going to England, but I am still confused about the journey. I seem to think somehow we lost a day. It was certainly dark when we arrived at the house in Brighton where we were to live. I remember standing in front of a terraced house. There was a low wall in front and a wood across the road. The stars were shining and I looked up at a bedroom and knew this was going to be my home. I knew I wasn't going to see my mother again, but didn't quite realize what that meant. I wasn't scared, it was just a matter of fact.'

The young Kriss must have been prepared well for the moment of separation. A year or so earlier he had been very frightened by the experience of losing his mother in a large department store and had thought then that he would never risk leaving his mother's side again.

'I didn't enjoy Brighton. I think we stayed at two places. At one there was an old lady who didn't care for us much. She had a son who would abuse us and we had no recourse. I think she was ill. She didn't come downstairs a lot. It was an unhappy time there. Something happened, I think she died. I remember doctors coming to the house and then we were moved on. We went briefly to a place like a play school. We must have also slept there and I enjoyed it, in stark contrast to living with this old woman. It was though very much an interim place, we were only there while they found us somewhere else to go. It was there I first discovered how to clean my teeth.'

A small achievement perhaps, but for Kriss an important one. He enjoyed practising his new skill so much that he brushed his teeth over and over again. He was even reluctant to leave his toothbrush and tube of toothpaste to go and play with the other children, even though at his new 'home' he and Riba had, for them, the novel experience of having a whole collection of toys to choose from. When, in June 1965, Kriss and his brother were moved on, Kriss yearned to return. Unlike the other foster homes it had been a lively place which had suited Kriss's outgoing and inquisitive personality.

Riba too has never forgotten the old lady in Brighton. 'If we made any kind of noise she would hit us over the head with the butt of an air-rifle. I was, I believe, about three then, I hadn't started school. I didn't cry much. I didn't like to show that emotion. I don't know why, I didn't think it was necessary.'

'I don't think I had any close bonding to my parents,' Kriss recalls. 'My mother and father must have been away a lot when we lived in Nigeria and we were looked after by a number of different people. So when we went from foster home to foster home in England it just seemed to us the way life was. We adjusted to each new place even though we might not have enjoyed it. That was the way things were. This was life, this was my experience. We went to so many homes. I don't recall settling in anywhere. We were always moving on. I didn't even have a favourite toy to take with me. There was nothing I remember holding on to. I do not ever remember, at that time, having an intimate relationship with anyone, never . . . not like father to son. Not even with my brother, not really. He was just around me all the time. Though I was always glad he was there, just for the sake of consistency.'

The two boys would from time to time receive a visit from Daniel's younger brother Cypril. He was a very gentle man, says Kriss, and spoke very quietly, 'a nice guy'. He was a student in London at the time and it was Cypril who rescued Kriss and Riba from the tyranny of the 'Spanish lady'. She was one of their many temporary foster parents and lived, so the brothers recall, in the King's Cross area of London.

'She was monstrous, she did some evil things. On more than one occasion—I think I might have wet myself—she made me drink urine. I think I was five or six at the time. What happened with the Spanish lady changed my relationship with Riba. We lost any intimate relationship, although I retained a lot of affection for him, as I knew it.

'I remember being very sly and realizing pretty soon that if I said nothing and just accepted my beatings I would be OK, she would just leave me. If I didn't answer back and just cried, I wouldn't be beaten as much. But my brother was much more stubborn and would answer back and wouldn't cry. So he got a lot more beatings. I remember standing there and this woman beating us bad. I said nothing and then cried, but my brother was stubborn, he answered back and was beaten and beaten and beaten. I knew that I should really be looking after him, but I said nothing. I found I was really looking after myself. I even found that if I owned up to doing something wrong, it was a form of protection. I would be accused of trying to protect "the little one" and he would then be thrashed. It was perverse. I wanted to protect him, yet I knew the more I tried to the more she would beat him and the less she would beat me. She hit him with a belt, with a wooden ladle and he'd be bruised. But there was no one from the social services in a position to spot what was going on. I think we must have been unofficially or illegally fostered.

'We didn't need to do anything very much wrong to be threatened with the belt. The Spanish lady had a daughter, she would often accuse us of doing things we hadn't done. Once we had a severe beating for eating some brown sugar which was on the table. The girl had some too but didn't get punished. Then she continued to steal sugar and blame us. The mother was a very hot-tempered person and when things were going wrong, we got licked. It was a horrible time. My uncle would come to visit us and when he was due the Spanish lady would clean and tidy us up. She would sit in the room while he spoke to us. She wouldn't move. We wanted to say that we wanted to leave and that we hated the place. He would say, "How are things, Kezie?" and we would say, "Fine, yes, fine," all the time thinking, "Take us away from here." Finally we told him, things are not good with this woman, and he took us out that day and we moved on.'

It was at the Spanish lady's house that Riba and Kriss had their first major fight. It was over a jar of peanut butter, and for years Kriss carried a scar from Riba's small sharp teeth.

'Almost all the places we went to we seemed to have problems. I don't know if we were difficult children, or what. But the Spanish lady was definitely the worst.'

Kriss now has no recollection of how many foster homes he and Riba were sent to. Normally they arrived late at night and on the first morning they would go excitedly to the bedroom window to see where they were, always hoping that the new home would be a happy one where they could settle for a while.

'One thing that did happen wherever we went was that I would be told to keep quiet. I always talked a lot and was frequently told that children should be seen and not heard. But I talked and talked and was forever being told to shut up.'

There was however, during this time, one settled period which Kriss and Riba now look back on with gratitude. It was spent in Southsea in Hampshire with Auntie Morgan and her husband Bert. Southsea is part of the Portsmouth conurbation sited on the south coast peninsula known as Portsea Island. Auntie Morgan, as Kriss knew Mrs Dorrien Morgan, was a highly experienced foster mother, once described by her local paper as a 'super mum'. In her time as a foster mother she looked after no fewer than 136 children. Before marrying she was a nanny, and the young Joan Collins, now the celebrated actress, was one of her charges. Kriss describes the home Auntie Morgan kept as strict, but fair. She remembers the two brothers arriving from Brighton. She had been recommended as a good foster mother and the arrangement was that she would look after the two boys for two pounds ten shillings a week.

They arrived in October 1965, with very few possessions, not even their medical records and papers. There was even some uncertainty as to who was who. Eventually a doctor determined which was the eldest by looking at their teeth.

Mr and Mrs Bert Morgan still live in Southsea, though since retiring from being foster parents they have now moved to a flat in Eastney Road, leaving the house in Trevor Road which Kriss and Riba knew. They follow their now famous foster child's career with interest and keep in touch, even remembering his birthday. Kriss visits them when he can, and they have met his own children. His outward personality, they say, is still recognizably that of the little boy they looked after. They talk of him 'running like the wind' when sent on errands. 'He would be back before you sent him,' says Bert Morgan, though at the time Riba seemed the more athletic. They recall seeing Riba shinning up ropes at the local school with great agility. Kriss, or Kezie as they knew him then, was however the more outgoing; his younger brother was quiet and withdrawn.

On Sundays, Kriss, Riba and two girls who were also being looked after at the Morgan's home were sent to Sunday School. Kriss does not have any clear memories of the local church, but even if Sunday School meant little at the time, it would have been the place where he heard many of the familiar Bible stories for the first time.

It is strange how small incidents can lodge themselves in the mind, and leave a pleasing and lasting impression. One Christmas, such an incident occurred which Auntie Morgan still cherishes. 'I had given Kriss some fruit and some nuts and told him to go back to the playroom to play. As he was going down the corridor he turned round with a big smile on his face and said, "You know, this is the best Christmas I have ever had."'

It was in Southsea that Kriss had his first settled period at school and he learned to read and write at Abbey Road Primary, the local school just around the corner from their home.

At the age of four, Riba too started his formal education. 'I was very excited. I did all sorts of things at school. I was in the Christmas play taking the part of Santa. When I came down the chimney I banged my nose on a beam and my nose began to stream with blood. I didn't cry.

'There was a time I did cry when I fell over and grazed my leg. It was stinging me, but I was mostly crying from the shock. An older boy who was next to me had a very bad cut from some glass. He didn't cry. And the teacher said, "Don't cry, look at him. He's much worse." I stopped crying instantly, just like that.'

It was at the primary school in Southsea that Kriss had to start to understand what it meant to be black in a predominantly white society. Although all the children living at that time with Auntie Morgan were black, there were very few other black children at the school.

'One day I was just about to go home and a black woman waiting at the school gate stopped me. I had often seen her and listened to her speaking in her own dialect.

' "Where do you come from?" she asked.

' "From near here," I replied.

' "You are not English," she said. "You are African."

' "No, no," I insisted. "I'm English."

' "No you are not, stupid boy, you are African, and you can't even speak your own language. Shame."

'And I remember then thinking, yes, maybe she is right. I am black, I am different.'

It is a memory which ties in with a recollection from his days with the Spanish lady. Kriss does not now know what triggered the idea, but he recalls wishing and hoping that he was not black. Perhaps it had been something the Spanish lady had said to him, or a remark made to him by another child.

'I didn't want to believe I was black. I looked in the mirror and saw myself and realized I was black. I went to bed and prayed and prayed, "Please make sure I'm not black in the morning."'

He would not have then thought of it in these terms, but it was after that meeting with the African lady at the school that Kriss realized he had no identity.

'Mr and Mrs Morgan were white. Almost everyone I went to school with was white. Something was different, but I didn't really know what it was. I am sure people made remarks, though nothing worried me on the outside. But deep down? There must have been some reason why I didn't want to be black. I went through a period when I was hoping and hoping and hoping I wasn't black. And then I realized I was black and yet didn't know what it meant. As the black woman at the gate had said, I couldn't speak my own language.

'I wasn't ashamed, just very self-conscious. So who was I? I wasn't fully part of white society and yet at the same time I wasn't even aware of any other culture. I was confronted with the reality that I was black and yet didn't even know how to speak my own language. I was saying I was English and denying my African heritage. I was just six or seven at the time.

'It was about then that I started telling people about elephants and how I had seen them in Nigeria. I was sitting at the table and these people were saying, "Are you sure?" and I said, "Yes, yes," claiming I was an expert on elephants.

'It was about that time I also fabricated a story about being racially abused at school. I was taken seriously and I got very frightened about the consequences. I think I had implicated one of the teachers. I don't know what happened from there. I think I broke down and admitted I had made it all up.'

Auntie Morgan and her husband became very fond of the two lads. They took them on outings in their wooden-framed Morris 1000 Estate, and on family holidays, including a visit to Wales. Kriss retains a clear memory of crossing the Severn Bridge and being excited that he was going to stay in a new country. Bert and his son Barry also played football with Kriss, and Kriss enjoyed helping with jobs around the house and garden. Many years later Auntie Morgan was to say she wished Kriss had been her son too, she was so fond and proud of him.

However, the fostering arrangement that Mr and Mrs Morgan had with the boys' family was entirely private. To begin with money came and it looked as if Kriss and Riba could look forward to a period of good, settled care. But then circumstances intervened which were to plunge the two boys back into a life of uncertainty.

In the 1960s Nigeria was torn apart by civil war. The Ibo people, who made up the majority of the population of the short-lived independent state of Biafra, suffered in particular. There were massacres and, in many parts of Nigeria, mass starvation. Vivid reports of suffering were despatched by journalists. William Norris of the *Sunday Times* wrote in 1968, at a time when the suffering had become acute and established, 'I have seen things in Biafra this week which no man should have to see. Sights to scorch the mind and sicken the conscience. I have seen children roasted alive, young girls torn in two by shrapnel, pregnant women eviscerated and old men blown to fragments. I have seen these things and seen their causes. High-flying Russian Ilyushin jets dropping bombs on civilian centres throughout Biafra.'

It is not necessary here to explain the bitter politics of the time. Suffice to say, as in any war and during any bloody political struggle, many innocent people were caught up in events which were not of their making. It was early on in that period of bitter confusion and conflict that the money being paid to Mr and Mrs Morgan failed to arrive. It was due no doubt to the war, but also, as Daniel was later to learn, from problems with his property investments in London. He describes how the properties he then had were acquired by the council without, he claims, compensation. His brother was left without the means to support the boys. Normal communication between Britain and Nigeria had become very difficult. Some parts of Nigeria were almost totally cut off from the outside world. Mrs Morgan could no longer keep Clara and Daniel Akabusi in touch with their sons' progress or send them photographs or give them news. All contact ceased.

There was another factor involved too, which Clara's brother, Tony Adams, was to tell Kriss about twenty years later.

'My uncle told me in a letter about how my mother had been under much stress and pressure during that period. Her marriage had been under great strain and during the time she lost contact with us, she and my father had separated. They went to court and my mother spent all her money on court fees and paying lawyers. It was some time before she got work in Lagos and then, just as she was settling down, the civil war drove her away from Lagos to Enugu. She was out of work and went to stay at home with her mother until the war was over.'

Clara describes Nigeria at that time as being in 'great turmoil. There was much unrest in the country. There was disorderliness in the affairs of state. There was great hatred and discrimination against the Ibos, the tribe we belong to, by the other tribes in Nigeria. They would not give employment to Ibo men. Ibos are very wise, hard working and resourceful. This is why other Nigerians hate them. At the height of the political crisis there was massive destruction of lives and properties. They looted the properties of Ibos living in other parts of Nigeria. They killed Ibos, even pregnant mothers, so that there was an exodus. There was a massive return of Ibos from all over the Federation of Nigeria to their own eastern region with Enugu as headquarters. This was when we left Lagos, losing contact with Kezie and Zeribe. You can imagine the agony we went through when we knew not their fate.'

Riba has since tried to talk to his mother about his childhood, to find out how he and Kriss came to be left with so many different foster parents in Britain, and how all contact was eventually lost. He has not, however, pursued the subject. He says that his mother gets very heated and bitter when the matter is raised and it makes him feel very uncomfortable. Many of the issues involved are concerned with the breakdown of the relationship between Clara and Daniel.

'She is a very capable woman,' Riba says. 'What went wrong must have been disastrous.'

The Biafran War was not one of the many recent African wars which the developed world has ignored. Pictures of massacred civilians and starving children touched the hearts and consciences of many people around the globe. In Britain there were those who felt a deep sense of anger and guilt and accused their own country and certain other nations of a partiality and responsibility bordering on complicity. The Ibos were admired for their courage, and their plight received much sympathy. Who can tell what might have happened to young Kriss and Riba had they too been caught up in the conflict? Despite all their unsettling experiences, they never starved or needed to shelter from gun-fire.

When money for the boys' upkeep failed to arrive from Nigeria, the Morgans approached the Nigerian High Commission for help, but with no success. Then one day Uncle Cypril came to Southsea to take his nephews on a trip to London. Mr and Mrs Morgan expected them to be away a few days. They never came back. As licensed but private foster parents they were used to children being taken away at short notice and had no right to protest. They had just bought a guinea-pig for Kriss and, when the boys failed to return, the new pet and its new cage were passed on to the other children.

Auntie and Bert Morgan had not only cared for, but had grown very fond of Kezie and Riba. Many months passed before they heard what had happened to them.

2

Village Road

The exact sequence of events which led Kriss and Riba from their secure foster home to the police station at King's Cross is unclear. They share a confused jumble of recollections, some of which tally with each other's impressions, others which, although substantially the same, contradict each other in important detail. The following reconstruction of events seems, on available evidence, to be the most likely.

When Uncle Cypril collected his nephews from Mr and Mrs Morgan in Southsea, he knew he himself could not afford to meet the continuing costs of fostering. But what was he to do, as the boys, only contactable relative? He was living at the time in a basement flat in London and, although it might have been possible for Kriss and Riba to have stayed there for a few days, it was far too small a place to be a permanent home for two lads, one aged six and the other eight. Especially as Cypril was in London as a student and, even if he had had the resources, could not have afforded the time to look after his two active young nephews. It was a difficult problem. As Daniel was to describe later, 'My brother was left in a state of dilemma. No contact with Nigeria, no rents from the houses, no compensation paid for their acquisition and no way out for the keeping of the two boys. And that is how they all from the ancient Akabusi family of Nigeria waited for their gods, their angels and the councils to come to their rescue.'

Cypril had in the past had the two boys to stay briefly at his home in Rosebery Avenue in London EC1. Riba can still conjure up a mental picture of the place with its iron railings, and in his mind's eye can still see his uncle studying. Kriss felt a keen responsibility for his younger brother and would make sure he was comfortable and that there was nothing to hurt or disturb him. Riba was often nervous and would scurry under his bed if he heard a strange noise.

To Riba life seemed very insecure and strange. As young children do, he detected that something was amiss, but did not know quite what. He would often not get to sleep at night. Kriss would stay up to reassure him. Riba recollects that having had the boys in the flat for a week or two, Cypril decided that looking after them himself was no solution. He did not know when normal contact would resume with Nigeria and if any more money would be forthcoming from Daniel or Clara. Kriss and Riba would have to become the responsibility of the local authority.

Looking back to the events of over twenty-five years ago, when Riba and Kriss were very young, they recall incidents rather than any clear sequence. The outcome was that they found themselves being taken, late one night, in a police car, to a children's home.

They do not blame their uncle in any way for what happened to them. Riba, as an adult, has visited Cypril in Nigeria and has got on well with him, although they have not discussed Riba's childhood recollections in any detail.

'He put us on a train,' Riba recalls. 'He gave me a large bar of Cadbury's Bournville plain chocolate and Kriss a large bar of milk chocolate, which we swapped. I didn't, at the time, like plain chocolate. I don't remember exactly what our uncle said, but it was some sort of explanation. He was experiencing difficulties and we were too much of a strain for him and then he said something about there being protection for us at the end of the rainbow. Somebody would meet us when the train stopped, a relation.

'We just went on until the train stopped and took it upon ourselves to get out, and we walked around King's Cross for a while. We didn't have any luggage that I can remember, just the clothes we had on. We ended up in a police station, in a cell, saying that we were lost. Nowhere to go. They made us wait for a while. They took our names and details, Kriss was very good at that, he seemed to know where we were from and that we had some kind of background.'

The time spent in the police station is what Kriss recalls, although his memory is hazy when it comes to trying to recollect how he and his brother arrived there. They were taken there he thinks, but whether by someone who found them wandering, or by his uncle, he does not now know. The record kept by the Islington Children's Department reports the two boys being taken to the police at King's Cross by their uncle on the evening of 22 March 1967.

Once at the police station Kriss and Riba were put down together on a bench. Kriss remembers swinging his legs backwards and forwards, over and over again, while a woman police constable tried to work out what to do with the two boys who had turned up out of the blue. They were still eating chocolate, and Kriss was feeling pleased with himself that his plain chocolate would be all for him, as Riba refused to eat it. Kriss did not, however, feel frightened. Uncertainty was part of life and he knew that in the end an adult would turn up from somewhere to take them to a new place, where there would be a bed and food to eat.

For over three hours the police discussed the case with the social worker who was on duty that day to deal with the sudden emergencies that a busy inner city social work department often finds itself facing. That evening, finding a place for two homeless boys was his priority. It is not uncommon in central London for homeless youngsters to be found at the busy railway stations, even though children as young as Kriss and Riba then were are not often found alone.

King's Cross is on the boundary of two local authority districts, Islington and Camden. If the boys had found themselves at a police station just a few hundred yards away in Camden their whole life story might have been very different. They might not have ended up in the house at Village Road in Enfield, which was to be their home for the next eight years, or have met the various people who were to have a considerable influence on their lives. They settled in well, and no major signs of deprivation were noticed in their behaviour. Contacts with Cypril were maintained, but thoughts of sending them to their mother in Nigeria quickly abandoned as risky and unpractical.

Today, had Riba and Kriss been taken into care in similar circumstances, their story would have been different. Child care policy has changed over the years and now two boys in such a position would have been found foster parents and possibly even adopted. The boys would also, if possible, have been placed with a black family.

Steve Longworth, who in time was to become Kriss's social worker, says that the boys were happy in the children's home at 16 Village Road, and were a 'success in terms of child care practices of the time'. He, and his wife Joycelyn, have stayed in touch with Kriss and Riba and become good friends. When a teenager, Kriss had enjoyed visiting them at their home, particularly, Joycelyn feels, because she herself is black, coming from Antigua in the West Indies, and Kriss and Riba were living in an environment largely inhabited by people who were white.

A number of years later when Kriss brought his then fiancée, Monika, to England for the first time, one of the first people he introduced her to was Joycelyn. Still conscious of and a little embarrassed by his lack of a family, he introduced Joycelyn as his sister.

The children's home, in Steve's words, was run 'in the old style', but Brian and Shirley Martin, who were in charge for much of the time Kriss and Riba were there, were successful in creating the atmosphere of a large family. Brian and Shirley were in many ways substitute parents to the boys. The helpers, the uncles and aunts, came and went. At any one time there would be about a dozen staff working at the home. There would also be a steady turnover of children, with up to sixteen boys and girls, between the ages of two and eighteen, living at the home at any one time. But Brian and Shirley built up a special relationship with the two boys which has survived to this day. They took them on family holidays to Yorkshire and, even after leaving the home, helped guide the brothers through their early adult lives.

Kriss has fond memories of the Yorkshire holidays. In particular he enjoyed the opportunity to belong to a family, and he resented one holiday when other children from the home came too and once again he was one of a group. He felt it was an intrusion. He even had to share a bed!

Not that the relationship with Kriss and the Martins was always easy. When Kriss was young, both Brian and Shirley had on a number of occasions to discipline him. Corporal punishment was not ruled out, although Kriss well recalls the day Shirley found he was too strong to slap. He was in the kitchen and disobeyed her. She went to strike him and he caught her hand and restrained her. Both realized that their relationship would have to be different from then on. When Kriss was beaten by Brian or Shirley, he recalls, he had usually done something wrong. Earlier in his childhood he feels he was, more often than not, just beaten 'for being a kid. For being too loud or under an adult's feet'.

Early on in their time at Village Road, Kriss realized that he and Riba were unusual. Many of the other children were there, not because they had no parents to look after them, but because they had had to be taken away from their parents. Many were there because of the way they behaved or because of the crimes they had committed. Kriss knew that he and his brother were not to blame for the circumstances in which they found themselves.

'We had done nothing wrong, we were only there because our parents weren't around. Some of the others had had some awful things done to them. Victims of incest, sexual and physical abuse. What surprised me when I got older was to hear how these children still loved their mums and dads. Whatever had happened to them they wanted to see their mum and dad.

'They kept many of their problems to themselves but we usually knew what had happened to them. Sometimes we would talk amongst ourselves, we had a den up in a tree house, and perhaps ask, "Why are you here?" and get the answer, "Oh, my father played with me." Then we might be in a gang and swear we wouldn't have any secrets from each other. There were a lot of people there who had a lot of problems.'

There were children of different races and nationalities, but the ethos of the home and the environment was essentially English. The staff and most of the children at the local school were white, as were the people living in the district. They spent many weeks in the summer in Yorkshire and Kriss's interests in football, pop music and television programmes were those of any other British youngster.

Through his friends, his school, his watching of television programmes, Kriss absorbed the norms and values of British society, including those covert attitudes which have led to cultural racism through eroding the self-esteem of black people.

Ann Davis, who was Kriss's social worker for two years, saw evidence of the way in which Kriss was affected by this subtle undermining of his sense of worth. What messages, she now asks herself, must he have been taking in as one of a few isolated black children in the care system? At thirteen and fourteen he was asking her a number of searching questions. Why was it that on average black people had a lower I.Q. than white people? Ann had to explain about the built-in bias in the testing. Was it true that when human beings evolved, black people evolved first? From somewhere, Kriss must have picked up a juvenile pseudo-Darwinian argument about black people being a link between apes and modern white man. Playground racial taunts had obviously had a subliminal effect.

Joycelyn Longworth observed that Kriss and Riba had 'caught onto the idea that being black was not good. They had picked up on the inherent racism in the system that made black things inferior'. His indifferent results at school could well be accounted for by the way society's attitudes tend to undermine academic self-confidence in young black pupils. Only later in life did Kriss discover the joy of learning and have it confirmed to himself that he possessed a sharp, capable mind.

'If you go through a childhood like that of Kriss,' Ann now says, 'it either damages you, or opens you up.' Ann also considers Kriss's later success as an object lesson for all social workers who tend, too easily, to write off the youngsters in their care as being underprivileged and therefore with no hope in life. But there was no way, back in the seventies, of telling that the engaging and rebellious teenager, Kezie Akabusi, would succeed. Even Brian Martin confesses to thinking, then, that Kriss showed no real potential for anything. Not even sport.

Kriss had lived with questions of identity since his meeting with the black woman in Southsea, but it was not until he was in his early teens that he became aware of a vibrant black culture which was not only an alternative to white culture, but also accessible to him. He began to listen to Reggae music and visit parts of London where black people were in the majority. Two young black teenagers came to live at Village Road who introduced Kriss to West Indian culture. He envied their sense of identity, and would imitate the way they spoke. It was not 'cool' in those days to be African, and so Kriss invented a Jamaican background when he went out with other black youngsters. He listened to others talking about Jamaica and made up his own stories about where in Kingston he came from.

'I wanted to belong to a group of people. In my early days I wanted to be white. As I grew older I realized I was far from being white and could never be white. And people would always let me know I wasn't white. Once you accept that, you then start looking for your own identity, or something you can affiliate to.'

In a letter written to Ann Davis in 1983, Kriss reminded her of an incident from his teenage years. Ann used to take him and Riba out to the cinema or football matches, and they stayed with her and her husband at their flat. They were with her once when they were stopped on Enfield station by, to quote from the letter, 'another black guy who told me off for (one) not combing my hair and (two) going out with white girls.'

There were a number of times Kriss felt conspicuous. His

skin said that he was black and yet his actions suggested he was white. In the growing up years, youngsters are prone to feeling acutely aware of their appearance and there would be moments when Kriss would look around him and see all his white friends and realize he was the odd one out.

The home, particularly during school term, lived by its daily routine. The morning started with Brian, or one of the other uncles or aunts waking the children. There would then be a mad dash and scramble for the bathroom, followed by a noisy breakfast. Kriss would then always walk to school by himself. He went to Edmonton School in Little Bury Street in London N9. In later years he would watch some of the other boys set off and then switch clothes, hide their school uniforms in a bag behind a wall, and head for the West End. Kriss never joined them. He was always popular at school and enjoyed the companionship, if not the lessons.

After school Kriss went home and changed. He then did his allotted chores, which always included cleaning his shoes, which he hated, and went outside to play. Riba, on the other hand, would change and go to his room alone to study. Riba went to a different school because, when the time came for him to join Kriss at Edmonton, the school catchment areas were altered. At school, on the sports field, Kriss was keen but not outstanding. David Williams, the sports master at Edmonton School, confesses to thinking at the time that Kriss had no athletic potential! What he remembers of Kriss is his smile and enthusiasm.

From eleven to thirteen years old, Kriss was small for his age and not particularly strong. Nor was he specially fast on the track, never being more than a second string choice for the 400 metres. Because he was light, David Williams encouraged him to learn the high jump. Once he had mastered the technique, Kriss became the best high jumper in the school. On sports days he would strip off so methodically, and take so long preparing for his jump, that the judges would grow impatient and tell him to get a move on. Although Kriss did not have a track suit and certain other items of kit, David Williams says that Kriss did not appear to mind.

But Kriss was always conscious of being a boy from a children's home. On sports days and open days, the other children would have parents coming to the school. He did not. Once, when a school football trip to Belgium was being arranged, the school and the children's home between them raised the money for Kriss to go. He was grateful, but aware of the special effort that had been made for him. Unlike the other boys, he had no parents to provide the money. He often felt out of place. To compensate, he would tend to be more aggressively competitive, to prove to himself that he was as good as any of the other pupils at the school. He wanted to be different and to be noticed because he was good, not because he was poor.

Riba too was aware of being different from the others at his school. His response was to immerse himself in his academic work. Also, as a gifted all-round sports player at school he had no need, and it was not in his nature, to behave extravagantly in order to be noticed. At his senior school he was quietly good at everything.

Kriss also played football and Brian Martin arranged for him to have a junior trial with a league team. But the Leyton Orient scouts watching the trial were not sufficiently impressed to sign him up. Brian remembers Kriss losing interest in the idea of a professional football career when it was suggested to him that he would be more likely to be a defender than a goal scorer. He only played for the school second team and was not someone who regularly attended training sessions.

The picture that emerges of Kriss at school is of a boy with a charming manner and smile who did not show a great deal of evidence of his promise. Another teacher, Hugh Prosser, says Kriss was a memorable individual, but also a 'constant irritant'. He was continually naughty, though without being malicious. As he approached his teens and moved from the lower to the upper school, the staff detected a change in attitude. He appeared more worried about his lack of a normal home background than he had been before and showed far more awareness of being black. As the time approached for him to leave school, the staff became increasingly worried about him. A case conference was convened involving the school and the social work department.

Kriss, living from day to day, was not aware of the behind-the-scenes work which his 'case', and that of his brother, involved. He lived in his own world which centred round Village Road and the school. Although many aspects of life were organized and arranged, many other areas were left unsupervised. He and his gang of friends devised their own codes of conduct and had to learn what was right and wrong on a pragmatic basis. On a number of occasions Kriss could have been lured into crime, or deeper trouble. He often hovered on the edge of danger but always pulled back. Or was he pulled back? Certainly he had the watchful eye and wisdom of Brian Martin to thank on one occasion.

Kriss and his gang had a game called destination. One of their number would perform a task, climbing a difficult tree or jumping into a holly bush and, with the shout of 'destination', challenge the others to follow. This game evolved. Soon the gang were going shop-lifting and challenging each other to steal more often and more blatantly. One of their number went into a shop and calmly walked out with a large rubber dinghy. Kriss admits to stealing carpentry tools. One day Brian became suspicious, and caught Kriss and the gang admiring their stolen goods.

Kriss's version of the story tells of how the police were called and he got very worried about the consequences of what he had done. Brian says he made no official report but called in a friend, who was a policeman, and who stood 6 foot 6 inches tall, to come and put the fear of God into the boys. In Kriss's case the tactics worked. In many ways he was glad to have been caught. He knew what he was doing was wrong, and was looking for an excuse not to continue.

Stealing, to the gang, had been a game and a test of their courage in the eyes of their peers. At one stage Kriss would only allow newcomers to join his circle if they proved themselves by stealing from a local shop. Yet there was, as always, honour amongst the thieves. Stealing goods from a commercial enterprise was considered fair game, stealing from those you knew was not. Brian Martin recalls an occasion when a boy came to see him with a bleeding nose. He had been roughed up by the gang for taking fifty pence belonging to Shirley.

Kriss's loyalty to Brian and Shirley, his sense of honour and his early leadership skills came together when he organized a protest march. The tale has grown with the telling and Steve Longworth cannot be certain it is not apocryphal. The story goes that Brian and Shirley wished to adopt a child and the authorities said no. Kriss and the other children at the home were so incensed by this that they went on a protest march to the town hall. Their message was that of course Brian and Shirley should be able to adopt a baby, they were already looking after sixteen children and doing it very well. Brian's version of the story is the more reliable, but it still shows Kriss in the same light. He and Shirley were hoping for an extension to their living quarters at the home when their newly adopted baby daughter arrived. The authorities decided to schedule various extensions and improvements to the house—some of which, Brian believes, were quite unnecessary—but not the one they needed. Kriss, on his own initiative, went to the social services department to argue their case, taking most of his friends with him to back him up.

From a very early age Kriss had had to take important decisions relating to himself and Riba. He devised a way of balancing the pros and cons of any course of action by holding a conversation in his head. It was almost as if he could listen to two protagonists arguing. Often he would stand by a favourite tree in the garden at the home to hold his debates. On one occasion he had a debate in his mind as to whether it would be better for him to be the quiet, introspective type of person, or the lively extrovert. He decided to try being quiet, but after a few days he found it too difficult to keep up and so became the outgoing joker in his class at school. The lively personality Kriss Akabusi displays today comes naturally to him, but it grew from a decision he took as a boy to allow that side of him to develop.

Much of Kriss's time at Village Road was spent proving that he was 'one of the lads', but inevitably his interest in the girls at the home grew as he himself got older. Much of his early knowledge of 'the facts of life' was learned from the girls, many of whom, because of their own experiences, were sexually precocious. Kriss was himself quite late to mature physically, but when puberty came he was as excited and curious about the changes happening to him as any boy of his age. Even before puberty he was curious about the way the bodies of the girls he knew were changing, and some of the girls were not slow in satisfying that curiosity.

At school Kriss was always popular with the girls, not for reasons of physical attraction, but because he made them laugh. Interestingly, the one girl in his class who did fall more deeply for him was the only black girl. Kriss however, in his early teen years, was not moved, preferring the company of the white girls.

Like all boys at some stage in their development, Kriss experimented with alcohol and tobacco. He and his friends, when they were still under ten, bought cigarettes for tuppence (old coinage) each and smoked them at school. Kriss hated the taste of Woodbines but joined in as it was expected of him. After a few weeks he gave up smoking. It was quite ridiculous, he thought, to be spending money doing something he did not even enjoy and which made his breath and clothes smell foul.

A few years later, at the age of thirteen, Kriss and a friend turned to alcohol. They would leave school at lunchtime to go to the friend's home to sample his parents' homemade wine. They would return to afternoon lessons in merry mood. One day their taste for alcohol went further and they found their way into the back of a pub. They began drinking sweet sherry from a case and forgot the time. Not only did they fail to return for afternoon school, but worse was to follow. The effect of the drink gradually caught up on them and Kriss began to feel very strange. His head began to spin, his legs crumpled and when, by some miracle, he got home, he went straight to bed. He then vomited all over the bedclothes. He had learned about the downside of alcohol the hard way, and has not touched sweet sherry to this day.

By staging debates in his mind, standing by his favourite tree, Kriss took many decisions which were to be crucial in later life. If he had opted to become a smoker, he might not have been an athlete. On a number of occasions he could have chosen a life of crime, or to have played truant and gone to the West End, but he refused to join in when it was suggested. Although Kriss liked to be popular and to conform, there was also part of his nature which placed him apart from his peers. He would refuse to go along with the crowd, as a way of demonstrating that he was his own person. Although his school results did not show any evidence of it, Kriss was convinced he was intellectually the superior of most of those around him, especially those in his immediate social group. He was also convinced in his own mind that he had a special destiny in life. He believed both in choice and in fate. He believed in providence. Today he looks back on his precarious youth and is certain the guiding hand of God was at work.

A telling incident stands out in his memory, one which he has often reflected upon and one which has caused him some anxiety. A Swedish woman came to work at the children's home who claimed clairvoyance through reading palms. One day, when he was about fourteen years old, she took his hand and looked at it. 'You will be very successful,' she said. 'But you will not be the best. You will get married and have two children. You will change your job on various occasions and be involved in sport. You will do very well but not be famous.' Reflecting on these and other predictions, Kriss acknowledges their accuracy. As to the reference to fame, he asks, 'What is fame?' He might be famous in Britain, even Europe, but he knows he is not a household name worldwide. It was the end of the palm reading which had Kriss curious and which worries him to this day.

'She got to me being aged thirty-four, thirty-five and stopped. "I can't go on, I can't do any more." She refused to go on. I pleaded with her to continue and she refused absolutely. "That's enough, don't ask me any more." Was I going to die? Was something so dreadful going to happen that I couldn't be told? She has left me wondering. All through my life I have believed her. This woman read my palm, read my life. Things she predicted happened. I do believe people like her can have insights into people's lives. Now, I believe Satan can use a medium like the Swedish woman. I used to read my horoscope and it determined my life! I would read that a Sagittarius was an outdoor person and an extrovert and mould my life accordingly. A lot of the traits that are me I took aboard from reading my horoscope.

'I cannot now put that palm reading out of my mind. It might have been that she saw I was going to be so successful she couldn't believe what she saw. What I believe now is this. All of a sudden she saw me being involved in Christianity. She saw a spiritual battle. I now wonder, will I be martyred for the gospel? It could be that something catastrophic will happen, or it could be that she got to a spiritual barrier and she couldn't see any more. She stopped so abruptly. She was telling me about changing careers and living in a foreign country and then it stopped. She wouldn't tell any more.'

From the moment the two brothers became the responsibility of the Islington Borough social work department, attempts were made to trace their parents. Letters sent to them in Nigeria were returned and searches made by the international social service agencies proved fruitless. Around the age of nine or ten Kriss would often wonder about the mother and father he could barely remember.

'Mums and Dads always came to take other children away from the home, even those who'd been sexually abused. Sooner or later they came. My bedroom was just above the drive and if a car rolled up I would think, is this my mum and my dad come for me? It was never to be. I would listen to the wood pigeons cooing and think, next time, soon, I won't be listening to you, my parents will have come for me. At night I would sometimes think about my parents and if I couldn't get to sleep would hum a silly rhyme to myself. "Lloyd George knew my father, father knew Lloyd George." Why, I don't know.'

Kriss knew about the war in Nigeria and recalls one time when his uncle, who paid occasional visits, got annoyed when his two nephews were referred to as orphans. Cypril was also displeased when he saw Kriss taking part in a play as a 'native prince': he considered the part demeaning to his people and his heritage. Kriss did not at the time realize the significance of what his uncle was saying.

Kriss would pray about his parents. 'Heavenly Father, if my mother and father are still alive, I pray that you will look after them. But if they started the war, I would be happy if you kill them.'

It was on one ordinary working day in 1972 that Ann Davis went into her office in Finsbury and saw that she had a letter from International Social Services. It was not unusual: they were frequently writing to let her know that they had drawn another blank in their search for Kriss's and Riba's parents. She was astonished, she recalls, to open it and find not only that the latest line of enquiry had been successful, but that both parents had been found simultaneously in different parts of the country. She admits to having been stunned by the news. From having been worried about the boys having no contact with their parents, she now became concerned about how the boys would react to learning their parents had been found.

Ann believes Riba was more excited to hear the news than Kriss. Perhaps Kriss had by now decided in his own mind that there was no point in holding on to the Nigerian dream. He had his own world and way of life which, perhaps, he did not want to see unsettled again. Possibly he felt that he did not want his problem of identity complicated by new information about his Nigerian roots.

Clara wrote to Ann Davis, thanking God and the social services for keeping Kezie and Zeribe safe. She sent photographs of herself and the boys' younger sister Chioma. She also sent Ann a present of a bead bangle. Before long she wanted photographs taken of her sons in Nigerian dress and was enquiring about her sons' education and future plans. Kriss was not keen on having his photograph taken, and only agreed on sufferance. Riba, however, was very willing to comply with his mother's wish.

Up until that time the local authority had assumed that the two boys would be their responsibility until they were adults. The time had passed when they might have been of a suitable age to have been considered for fostering or adoption. They had once been considered for fostering and Kriss has a vague memory of a white couple coming to 'inspect them', but nothing further came of the meeting. Steve knew that, now Clara was in touch, the social worker's responsibilty for the boys could be terminated at any time and with no warning. Since the boys were in voluntary care, Clara was within her legal rights to turn up and remove the boys from the home whenever she wished. This was not, of course, an immediate possibility. Clara had made contact, but she did not have the means to fly to Britain to make her claim to resume her role as a mother.

Although this was the first contact between Clara and her sons since the start of the civil war, when normal communications between Nigeria and Britain had broken down, the home had earlier received an indirect intimation of her wishes concerning the boys' religious education. Exactly how these instructions were conveyed, Kriss does not know. He believes he was aged ten or eleven at the time. What he does know is that the result of that contact was unfortunate: Kriss became estranged from the Christian church throughout his teenage years and for most of his twenties.

For a number of years it had been part of Kriss's routine to go with some of his friends to one of the local churches, usually the Congregationalist or the Methodist. He played the bugle in the Boys' Brigade, enjoyed the sports and went to Sunday School. 'Then one Sunday I came back to the children's home and was told that Riba and I couldn't go to those churches any more. It seems my mother had written and was upset that we were not being brought up as Catholics. All of a sudden she had come into my life. Before that, I had had no contact with her at all, not even a birthday card.

'So I went to the Catholic church and hated every minute of it. There was no fun. On the Saturday morning we had to go to the convent. We had classes. They were a bit like the Sunday School but a lot stricter. There was no laughing and joking. This was learning things. I didn't enjoy learning things at school and certainly didn't enjoy learning things on a Saturday at the convent. On Sunday, my brother and I had to sit through the mass. None of our friends were there and I didn't understand a word of what was going on. The only things I liked were the smell of incense and the sound of the people singing. Otherwise it was a very boring time. I couldn't wait to get out and go home. I do remember, however, yearning to take the bread; but I hadn't gone through all the preparation and so couldn't.'

The time came when Kriss and some of his friends, who were still going to the other church, began to question the need to go to church at all. In Kriss's case he was beginning to find the Roman Catholics were restricting his enjoyment of life. Too many of the things he enjoyed doing were deemed by the priest to be sinful. They raised the matter with Brian. Brian said that they were now of an age to decide for themselves. That night Kriss prayed, 'God, I don't know if you're out there, but I want to have a good time. I'm still going to pray to you, but I'm not going to go to church.' The next day he told Brian what he had decided. To begin with Kriss felt twinges of guilt, but these soon faded.

One of the results of the renewed contact with Nigeria was that Clara could be in touch with other people she knew in London. She wrote to relatives from her home village of Esmoha and asked them to visit her sons. Dennis Agbugba went to Village Road and recalls his first impression. The boys were engrossed in a game on the billiard table. He invited them to lunch and they went to see him and his wife Ann, one weekend. It was the first of a number of weekends, when the boys were introduced to African food and Dennis and Ann were able to tell them about Nigeria and their family.

Weekends away from the home were not uncommon. When children did not have parents or friends to take them out, Brian and Shirley arranged numerous diversions. They also had holidays at Butlins and were taken out to the parks and Epping Forest. At Christmas they went to the pantomime, visited Santa Claus and had toys to unwrap. Inevitably, the treats were communal. Kriss remembers the many times the children would be piled into a bus to go somewhere and he would feel embarrassed that to the outside world it was obvious they all came from a children's home. There would be moments too when outsiders treated them in a kindly but patronizing way as the 'poor little boys and girls' from the home. Kriss and Riba, despite their clear, developing personalities, were all too often seen by outsiders not as individuals but as one of a group.

Brian and Shirley gave Kriss and Riba as much individual attention as they could, but their time had to be shared with the other children, many of whom were seriously disturbed. Ann Davis and Steve Longworth did their best to form a good relationship with the boys, but they too, as social workers, were responsible for many other children and families. Kriss and Riba never wanted for anything, physically, but they needed more. It was the giving and receiving of affection which they lacked. They had each other and felt a concern and affection for each other, but not in any demonstrative way. Kriss recalls just once, during their time at Village Road, putting an arm round Riba to comfort him after a fall and feeling very awkward. 'Do I really feel like this towards my brother?' he asked himself at the time.

Kriss now feels that because he never learned how to give and receive affection in a natural way, he found it difficult in later life to learn how to be spontaneously loving with his own children. Kriss also discovered a way to cope with rejected affection. From an early age adults came into his life and then went again so quickly that he soon realized it was not worth investing too much time and love in forming a relationship. The best way to avoid being rejected was never to offer too much by way of affection in the first place. And if a relationship did form, and then seemed threatened, Kriss devised ways of standing aside from his emotions and withdrawing from events.

'We were never badly off when it came to the material things. Everything was provided. Food was excellent. There was so much activity and so many opportunities to be doing things that I didn't notice this lack of intimacy. It is looking back I realize. There was nobody I could go and lean on and whose shoulder I could cry on.'

Perhaps Riba felt the lack of intimacy more acutely. He was two years younger, and links with his mother had been severed at an earlier age. There might have been other reasons. He caused Kriss, Brian, Shirley and the social workers concern by his long periods of silence and withdrawal. As when he was very young and being beaten by the Spanish lady, he could be very determined. If he decided not to eat a meal he would sit in front of his plate for hours, refusing to take a mouthful.

Kriss would sympathise with Riba and tell him he understood how he was feeling. Only towards the end of Kriss's time at the children's home did he begin to realize that Riba's personality problems could have their roots in mental illness. Around the age of twenty Riba developed pyschiatric problems which led to a period of hospitalization. At the children's home he was not gregarious like his brother. He took his school work seriously and also studied judo, but was never 'one of the boys'.

Kriss attributes his own extrovert nature to being the older brother. When the maternal link was severed he was just old enough to find a way of coping. 'By being louder than loud, I could pretend things were not too bad. Riba knew things were bad. He lived through events and I blame a lot of his problems on the Spanish lady and the times he was beaten and yet refused to cry.'

Shortly before Kriss was due to leave school and also leave the children's home, he and Riba heard that their mother was to visit England. It was the summer of 1975. They were then told the day she was expected at the children's home. Kriss remembers feeling curious but unexcited at the prospect of being reunited. He had passed the stage of longing for her to arrive and was by now planning for his future, a future he assumed would be in Britain.

Clara arrived, wearing full traditional Nigerian dress, one Saturday, just as Kriss was playing football in the garden. He saw her arriving from a distance and knew instantly she was his mother. He watched her walk up the drive and go into the house, yet he carried on playing football. In due course one of the staff came out and told him that his mother had arrived: would he like to come and meet her?

'Riba and I went into the office. She was smiling. I looked at her. We then went into the playroom and sat down on the big sofa. I don't know what I expected. I just looked at her, thinking, "This is my mother, this is my mother." I could see the resemblance, and she started telling me about things I had done when I was small and about life in Nigeria. But I wasn't listening.

'For years I had venerated my parents from afar and had a fairy tale idea about their return. Yet I didn't feel any emotion or any bond with this woman who I knew to be my mother. I had hoped for an instant bonding, but it wasn't there. I told myself, "Kezie, this is your mother," and then I thought, "So what?" In the end it was very much, what can I get out of her, "Have you brought any sweets, any presents?"

'Again, no intimacy.'

Perhaps the protective mechanisms Kriss had devised to spare himself from emotional rejection were now too automatic, even when meeting his own mother.

If he felt no great joy, neither did he feel any resentment. He bore no malice towards this woman. It was a sterile meeting of two strangers, and afterwards Kriss carried on with his game of football. He discussed the day's events only briefly with Riba and then just in a light-hearted manner. Riba remembers one of the small details of the day. Clara was given some bread and butter, which she dipped into a cup of sugary tea. Riba's impression of her was that she was a self-confident woman, big and attractive, and someone who was used to taking responsibility. She was a nurse and midwife and ran her own hospital. Yet he could not help but think that this image was somehow contradicted by his own impression of her irresponsibility, in having left him and his brother in England to be fostered.

The social workers might have been concerned for the two brothers and how they would cope with such a major event in their lives as being reunited with their mother after twelve years. Riba and Kriss were far less worried. The day of the reunion was just another day to them. They looked to see what they could get from her and she asked them if she could have a gold ring given to Riba by a school friend as a momento. Kriss handed it over.

The years before that meeting Clara describes as agony, not knowing what had become of her sons. When she knew she was to be reunited she thanked God, first, and then the British authorities for their care and loving kindness. Her recollections of the reunion of sixteen years ago inevitably differ in detail and perspective from that of her sons.

'The year I found myself in the aeroplane to London, I could not believe it. I arrived at Uncle Dennis Agbugba by 3 p.m. Dennis telephoned Kezie, telling him of my arrival. I spoke to him and reassured him of my seeing them next morning. After I had been to the home, we invited them to come and spend the next day with us. Mrs Ann Agbugba prepared a sumptuous meal. The boys enjoyed eating the native dish with their fingers for the first time. Towards the end of my holiday Kezie hinted me of his intentions to enlist in the army. First I did not like the idea, for I would have preferred him to go to university and read law, medicine or engineering. God's will be done. Today I have no regrets.'

Over the next two or three weeks they met again on a number of occasions and Kriss experienced the same indifference. They went shopping and Kriss was interested in little more than what he could get his mother to buy him. Conversation eventually turned to Nigeria and the return of the two brothers to their homeland. Kriss did not take the talk seriously until Clara persisted with the suggestion: then he became worried. He explained that he was happy in England. She persevered, explaining that they had a family in Nigeria and they were important people. Kriss agreed that one day perhaps he would make the journey. Clara took this as a sign of Kriss's willingness to adopt Nigerian ways. It was Clara's aim to persuade the boys to come back with her, but, as Ann Agbugba recalls, Kriss had already decided what he wanted to do. He was saving money from a paper round to buy a motorcycle, he intended to go into the army and learn a trade. Ann was impressed by his mature approach.

Kriss's values and expectations were now very western. When his mother suggested he dress the Nigerian way, if only for a photograph, he refused. 'Oh my dear! We had this hat and all these wrappers and a thing that looked like an animal's tail. No way was she going to get me into this Mickey Mouse gear.'

When Kriss expressed concern to Steve about his mother's intentions he was reassured that he would not be made to leave and go to Nigeria against his will. Riba too was keen to stay in England and complete his school work. While trying not to convey his anxieties to the boys, Steve had also been concerned that Clara might exercise her legal right to take her sons away from the children's home. He had gone so far as to consider applying to the courts to have Clara's legal rights removed and transferred to the local authority.

Despite his unwillingness to abandon English for Nigerian ways, Kriss nevertheless found his interest in Nigeria stimulated by his mother's visit. He asked more questions of the Agbugbas about his background. He came to enjoy their spicey African food, made from ingredients such as dried fish, goat meat, maize, rice, okra and peppers. He was also told more about what his mother meant by saying that his family were people of importance. His father had a position of authority and high status within his region, the full significance of which Kriss did not come to appreciate until he visited Nigeria a number of years later.

'They could have told me I was the Queen of Sheba,' Kriss recalls, 'but without any evidence of the wealth and power, there was no way anything I was told meant anything significant. The reality was that I was the boy from the children's home.'

Real life for Kriss meant the routine of school, meeting his friends and living alongside the other children at the home in Village Road. As he entered his last year at school and began to discuss possible careers, it also slowly dawned on him that this familiar pattern of life would soon be coming to an end. Once he had a job he would have to be looking for a new place to call home, and he dreaded the thought of living alone. He did not feel confident that he could survive without the backing of an institution, although he had by then almost outgrown the children's home environment.

He was strong and stroppy. He had grown very friendly with another boy at school and spent a great deal of his spare time at his home. Steve McGilchrist and Kriss had much in common. Steve's father was black and Steve, like Kriss, was keen on all sports. They discussed the possibility of Kriss moving into the McGilchrist home and working at a nearby factory. He also applied for a job with the gas board, but they turned him down. One of the staff at the home felt he was rejected on the grounds of colour and Kriss agrees it could well have been a factor.

Kriss had by now, however, developed a new idea—as he had told his mother. Attracted by promises of sport and travel he applied to join the army. Brian Martin had been in the Royal Corps of Signals and encouraged him to follow in his footsteps. They had often talked about Brian's days as an army dispatch rider. Brian accompanied Kriss to the recruitment office, and wished him luck when the time came for Kriss to go away for a weekend to take a series of aptitude tests.

Kriss was especially keen to persuade the army to offer him a trade apprenticeship. The idea of data-telegraphy appealed to him, although he knew nothing about what it involved. He liked the sound of the words and the image of working with computers and modern communications equipment. Kriss was also reassured by the thought that the army would provide him with a continuation of the type of community existence in which he felt comfortable.

A number of the people officially responsible for him were growing anxious for his future. So Kriss's decision to join the army provided the solution his social workers and school were looking for, despite a number of misgivings. Those who knew the impulsive, erratic, ill-disciplined side of Kriss's character were seriously concerned about how he would cope with military life. It had to be Kriss's decision, but he was presented with some of the arguments against joining the forces. One of the staff at the home in particular was against it. He warned Kriss about the dangers of forfeiting his identity and becoming cannon-fodder in the event of a war.

Kriss debated the issue in his mind and judged in favour of joining the forces on the grounds that an army career would provide him with a trade. The idea that he might have to fight was so unreal that it hardly weighed in the argument. Yet getting into the army to do exactly what he wanted to do was not a straightforward matter. After passing his aptitude tests, both the written and practical, Kriss was offered a number of possible trades. He was adamant: only an apprenticeship to learn data-telegraphy interested him, otherwise he would not join up.

In the end, Kriss was offered a certificate stating that he would be enlisted as a junior signalman to study data-telegraphy. Only much later did he realize that he had not been offered a place at the apprentice college. If he had known that then, he would not have signed the papers: the army would have lost a young recruit and Kriss's future would have been very different. On 7 August 1975 he took his certificate to the recruitment office in Finchley and officially became a member of Her Majesty's forces. In Kriss's mind there might have been some misgivings, some qualms, but he convinced himself there was no going back.

3

The Army's 'Flyer'

It was the morning of 9 September 1975 when an excited but slightly apprehensive Kriss stood on the platform at King's Cross station in London waiting to board the Newcastle train. He had with him his suitcase packed with the latest fashionable clothes, which he had bought on his last shopping outing from the children's home. He realized the day was a watershed in his life. From that day he was no longer a child but a man.

He looked around him, at several other neatly dressed and nervous-looking sixteen and seventeen year-olds, and guessed they too might be on their way to become junior soldiers. It was only when the train began to move slowly out of the station that the full truth dawned. As he waved goodbye to Steve and Joycelyn he realized that he was leaving them and his old life behind. It must have been to make the break easier that he did not, as Riba recalls, even say goodbye to his younger brother. Riba only realized that he had left when, after a few days, he noticed Kriss was no longer around. His brother's absence felt strange to Riba: it made him feel, for a while, less secure about life.

As the train gathered speed Kriss went to his seat in a reflective mood. He was off on a new adventure, but it was a journey of uncertainty. He had a job to go to and a new skill to learn. He had new friends to meet and new opportunities ahead, and this time he was on his own. Although of late he and his brother had been at different schools, and their lives and interests had diverged, Kriss was always aware of Riba being around, the only constant presence he had known throughout his childhood.

Kriss also had the question of identity to sort out. He was

black, both irreversibly and proudly so. By now he had made many black friends, both youngsters and adults. He had met his mother and knew something of his background. He had been influenced and impressed by his contacts with London's West Indian black culture. And yet he realized that he thought and reacted to events more as a white English teenager. But it was an undeniable fact that his name was African: he was Kezie Akabusi.

It was on his journey north, as he was mulling over past events and thinking about the future, that he took an important decision. In his new life he would no longer be known as Kezie. His father had given him the English Christian name Michael, and for a while Kriss signed himself K. M. Akabusi, but he now wanted to make a symbolic break with his past. He decided from this time on to introduce himself as Kriss. And why Kriss with a 'K'? He did not want to deny his past completely; to avoid complications, he wanted his name to keep the same initial; and the extrovert side of his character wanted a name which people would remember, something a little different.

It was a long journey and Kriss remembers passing Peterborough, York, Darlington and Durham and thinking how far he had come and yet how much further he still had to go. He fell into conversation with two other lads on their way to become junior soldiers. They had a friendly argument about local radio stations and which was the best.

It was mid-afternoon when the crowded train slowed to cross the bridge over the River Tyne and enter Newcastle central station. Kriss and his two new friends followed the crowd off the train and along the platform. They saw a man in army uniform shepherding a large group of others of their own age onto another train. They joined it and the new recruits soon found themselves heading slowly westwards out of the city.

The carriage was full of young aspiring junior soldiers, laughing and joking and introducing themselves to each other. They were from all over the country and Kriss was intrigued to hear the various regional accents. This second train journey was much shorter, only about fifteen miles. Soon they arrived at their final station and suddenly Kriss's excited chatter stopped. Instead of a comfortable coach to take him and the others on the final leg to the army camp, there were two large military four-ton trucks. Kriss knew then that he was in the army.

He and the lads piled into the back and sat on the hard benches under the canvas cover. As they drove along, some of the new junior soldiers began singing songs they had learned as army cadets. Never having been in the cadets, Kriss, for the first time, felt out of his depth. He looked around and realized he was the only black person there. He tried to join in with the singing, but not knowing the words felt awkward and different.

The trucks drove north from Prudhoe to Albemarle Barracks at Ouston near Stamfordham. Each new arrival signed in at the guard room and from that moment every minute of every day was organized. They were allocated billets, shown where to put their cases and then marched in a compliant but erratic formation to the dining-hall. There they received further instructions and also had to fill out a form giving the army information about themselves: name, date and place of birth, address and religion.

'But I'm not religious,' said Kriss, not being difficult, just honest. The army, however, when it asks a question, needs an answer.

'Are you Church of England, Methodist, Catholic?' he was asked.

Catholic struck a chord with Kriss and for the purpose of army records and future church parades, he was listed as a Roman Catholic.

His first hours as a junior soldier were spent being allocated uniform and kit. Having attended to all the formalities of joining up, Kriss and the others were told to return to their billet and line up by their beds. Each dormitory slept twelve. Then a sergeant arrived and his first instructions involved how they were expected to make their beds in the army.

They had a trial run and Kriss, having been taught to make

his bed the same way in the children's home, was the only one of the new intake to get it right. The sergeant praised him for being the single individual to have been listening properly. Slowly it occurred to Kriss that his past experience of life might now give him a certain advantage over the others who had come from more normal home and family backgrounds. He knew he was better equipped than most of his fellows to survive an institutionalized existence under a disciplined and ordered regime. Some of the lads were little more than boys, away from their mothers for the first time. It was not unusual for them to be reduced to tears by the unfamiliar harsh and spartan conditions. Kriss realized that their weaknesses showed up his strengths.

As September turned to October Kriss became settled into the routine of 12 troop. There were classes to attend: first-aid, communications, signalling skills, fieldcraft and weapons instruction. It was only the drill that Kriss hated. By now the weather was cold and the mornings getting darker. Out on the parade ground there was nowhere to shelter, and no way of running indoors to warm up as there had been at the children's home in London. But Kriss did not give up. The psychology employed by the drill sergeant to drive the young junior recruits on was just what was needed for Kriss.

'Over the next few weeks,' the sergeant said, 'the wimps will give up. Out here, I'm God. What I say you do. When I say go, you go. When I say stop, you stop. If you're a wimp you can fall out now.'

There was no way the sixteen year-old Kriss Akabusi was going to allow himself to be numbered with the wimps. How would he be able to go back to London and face his friends as a failure? Every week a list was posted naming those who had failed. Kriss saw them going home, some relieved, but others crestfallen and disappointed. And as every week passed and the name Akabusi did not appear on that list, Kriss knew he had chalked up a success.

For the first six months junior soldiers can leave at any time. During that time the army too can tell anyone who fails to come up to scratch that he is no longer required and is free to go. So Kriss had an added incentive to complete the drill and do well in all other spheres of junior army life. To have been dismissed would have been as ignominious as quitting.

Another shameful option was to be back-squadded, told to start the course from scratch again with the next new intake. This again Kriss was keen to avoid. Fortunately his natural competitive spirit stood him in good stead. He now estimates that fewer than fifty per cent of his original group successfully completed the first thirty weeks of basic training without a set-back, and he was one of them.

One of the main causes of failure was lack of physical fitness. Many of the teenage lads were weak and unused to real exertion. Kriss had played a lot of sport, and although not strong in the upper body was agile and enthusiastic. He was competent, if not always tidy, and while never the best at anything was always one of the most able. He was generally popular. He laughed and joked and was eager to please.

The highly regimented life did however come as a shock to his system. Not only were there frequent parades, there were parades for parades. Breakfast was at 7 o'clock and reveille half an hour earlier. But 6.30 a.m. was not the time the bleary-eyed juniors rolled out of bed. When the troop corporal arrived at 6.30, the room had to be clean and tidy for inspection. So cleaning had to start at 6 o'clock and for that Kriss and the others had to wake, get up, wash and dress at 5.30, when it was still dark. By 9 o'clock, when Kriss was out on the drill square, he would reflect that, while a sizeable chunk of his morning was already behind him, Riba and his old friends were only just arriving at school to start their day.

To his surprise, he found that as a junior soldier he could apply his mind to classroom lessons in a way he had never done at school. It was all part of that drive to prove he was the equal and the better of those around him. He was spurred on as well by a need to confirm his place on the data-telegraphist course. He needed a good report for everything. So he even listened attentively to the Padre's hour and the talks on the army in the contemporary world.

He now remembers with some sympathy the young teenagers in uniform who failed to keep up or conform, however hard they tried. Not only were they bullied by their peers, but they also had to suffer the official extra duties and punishments which came with being disorganized and incompetent. They were the butt of every joke. Consistent with human behaviour in other walks of life, the junior recruits as the lowest form of army life had in turn to find someone even lower to bully and despise. Kriss remembers how one of their number was thought not to have washed and was thrown into a bath of water and scrubbed with brooms. As one of the macho mob, Kriss joined in. Life at the time was governed by a crude masculine bravado and an extraordinary attention to detail. Berets had to be a certain shape and this shape could only be achieved by soaking them in water. Uniforms had to be immaculate and conform exactly to army regulations. During their off-duty moments the young men would boast to each other of their sexual prowess and pass pornographic magazines around. Even Kriss, who had been aware of his sexuality from a young age, was surprised, even shocked, by some of the things he heard. It was however mostly talk, and typical of the behaviour of any group of sexually charged young men confined to barracks and their own company. It was commonplace to swear, and Kriss was frequently at the receiving end of racial abuse. It did not however worry him, as everyone at the time was addressed in vulgar, derogatory terms. When it came to trading personal insults, Kriss was as good as any of them. There were sometimes fights and, again, Kriss could hold his own. He was acknowledged as one of the hard men of his troop, well respected by all and popular because of his ready wit and sense of fun.

The N.C.O.s found 'Aki' or 'Akismith', as they called him, enthusiastic and keen to make a good impression. Life was physical and rough and the men in charge of the lads were generally bigger and stronger. The sixteen and seventeen year-olds were still growing and gaining muscle and bulk. Games tended to be tough and hard but were normally played in a good spirit. Kriss remembers only one of the N.C.O.s being unnecessarily aggressive. Regrettably, one troop sergeant took advantage of his position of authority and Kriss's naive willingness to curry favour. He fancied a set of mugs which Kriss had brought with him, one of his few personal possessions, and persuaded the young soldier to hand them over, much against his will.

The troop sergeant of number 13 troop, however, was a very different character and became not only a genuine friend but also a major influence in Kriss's life. Ian Mackenzie was the athletics officer and he noticed in the junior signalman a raw talent for running.

Ian Mackenzie himself was a good athlete and the 400 metres was his distance. One day in the early spring of 1976 he was out running on the airfield when he was joined by Kriss. They ran for a while shoulder to shoulder, chatting, when Ian Mackenzie decided to get down to some serious training. As he accelerated off, he expected to leave the youngster behind, but Kriss ran ahead of him.

Somewhat surprised, the sergeant called out, 'Akabusi, what do you think you're doing? I'm supposed to be the fastest round here.'

A little later they had a more serious talk. 'Listen sunshine,' he told Kriss, 'you have got the potential to win the army championships.' And he even entertained the thought that the Olympics were within Kriss's grasp.

In time, Kriss and Ian Mackenzie got to know each other well. Kriss would go to his home and stay with him and his wife Pamela. Initially Kriss was reluctant to let on about his background, but in due course told his story. It was Ian Mackenzie who first convinced Kriss that whatever he wanted to achieve he could achieve. 'You can be number one,' he said.

Kriss began to believe in himself and his future. He had confirmation of his feelings of destiny. And Ian Mackenzie advised Kriss, should he reach the top, not to let his natural personality change. 'Don't forget, you owe it to yourself and your sport not to think yourself too important to go and talk to youngsters and encourage them.' And it was Ian Mackenzie who first said to Kriss in no uncertain terms, 'Don't drink, don't smoke and if ever I catch you taking drugs I'll cut you dead.'

Kriss sampled a first real sense of achievement when, at the end of their initial training, he and his troop prepared for the passing out parade. They had completed some rigorous tests, including the one which Kriss found particularly unpleasant, the training for nuclear, chemical and biological warfare. He had to wear a cumbersome protective outfit, or 'noddy suit' as it was known, and learn how to use a gas mask. Then, suitably kitted out, he and the others were told to go into a building filled with CS gas. Kriss held his breath as long as he could, as he did not trust the mask, and soon found himself coughing and spluttering with his eyes watering.

Standing on the parade ground on 9 April 1976, in his best military kit, his Number 2 dress, performing drill to perfection, Kriss felt immensely proud. One familiar sensation, however, slightly marred the occasion. All the others on parade were being watched with equal pride by their parents. Kriss, despite his many friends, was essentially alone.

When it came for the usual parental report to be sent out, it was addressed to Riba as next of kin. The report, headed Junior Signalmen's Wing, 11th Signal Regiment, described Junior Signalman Akabusi, Number 24354835, as a hard working, cheerful and reliable soldier. His team spirit and physical stamina were listed as outstanding, with determination, self-confidence and ambition as above average. In all his subjects he was graded as average, above average, or excellent. Only his weapon handling was described as weak, and in the section on his academic work it was noted that he could be carefree to the point of being careless.

After passing out, the junior signalmen were due some leave. Kriss watched his friends pack and prepare to go to their various homes. But where was he to go?

His Christmas leave had been spent at the children's home, and, with the money he had saved from his army pay, Kriss had had much pleasure in buying Riba an alarm clock/radio. It was the first time he had ever been in a position to buy his brother an expensive present. He told all his friends about life in the army, about firing weapons and sleeping out on the moors during exercises, often exaggerating and stretching the truth to make the maximum impression. It was the last time he was to stay at Village Road.

By Easter the children's home had closed and Riba had been moved to a new home in Cuffley, just north of London, where there was no room for Kriss.

So now there was some concern, and the army's caring side came to the fore: one of the N.C.O.s and one of the officers offered to look after him. Kriss was grateful for both invitations but hesitated to accept. Although they had now left the children's home, Kriss was still in touch with Brian and Shirley Martin, and when they suggested he come and stay with them Kriss was delighted to take up the offer, and so he headed south to London.

After a six-week break, Signalman Akabusi reported to Catterick in Yorkshire to begin his training in data-telegraphy. He was taught to type, operate a teleprinter, use a tape relay machine and decipher codes. He had to learn how to handle classified information and how to address messages in correct standard army style. Kriss was quick, and discovered what it was like to be excited by learning.

He was not entirely office-bound during this period. Military training continued with drill and exercises, and Kriss spent a lot of time playing various sports. In particular he was still keen on football and basketball. Yet word had reached Catterick that Aki was a runner. And no ordinary runner, but a 'flyer'.

While still a junior, his promise and potential as a 400 metres runner had been spotted both by Ian Mackenzie and the senior physical training instructor at Ouston. They had put him in for his first race and when Kriss had not appeared too keen on the idea he was told in brusque military fashion by his troop sergeant, 'Akismith, don't argue. YOU WILL RUN!'

At the time, Kriss preferred the sports where there was more competitive fun and a greater chance of taking things easy between bursts of activity. Running, especially the hard training that went with it, could hurt. To have protested would have got him nowhere, however, so he took his place at the start of the 400 metres in a pair of borrowed, standard issue army spikes. When the gun fired, he set off. He ran without any undue exertion, and won.

'Aki, you went like the wind,' they told him afterwards.

Catterick, in the summer of 1976, was Kriss's first season of competitive running. To begin with he did no serious training and looked on his running as just one of his many sporting interests.

Before long, and although only seventeen and eligible to run as a junior, he found himself racing against a number of very good seniors. Ian Mackenzie, who by this time had also been posted to Catterick, warned him to be careful as he entered this new league.

Kriss was still not an enthusiastic runner, but he enjoyed his growing reputation, one which was to become firmly established amongst those who knew him at Catterick, following his race against a formidable and very experienced Kenyan. Although Kriss did not win, he was impressively close, crossing the line in just over 51 seconds, taking 2 seconds off the time he recorded in his race at Ouston. Despite his lack of formal training, he was fit and had a fluid natural style and long stride.

Ian Mackenzie took him in hand and at weekends invited him to his home at Bedale where, on a school football pitch, he put him through his paces. By this time Kriss had qualified to compete at the Army Junior Championships and had a target to aim at. And when the day came for Kriss to travel down to Aldershot he took with him a special present from Ian—a new pair of yellow Adidas spiked running shoes.

He was not yet eighteen and running against soldiers who

were a year his senior. Inevitably he was somewhat overawed by his surroundings, but he did not let his emotions or nervousness effect his performance on the track. Perhaps, as was to happen so many times later, his performance was lifted by the occasion itself. He won and became the army 400 metres junior champion, the first of many athletics titles he was to hold. Ian Mackenzie recalls seeing the sheer joy in Kriss's face when they met for the first time after the race.

Away from the track Kriss was learning some of life's lessons the hard way. Kriss was very careful with money, almost to the point, he now admits, of being miserly. It was a form of security to know that his army pay was mounting up. The army provided all his food and accommodation and he had little need for anything more than basic pocket money. By the time he was at Catterick he had saved hundreds of pounds. As the army kept his bank book, one of the N.C.O.s, who was heavily in debt, approached Kriss for a loan. Kriss was, as usual, eager to please and completely trusting. He knew nothing of the man's money problems and was confident he would see his money returned shortly. Weeks passed and no effort was made to return the cash. Eventually—after Kriss had been posted abroad—he raised the matter with his troop sergeant, who was appalled to learn what had happened. As the N.C.O. who had borrowed the money was now in Northern Ireland, his commanding officer had to intervene to insist the money was returned.

Social life for Kriss was centred on his army friends and occasional forays into the local towns. He remembers meeting an art student at a disco in Darlington. After a good evening, he offered to take her home. She demurred, saying it was quite unnecessary, but Kriss insisted and accompanied her on the train from Darlington, via Middlesborough, to Saltburn-by-the-sea, arriving on the evening's last scheduled service. He escorted her to her house and waited to be invited in. 'Goodnight,' said his evening's partner firmly. Kriss spent the night at the railway station.

Life at Catterick, although still disciplined, was a little easier for the junior signalmen than it had been at Ouston. No longer were they required to get up at 5.30 in the morning. As they got to know each other better as individuals, they felt less need to indulge in their overtly macho barrack-room chat. Kriss and his fellow trade trainees continued to rate their status according to the number of weeks or months they had been in the army and there was a high quota of swearing and ragging, but, by and large, life was generally less harsh.

Kriss willingly absorbed army lore and, because of his success on the track, continued to be respected and well liked. The masculine, chauvinist ethos of the barrack room appealed to him and he to it. He did not normally drink to excess, as many others did, and he now prefers to forget the one evening when he had consumed too much vodka and was publicly embarrassed by a stripper at a party. In general, however, he was becoming more mature in his outlook from meeting and talking with the many experienced soldiers who passed through Catterick for short refresher courses. He finished his training in December and now, eighteen years old and a legal adult, he waited to hear what the army had in store for him.

4

Lippstadt – and Monika

Kriss was hoping for an overseas posting. He thought of Hong Kong, Cyprus and Gibraltar. In the event he was sent abroad, but not to a country which could claim to have an exotic reputation or climate. He was sent to Lippstadt in Germany to join 22 Signal Regiment.

He was nevertheless excited by the prospect. The last thing he had wanted to do was stay in England. So, one Sunday in the new year of 1977 he reported to Luton airport with his kitbag and a suitcase of civilian clothes and personal belongings. The flight to Germany was his first trip in an aeroplane since early childhood. When the plane landed at Gutersloh, everything to Kriss appeared curious and new. He was intrigued and amused to see familiar signs and advertisements in a foreign language. The countryside was covered in snow and the bus to the army camp was driving on the righthand side of the road.

When the new intake arrived, they first had to report to the guard room. Kriss was told he would be in Juliet Troop. 'Where's Juliet troop?' he asked innocently. 'Don't ask stupid questions,' came back the reply. 'Look at the board.' Kriss had learned another important lesson in army life, he was no longer a beginner and was now expected to know things and think for himself.

He then discovered that to his mates in Juliet Troop he was the new boy. 'Hello, Sprog,' was the first greeting when he arrived. Somebody waved him in the direction of his room and the next words addressed to him were, 'Sprog, see you in the crutch at half past four.'

The crutch turned out to be a recreation area. There Kriss introduced himself to the others in Juliet Troop. Once they knew a few basic facts about his life, they returned to talking and laughing amongst themselves and Kriss felt out of things. He recalled what he had been told back in England. Once you have finished your basic training and trade courses you are in the real army and you have to fend for yourself, think for yourself. There will be no one to wake you up, tell you when it is time for breakfast or tell you to keep your kit and your living space clean and tidy. You will be responsible for yourself. You will be given duties and will be expected to carry them out, without being supervised.

For Kriss it was a new experience. With Juliet Troop Kriss was still sharing a room with a group of others and living a communal existence. Inevitably, given his cheery disposition, it did not take long for him to become more accepted, despite refusing to join in with the troop's drinking binges. If he joined them socially he would have only orange juice.

The day came when the troop decided that Kriss would have to learn how to drink alcohol with the rest of them. He was taken to a bar and his orange juices were laced with vodka. When the alcohol began to do its worst, the troop laughed. The worse Kriss felt, the more his colleagues laughed. He does not know to this day how he returned to the block. It was his initiation into Juliet Troop.

From that day on Kriss was allowed to be teetotal and was often the only one of the troop to return to the camp at night sober. He was accepted because he could be loud and excessive with the best of them, without needing to get drunk. He had not taken a moral decision to forswear alcohol, his decision can be attributed more to his wish to be one of the crowd, but at the same time stand a little apart from it. He was also very careful with money and saw booze and cigarettes as being an unjustfi-able waste of cash. Yet, once caught up in the spirit of a party he could be as bawdy as the next man.

At weekends some of the soldiers would drink through the

day and night, going from camp bars to local pubs. Perhaps the troop needed to let off steam, as military service in Germany could be predictable and tedious. The army was in the country for historical and tactical, but not active, reasons. The British army had been there as the occupying force since the end of the Second World War. Strategically, it was still there to deter any threat from the Communist east. In practice there was very little for the soldiers to do. Their main function was merely to be there and be ready.

Kriss was quickly disillusioned by army life in Germany. He had gone expecting the army to need his newly acquired skills as a data-telegraphist. He found he was given jobs sweeping the roads and painting the generators and army waggons. On top of that there was a lot of time spent doing nothing. Only the afternoons had any set pattern, when there were periods set aside for weapons training and practising nuclear, chemical and biological warfare defence techniques. To learn anything new, Kriss found he had to apply to go on a course.

'Unless there was a cleaning parade, no one forced you to do anything. Most of the time you were looking for things to do. I spent a lot of time asleep. I knew very little about why the army was there, although we were told about our particular role. We went out on exercises, but it was a bit of a chore. It wasn't as I envisaged it. We would be in the back of a waggon. If it was winter, it would be cold. I wanted to be in a communications centre, and I never was. I was out there digging trenches, camouflaging the waggon, moving locations. It was like playing a big game I wasn't interested in. Every Monday I looked forward to the Wednesday sports afternoon and the next weekend.'

Kriss had been at Lippstadt six months when he fell into conversation with a fellow soldier. He told Kriss about a discotheque called Sloopy's in the town of Bielefeld, some thirty miles to the north. He invited Kriss to drive there with him that Friday. After the crude masculinity of the camp social life, Sloopy's was just what Kriss was looking for.

'I had the time of my life. Saw all these attractive German

girls. There was music and I danced and I had a corker of a time! It was a magnificent long weekend. There were other black guys and no need to get drunk. From that weekend onwards I would go to Sloopy's, or one of the other discos. My whole lifestyle changed. I became one of the guys, one of the in-crowd. I even started spending money and bought a radio-cassette.' With some of his new friends he even adopted a West Indian speech pattern to give himself an authenticity.

Shortly after his arrival in Germany Kriss went on a basic German language course. It was army policy to train some of the troops to be able to communicate with the local population, should they need any help when out on exercise. At Sloopy's, Kriss's knowledge of practical German grew rapidly. There was no better incentive to learn than having to find the right words and phrases in German to impress the local girls.

At this stage Kriss had two main interests, his social life and sport. He enjoyed the periods of physical training and competitive sport. When the summer came and games were held at the camp, Kriss won almost everything in sight, including the high jump. He competed with athletes from the other bases in Germany and won again, and in the summer of 1977 returned to England to compete for the second time in the Army Junior Championships at Aldershot.

He felt fit and confident, despite a noisy, bumpy and uncomfortable flight in a military transport aircraft, and won the 400 metres with ease, knocking a huge 3.3 seconds off his winning time of the year before. In the 200 metres he had a tougher race and won by a narrow margin.

The army gave him permission to spend ten weeks in England that summer, concentrating on his sport. He trained with the army's senior athletes, having been selected for the inter-service team. To the impressionable young signalman these top athletes were legends and Kriss, in his new army tracksuit, could hardly believe he was training alongside them. His wide-eyed enthusiasm could barely be contained when he was selected to run for the Army in the 4 x 400 metres relay against the Royal

Navy and the RAF, and the squad won.

Kriss had found many of his army duties back in Germany little more than drudgery, but this concentrated period of sport gave him a renewed motivation. When he returned to his duties in August, Kriss found his sporting success had won him the respect of his peers in Juliet Troop, although some others stationed with the unit at Lippstadt were envious of the privileges being granted to the athletic, but nevertheless very junior, member of the army.

It did not go unnoticed by certain people in authority that Kriss had missed important summer exercises. In addition, it was noted that he had been losing his sparkle and interest in matters military as his serious involvement in athletics grew. Excuses were found to give the loud, and rather lazy, young man, some of the less attractive duties. Kriss brought some of this extra unwanted attention on himself with his attitude.

However, in due course, the army took an imaginative decision. Kriss was given the opportunity to work at the camp gymnasium under QMSI Vic Bourgoise, a preliminary move leading to a possible transfer from the Royal Corps of Signals to the Army Physical Training Corp.

To begin with, Kriss had some reservations. He had found PT hard going during basic training, and wondered now if he would be able to cope with a higher standard. All the instructors seemed very much larger and harder than he was.

By the spring of 1978 Kriss had had enough of ordinary duties, particularly the double duties he was made to do to make up for the time he had been away. Whatever he did he could not, it seemed, please the lieutenant in charge of the troop and Kriss was always eager to please those around him. During the autumn and winter he had played a variety of sports—basketball, football, volleyball—and spent a great deal of time in the gym. He had grown to enjoy the company of the physical training instructors.

After comparing and weighing the options in his head, Kriss took a decision. He would give the gymnasium a try. It was a chance to be given responsibility, to hold a more respected job on the camp and to look ahead to a first promotion to lance-corporal. There were training courses to go on and a lot of hard work lay ahead, but Kriss now relished the challenge. He dismissed the thoughts he had entertained of leaving the army and looking for a new career.

But first there was the 1978 athletics season to negotiate. It turned out to be a season when Kriss lacked both success and direction. The army gave him every chance to succeed, and yet it was not a good year for him. Although a member of the Army Inter-Services Championships squad, he did not compete. All through his career Kriss has tended from time to time to experience seasons of little, if any, improvement. He will hit a plateau and need to find a new approach to training to put him back on the right path. 1978 was the first such season. In terms of statistics: in 1976 he had run the 400 metres in 52.4 seconds, had improved this to 49.1 seconds in 1977, but in 1978 could not run faster than 50.2 seconds. Before the end of 1978, however, Kriss was on the way to finding that crucial new approach, as an indirect result of an all-important meeting in a German disco.

The Atlantic Disco in Gutersloh specialized in playing soul music. Much of its unique atmosphere was the product of its exuberant clientele, and Signalman Akabusi, or Aki to all his friends, was its most exuberant customer. The regulars, mainly British and American soldiers and German girls, would say that the evening was never truly under way until Kriss turned up. He would arrive in a sporty car and park it right outside the main door. Then, dressed in a basketball vest, shorts and trainers, with a towel round his neck, he would make a noisy and conspicuous entrance. He would shout greetings to his friends across the room and no one could fail to notice his arrival. He would greet each of the girls he knew with a kiss, and the day any girl received a kiss from Kriss she knew she was in with the crowd.

Eighteen-year-old Monika was allowed by her parents to stay out until midnight. They knew she frequented the Atlantic

Disco, and it did not worry them unduly that it had a reputation for attracting soldiers, particularly black soldiers—as long as she returned home on time. Monika found the vibrant atmosphere and the steady beat of the music exciting. She would be taken to the disco by one of Kriss's friends, another soldier—a much quieter character called Tony. She regularly watched the extrovert Aki organizing the revellers and almost running the place.

Monika came from an ordinary German working family. Her father was an engineer at a local factory. He was in steady employment and over the years of Monika's childhood the family's basic standard of living became slowly more affluent. They lived in a four-bedroomed rented flat. Monika was the eldest child and had two younger brothers. From an early age she had been interested in dance, gymnastics and ballet, and was hoping to become a dance and physical education teacher.

One day Monika knew that Tony had to be away and that, once her father had driven her to the disco, she would have no transport home. So she approached his friend to see if, the next week, he would be able to give her a ride back to her house in his car. Kriss offered to go one better and pick her up as well.

'Everyone was welcomed to our house,' Monika recalls. 'My father would say, I don't care what colour they are as long as they come in here and behave themselves. So in Kriss walked. He spoke very little German and my parents did not speak any English. But he tried to make conversation and he is the sort of person who doesn't mind being laughed at if he makes a mistake.' (Today Kriss's German is good if unconventional. He can converse freely and even be interviewed by German television without problem, but Monika admits it sounds a bit common and he has picked up a number of slang expressions which are unlikely to be found in any phrase book.)

That first evening was a good evening, and others followed. Kriss replaced Tony as Monika's partner. He became a regular visitor to her home. She remembers how he would watch football on the television with her father and become so excited that he would slip out of his chair. 'What's the matter with this guy?'

her father asked. 'He can't even keep still long enough to stop himself falling out of his chair.'

Monika's parents did not take the relationship between their daughter and the young soldier too seriously. He did not, at first, appear to them to be someone who took anything seriously himself. He was always laughing and joking. But they found him kind and keen to help. They grew to like him. Their only reservation was his choice of dress. When not in his disco gear he would turn up in an old blue overall full of holes. This normally created no problem. But Monika's parents invited Kriss for Christmas—Christmas Day is also Monika's birthday. As the day approached, they became increasingly anxious that he might turn up in his usual garb. It was needless anxiety. Monika had a quiet word, asked Kriss to come in a proper pair of trousers, and he readily agreed.

Monika knew that Kriss had had many girlfriends. Kriss also knew that the beautiful blond German girl he was seeing on a regular basis would have no problems in attracting a replacement escort. After six weeks without a cross word between them, they had a disagreement. Monika reacted by saying that she had her doubts about the relationship and was not sure if she wanted it to continue. She expected Kriss to respond as earlier boyfriends had, by saying that of course they had a future together, and that he hadn't meant what he had said during their argument. Instead Kriss surprised her. He picked up his hat and walked out of her room. Kriss had called her bluff, and it was Monika who called after him, asking him to stay.

One of Monika's brothers was later to observe that the only reason Kriss and his sister stayed together was that Kriss would not let her play 'silly games' with his emotions. From long childhood experience Kriss was emotionally hardened.

The more Monika came to know Kriss, the more she heard from him about his childhood. It seemed extraordinary to her that he could have been left by his parents at such a young age. She asked him questions which Kriss was prepared to answer but he did not volunteer much information. It no longer seemed to him to be relevant. From what she did glean, Monika formed a very negative image of Kriss's mother. Meeting Clara later did nothing, in her mind, to dispel those images. To this day she fails to understand why Clara left her sons to be brought up by strangers.

Although Monika's childhood had been spent within the framework of a family, she discovered as she spoke more to Kriss that they had a shared experience. Both had, at different times taken on a responsibility for a younger brother. In Monika's case it was as she grew older, when her mother's health was failing fast. Her brother was then at his junior school, but he would sometimes come home and find his mother unable even to open the door to him. To the outside world everything appeared respectable and normal. Alcoholism is an illness, but not one which a family calls to the attention of the world. In these circumstances, Monika's father could hardly cope with his own emotional turmoil and stress, and so it was left to Monika to find the necessary inner resources and strength to manage affairs. Monika had to carry a heavy burden of responsibility, and the experience made her a tougher person. It also enabled her to understand more about Kriss and why he had constructed a tough emotional shell around himself.

As Kriss and Monika became an established couple, relations outside the immediate family came to hear of Monika's deepening friendship with a young black British soldier. A relationship, let alone an engagement or marriage, between a couple from different races is a direct challenge to attitudes and prejudices. Families and friends on both sides can feel such a union is wrong. That a black man should partner a white girl is a very threatening attack on the attitudes which still lurk just beneath the surface of the European psyche. It implies an equality of the races. Two generations ago, it was officially taught in Germany that the white, the Aryan, race was superior. Self-confidence in one's nation and oneself depended on believing that. For a black man to penetrate that shield of supposed superiority was a direct violation of the individual's and the nation's sense of self-worth.

Monika's grandmother, her father's mother, was outspoken in her opposition. She said to Monika's face that she could come to visit her but 'he is not to come through my front door'.

'She was a Christian and went to church regularly,' says Monika. 'But I was backed up by my parents and my father's brother and his whole family and they all told her how wrong she was. Obviously there was no way I was going to see her without Kriss.

'She is a person who had lost her husband during the war and had two little children at the time. She was, back in those days, very poor and starved. She had become very hard in herself and there was no way she could have coped with life if she had been too loving. She had also been brought up as one of the generation of Germans who'd had the ideas of racial purity preached at them from an early age. She had memories of black American soldiers entering Germany in 1945 and of how she was told they had treated German women.

'We did not go to see her for a long time, and she knew she was fighting a battle she was not going to win. Kriss was really good about it. "You have to understand." he said, "She is old. She has been brought up to believe all people of other races walked around with a knife in their pockets. I will prove to her I'm different, it's not like that." And he has certainly managed it. She absolutely adores him now. He is the only character in the whole family who will put his arm around her. She comes across as so hard and unloving, and Kriss ignores all that and treats her as you should treat an old woman, with love and respect. She feels so close to him now. It is quite amazing.'

Monika's other grandmother is now in her nineties, living in a home. 'When we go to see her and she is sitting in a room with other elderly people, she will say to me, "Did he really have to come? Did you really have to bring him? The others here will see him?" Kriss laughs. She is just so old, he understands. He still comes with me to see her.

'My uncles say he is welcome to their house but also add that they wouldn't want a daughter of theirs to marry a man from a different background. They admit it. While I feel offended, Kriss is far less so. They are at least honest about their feelings, he will say. Luckily my parents and my brothers didn't think like that in any way.'

Monika says she always knew her husband would be black. She has a stark memory of seeing a black man for the first time when she was a child of seven. She had been underweight and thought to be a sickly child and had been sent away for six weeks to a children's convalescent home. At the end of her time away she returned to her own home by train. She had arrived at her local railway station and was with her mother and grandmother.

'As we walked off the station I bumped into a black man. I had never seen one before. I was so shocked and frightened and scared. But this man was so kind to me. I don't know what he said, but I remember walking away from the station feeling so attached to him. I felt so drawn towards this man. I never saw him again, but from that day onwards I had black dollies and my special dolly Jenny was jet black. As I grew older I became drawn towards African and West Indian music, and the people. It wasn't a romantic image, it was just there, one of my feelings. I have always felt at home with them. They have got something white people haven't got.

'I used to think I would like to have been black. I would admire black women, they seem stronger and more expressive. I felt minor. When I was in a group with black women and I was the only white woman I would never feel superior because of my colour. But I have no crisis within myself about my colour.'

When Monika first met Kriss she could have had no idea that she was getting to know a potential world-class athlete. He was at the time a good, but by no means outstanding, army runner who had just had a bad season. He was not in regular training and although he had an enthusiasm for the track, his running was not his entire life. They quickly discovered they shared an interest in many sports, and physical education in general, and Monika persuaded Kriss to think about renewing the earlier contacts he had made with the local athletics club.

This was the important move Kriss needed to rekindle his interest and lift him off his plateau. Monika made the first approaches and Kriss started to attend training sessions with LG Gutersloh on a regular basis. He came to the attention of the leading German coach, Hansi Bohme, who told him to dedicate himself to his running. It was not satisfactory for him continually to turn up for training as an athlete carrying a variety of injuries from soccer and other sports.

Many international sportsmen and women are recording their peak performances at the age of twenty. Indeed swimmers have often retired from the pool by that stage in life. Kriss, in sporting terms, has been slow to reach his maximum potential. For four years, from twenty to twenty-four, he made good and steady progress as a 400 metres runner. He won many club and army races, but was not world class. He considered himself to be a professional army physical training instructor who ran well as a hobby. It was a hobby he took seriously, and one which gave him kudos in army circles, but he was by no means a full-time athlete. His achievements on the track and his colourful personality made him a popular sporting figure in Gutersloh. Wider recognition was yet to come.

Meanwhile it was his brother who was putting the name Akabusi before the public. Riba, the quiet one who preferred his own company to that of the crowd, had decided to become an actor. He made his acting debut in a film in 1977 and over the next three years was much in demand. It might seem a surprising decision for Riba to have taken, given his personality. Acting, however, is a form of disguise. It enables the actor to present a confident face to the public while in reality he, or she, is hiding behind a mask. Riba appeared in two films, *The Class of Miss Macmichael* and *Quadrophenia* and had parts in nine television productions. His appearances on stage in the London West End, in *The Rear Column* and *White Deer* were well received by the critics.

Kriss remembers the pride he felt in his younger brother's

success, on seeing his name displayed prominently outside the theatre where he was performing. He was pleased that Riba was making his own way in life. He had always encouraged Riba to follow his own interests and not to feel he had to copy or emulate his older brother.

During one period of leave, Kriss went to see him in the West End. 'He was good. I thought he was going places. He had the ability to be able to get into a part. In one of his films he played the part of a man who was mentally ill, and ever since that part he went like that. That could have been the final straw. He could really get inside the characters he was portraying.'

Riba's success did not, however, last. Acting is a precarious business and by the end of 1979 Riba was finding it increasingly difficult to get parts. The worry put a greater strain on his already stressed state of mind. The end result was a breakdown.

Meanwhile Kriss's life in the army was progressing well. His relationship with Monika had brought a stability to his life, and becoming an army physical training instructor had given him a new and necessary motivation. At the end of the summer of 1978 he had attended a six-week course in army physical training in Aldershot which qualified him to assist the experienced instructors in the gym back at base.

For two years, as an assistant instructor, Kriss would carry out the battle fitness tests, being responsible for a squadron— around 200 men—from 22 Signal Regiment. Every soldier is expected to maintain a degree of physical fitness in accord with his age and responsibilities and this fitness has to be tested on a regular basis. Typically, a group of twenty or thirty of the younger men wearing boots, denim trousers and a tee-shirt, would be taken by Kriss on a 15-minute run-cum-walk on roads and tracks around the camp. He would then have to time them back, giving them $11^1/_2$ minutes to cover the same distance. Kriss stayed with them all the way, running at the front to help the leaders and then falling back to encourage the stragglers, making sure he was always at the finishing line with his stop watch after $11^1/_2$ minutes precisely. His fitness, persuasive powers and enthusiasm were ideal qualifications for the job.

By this time Kriss was a lance-corporal, but he was still the junior of most of the men he took out for the test. He even had to accompany the colonel, although being an older man his test was less rigorous. N.C.O.s and junior officers would be taken out in a group, while senior officers were allowed to take their tests alone. For a lance-corporal to encourage his colonel to run or walk faster requires a certain tact. Kriss found the best policy was to keep him informed of the distance to be travelled and the time remaining, including a respectful 'sir' in every sentence.

Each man was expected to be self-motivated: Kriss was there to enable each soldier to do his best. Sometimes there were failures.

'I wouldn't tell a major that he had failed in front of a private. He knew he had failed and I knew he had failed, but we would wait until later to discuss it. I would probably suggest some remedial training which we would do to enable him to pass the test at the next attempt. At the end of the day he might have to be referred to the medical officer.'

Kriss found that the general standard of fitness in the army was good, and certainly much higher than the standard found in an equivalent civilian population. The younger and stronger soldiers also had to undergo a combat fitness test. They had to carry a weapon and a backpack, wear a helmet, and travel eight miles, at the end of which they still had to have the energy to climb into the back of a large army truck. Kriss also had to organize assault course tests and training.

Normally Kriss had to lead and encourage by example, although on the combat fitness test he was excused the backpack. In a busy period Kriss would conduct two or three battle fitness tests in a day. These could involve groups or single officers. In the same day he might also have to organize and demonstrate the tougher test schedules. In addition Kriss would be preparing soldiers to take or retake their various fitness exams. He would put them through their paces in the gymnasium, organizing circuit training and sports.

'I could bully the lazy and reluctant ones but was always careful not to embarrass people in front of other guys. I would make jokes and keep it light-hearted. But if I said I wanted someone for remedial training, that's where the real bullying could go on. I would push people up to their limits. I might have been just a lance-corporal but I had the authority of the Quarter Master Sergeant Instructor. They looked up to me. I might not have had the rank, but I had the authority. I represented the QMSI. If I was putting an officer through his paces, I had the authority of the adjutant. That was the military system. If I had a captain, I would call him "sir", but still tell him what to do. "Sir, that's not good enough. Go and do ten press-ups." He would have to do it. But most of these guys were pretty well self-motivated. To fail the battle fitness test would have brought shame on themselves and their regiment.'

One of the officers Kriss had to test was the lieutenant from Juliet Troop. He was not at peak fitness and failed his battle fitness test twice. Kriss had to put him through the appropriate remedial treatment, aware that while he, as a lance-corporal, might have the authority in the gymnasium, the lieutenant still had authority away from it and was responsible for writing the reports on Kriss which were important to his future career.

Kriss was an assistant instructor for two years and it was during this time, at the end of 1979, that he had sufficient confidence in himself and his chosen way of life to allow his curiosity about his family background to surface. He decided to make a journey to Nigeria, to meet his mother again, and to go to his father's village to learn more about the inheritance his uncle had first hinted at.

5

The Ibo Prince

By birth Kriss is an Ibo, or Igbo, a member of the Nigerian tribe of some fifteen million living in the eastern part of the country. This is the tribe which won the sympathy and admiration of the outside world during the Biafran War.

The early history of the Ibo people is unknown. It is thought they migrated to their present lands from the north. There is, however, one legend which claims the Ibo to be a lost tribe of Judah, and they have consequently been called by some the Jews of Africa. Place names such as Ubru, Ibru and Uburu have been said to have derived from the word 'Hebrew'. Male circumcision at eight days and the initiation ceremony for boys at the age of thirteen years, correspond to Jewish practice. It is even pointed out that blue eyes and a lighter skin colour are not uncommon amongst the Ibo. There is, however, no hard evidence to suggest that this Jewish connection is anything more than fanciful, but it illustrates a common idea that there is something special, or different, about the Ibo.

When Kriss arrived in the land of his forefathers, for the first time since infancy, he was approaching his twenty-first birthday. He had by then been in the British army for over four years. He had a German fiancée and a growing reputation as an athlete. He had been entirely educated in Britain. Not surprisingly, he came to Nigeria and saw his parents' country through the eyes of a European. His mother and father might have been expecting a returning son, but he arrived as a foreigner.

Kriss did not speak the language of his tribe. He did not have any understanding of the traditions, expectations and taboos which make up Ibo culture. The background assumptions shared by the Ibo concerning the patterns and purpose of life were entirely unknown to him. For it is almost impossible for any outsider fully to understand the subtleties and nuances of a society unless they have been steeped in it from early childhood.

In his book about the Igbo, the author Victor Uchendu writes:

'The Igbo world is a world peopled by the invisible and visible forces, by the living, the dead and those yet to be born.

'It is a world in which all these forces interact, affecting and modifying behaviour, a world that is delicately balanced between opposing forces, each motivated by its self-interest.

'It is a world in which others can be manipulated for the sake of the individual's status advancement, the goal of Igbo life.

'It conceives reincarnation as not only the bridge between the living and the dead, but a necessary precondition for the transaction and transfer of social status from the world of man to the world of the dead.'

The traditional Ibo view of the world is very much alive in Ibo culture today. Even Ibo who have a thorough understanding of western culture and the Christian religion will have many of their deeper attitudes coloured by the ancient Ibo view of this world and the next. And the world of Ibo culture would have been entirely bewildering, and possibly even seemed threatening, to a young British army lance-corporal.

Kriss might have had a chance to get his bearings, but for the fact that he had no way of standing back and being an observer of all the unfamiliar things going on around him. For it was quickly impressed on him that he was his father's first son and his father held a key hereditary position in Ibo society. Kriss was in fact a prince. Much was expected from him.

Ibo political, religious and social structures are closely intertwined. There is a hierarchy of chiefs. There are secret societies and priestly elders who embody, invoke and use the authority from the unseen world of the gods and spirits. Laws and customs concerning such matters as marriage and land rights are enforced through a fear of the supernatural, as well as physical or material punishment. There are oracles to be consulted about the future, which demand elaborate sacrifices.

Each person, it is believed, has a *chi* or guiding spirit. One's *chi* is part of a wider spirit world inhabited by deities, ancestral spirits and malignant spirits. There is the earth god; there are the forces of nature. Above all is Chukwu, the great spirit, the creator. He is described as unknown and wondrous, the origin of all things. Ibo say nothing exists or can exist without him. He sustains, protects and loves. He remains too distant for human comprehension and yet is close enough to understand our needs.

The early Christian missionaries found they could make the link between their God and the Ibo Chukwu. However, Ibo tradition dismisses the suggestion that Chukwu needs to be worshipped and praised. As he is the greatest, it is argued, only the greatest is suitable for him and acceptable to him, and human beings cannot provide the greatest. The function of prayer is merely to provide psychological satisfaction to the one who is praying, to help him or her off-load anguish. The enemy of Chukwu, the devil figure, is Ekwensu.

Traditionally, Ibo explain conception and birth within the framework of the spirit world. Conception, although biological in nature, also requires the consent of the deities and the willingness of a dead family spirit to be reincarnated. Children are returning ancestors, and parents normally hope that the returning spirit takes the form of a male child. A name has to be chosen for the child with great care. Kriss's Nigerian name, Kezie, means 'well formed' and his full name also includes the name of the great god, Chukwu.

Interestingly twins were considered an abomination, and an offence against the earth god. Only animals, it was said, reproduced through multiple births. In the past, twins were killed at birth. It was this practice which gave a first impetus to the acceptance of Christianity in Ibo society towards the end of the last century. The first people to be attracted to the new religion were social outcasts, including mothers of twins who had tried to save their children. The outcasts also included the Osu, a sub-group within the tribe, comparable to the Indian untouchables. They were a slave class which was both feared and reviled for religious reasons and may in the distant past have been the group from which human sacrifices were selected.

The Roman Catholic church took the missionary initiative, but progress was slow, perhaps because early converts had come from outside the mainstream of society. The church did not see any substantial growth in numbers of converts until the twentieth century, when it began to find some success through its policy of providing basic education. In 1906 there were fewer than 1500 Roman Catholics amongst the Ibo; by 1932 the total had grown to over 100,000.

The missionaries found Ibo culture and faith both strong and well-established. The Ibo were a spiritual people. It was not a case of missionaries coming into a new area and finding a belief-system in decline and waiting to be replaced. Indeed, where converts have been made it is arguable that Christianity has not replaced the existing culture, but added a new dimension to it.

A story is told of one of the Roman Catholic church's first baptisms. A man condemned to death for murdering an enemy had sought out the Roman Catholic priest. He asked to be accepted into the new faith. Just before he was due to have the sign of the cross made in water on his forehead he turned to the priest and asked, 'If I accept baptism, father, will it prevent me from seeing my enemy in the next life?'

'No,' replied the priest, 'I expect you will meet him in heaven.'

'Ah, good,' said the condemned man, 'then baptise me. I want to see him again, so that I can knock his head off a second time.'

Although Ibo political and social structures appear to form a hierarchy, they have also been described as embodying a democratic tradition. A village or district has a chief who acknowledges the authority of the regional figurehead. Yet in parallel there exist other networks of authority. Individuals can, through their wealth and achievement, gain titles. One of the achievements which could earn a man great status was to return from battle with the head of an enemy.

The various fraternities and societies were all instruments of government of a kind. There is also the age-grade system. Here, powerful organizations exist, open only to men of a certain age-group, and these can be substantially self-governing. There are too the masques, the performances of ritual and dance which wield power through the connections with the world of the supernatural which they are believed to have.

The spirits of the ancestors are never far away and they can approve or disapprove of what is done by the current generation. In traditional Ibo belief the soul or spirit of a person goes neither to heaven nor to hell but comes back to earth to join his lineage in order to fulfil his unaccomplished mission. The chiefs too are closely associated with the practices of spirit worship.

In his book *The Igbos of Nigeria*, John Njoku wrote, 'Igbo place emphasis on individual achievements and initiative. Individualism is rooted in a group solidarity.'

To maintain the cohesiveness of the group much emphasis was traditionally, and still is, placed on the arrangement of good marriages to form solid alliances between families. Senior Ibo men can have many wives. Kriss has a number of half-brothers and half-sisters from his father's marriages. Position in society is gained through the father's line.

Victor Uchendu emphasized the importance of acquiring that position. 'An Igbo without patrilineage is an Igbo without citizenship, both in the world of men and in the world of the ancestors.'

An Igbo man can have an extensive family, with children from a number of women. Living within the village compound, the children were traditionally a shared responsibility. They participated in the world of the adults. They went to market, helped work the land, went to funerals and feasts and took part in religious ceremonies. The compound is the traditional basic social and economic unit. It is made up of a number of independent, though interdependent, households, with a head who has ritual, moral and legal obligations. In an area where there are a number of compounds, one of the compound heads is the senior, according to his ancestral lineage. In many places he carries a branch from a special tree as symbol of his authority. He has a priestly function, in that he may sacrifice to the earth god, and has a presiding function when the group meets to debate issues of mutual importance; but he has no executive power.

Although Kriss, on his arrival, was able to speak English with his parents to discuss day-to-day matters, he had no way of bridging the cultural gap. It was as impossible for him to understand Igbo society as it is for a visitor to Britain to understand the complexities of the British legal system, the established church, the constitutional monarchy, the army, freemasonry and cricket.

When Kriss arrived in his father's home village of Umanachi, his grandfather was still alive. He was Duru Oji Aku the first. Clara Akabusi describes her memory of him as that of a cheerful old man with two wives and many children. No one knew exactly how old he was, but it was reckoned that he was over ninety, from the evidence of his memory and recollections.

Daniel Akabusi, Kriss's father, was the first son of his first wife. Being the first son of Daniel, Kriss is destined to be Duru Oji Aku the third. Kriss's grandfather was much respected for his age, and his position as head of a minor, but significant, royal lineage. Duru Oji Aku the first told Kriss about his ancestors, particularly his own grandfather Ojunwa, who had not only been a famous slave-trader, but had achieved great status within the tribe for taking the heads of his enemies as trophies. Ojunwa had also protected his own people from being taken slaves by making a deal with the other, more powerful slave-traders: if he provided them with slaves from other villages, they would leave his people unmolested. Kriss was told that he, Kezie, was the reincarnated spirit of his great-great-grandfather.

Kriss would sit with the old man outside in the open, with his second wife translating. He would bring his grandfather a cold beer and then settle down to listen to the tales of his ancestors. Duru Oji Aku the first was almost blind but could see just enough of Kriss's shape to learn to recognize the grandson and eventual heir he had not seen for eighteen years.

Kriss enjoyed the company of his grandfather and developed an affection for him, but he was too steeped in his British ways to enter into his family's culture. Everything seemed so strange, he could not relax. He was shown the kola nut ceremony whereby important visitors are welcomed to the village. The elders of the village break a special, bitter-tasting nut and pass the pieces around, in order of seniority, reciting proverbs and incantations. He could understand enough of this ceremony and its purpose to be able to join in.

However, he was repulsed and embarrassed by one special ceremony focused on himself. It involved Kriss slitting the throat of a goat and allowing, so he recalls, the blood of the animal to spill on his leg. On the morning of the ceremony he refused to go ahead. The sacrifice had to be made by proxy.

One can only guess at what the village made of the returning son. He would have been a curiosity for sure, but it would have been difficult for many to understand how this young man who looked like one of them could be so socially ill-equipped and unschooled.

Kriss in turn was quite bemused and amazed by his welcome. For much of his life he had been a nobody: the unwanted foster child shunted from pillar to post, the boy from the children's home, signalman number 24354835 in the British army. Now here he was, being treated as royalty. And it was no dream: he was a prince. Not, admittedly, the prince of a major royal line. Nevertheless, to several thousand people in the area around his family village in eastern Nigeria he was a man of high rank and birthright, a man of high prestige and honour.

'The first time I arrived at Umanachi I was astonished. The villagers were just going crazy, shouting "Welcome, welcome!"

Then a twenty-one gun salute went off. This totally set me back, as I hadn't realized how big I was really supposed to be out there. Women came out from all over the place. The square filled up with women. They were all dancing and singing traditional songs. This went on for a couple of hours and as news spread around people started coming with livestock, chickens, goats. Others shared kola nuts and gave me their blessings.

'I'm not known as someone who holds back. But I looked around and couldn't take in what was happening. I tried to associate with it all, but didn't have the same cultural roots and was left muddled and bewildered. Obviously I accepted everybody's greetings and gifts and talked to people. I was staggered that all this was for me. I kept saying to myself, "I'm a signalman in the army, this can't be for me." I had never been in this position of exaltation. It was a time of wonderment.'

Kriss enjoyed his three weeks in Nigeria, but knew his life lay with his British army career for the foreseeable future. He discovered, before he left, the down side of being held in high esteem as a royal figure.

'Within myself I was still a child, and I am a very playful character. In the children's home I had always been running around, playing with the guys. When I was at the village I tried to do the same thing. There were lots of children there from eight to sixteen and I would play football with them, and hide-and-seek—messing around with them in general. That was frowned upon. Listen, I was told, you are *Duru*. You don't mix with the people like that. That is not what is expected of you. You are educated. People want to see you come in your suit and speak articulately. You are the heir apparent. You are also the educated westerner and you cannot allow people to think you fool around and waste your time. It was frowned upon that I liked to play with the children.'

Kriss was taken by his mother to be presented to the senior royal chief of the whole region. He met many people and was told many things about his inheritance. He retained in his memory only part of what he was introduced to, and an even smaller part of that he understood.

From a country where the average temperature is 85 degrees Fahrenheit, Kriss returned to a European winter. It was to be two years before he returned. He had satisfied his initial curiosity about his background. Much of the way of life he had found alien, yet it was not until he revisited his Nigerian family with Monika that the cultural tensions surfaced. He was then no longer able to keep himself at an emotional distance from the inevitable clash of customs and expectations.

6

Athletics – and Marriage

'Inside—UK men's top fifty'. From the words on the cover of the 27 October 1979 edition of *Athletics Weekly*, Kriss knew that inside the magazine he would find the latest annual lists of Britain's leading athletes, compiled from their performances during the summer season. From the training and competition he had had in Germany, he knew his own times over 400 metres had improved by two seconds. He had taken that important step up from his personal plateau. But how did he now compare with other British 400 metres runners? What times had they recorded during the same period?

Heading the list of the top fifty 100 metres sprinters was Allan Wells. He also headed the 200 metres list. Below him were such familiar names as Daley Thompson, Ainsley Bennett, Mike McFarlane, David Jenkins and Steve Scutt. Many of the names also appeared on the official list of the top fifty British 400 metres runners of the year—plus a few others, including Sebastian Coe who had recorded a time of 46.87 seconds over the distance.

Kriss looked down the tally of names and there, at number 41, saw 'Chris Akabusi, 48.3'. The compilers had misspelt his name, but it mattered little. Kriss had it confirmed in print that he was one of his country's leading athletes.

He had certainly made a name for himself with his new club in Gutersloh. Not only had he been faster than any of his fellow team members by nearly a second over 400 metres, he had also been the fastest over 200 metres and run 100 metres in 11.1 seconds. By the end of the season his collection of medals, shields and cups had grown rapidly.

On returning from Nigeria Kriss settled back into a familiar routine. He was working at the gym, seeing Monika on a regular basis, training with the athletics club in Gutersloh. His three weeks in Africa had been a curious interlude. He had been intrigued by what he had discovered about himself and his past, but felt far more at home in the familiar surroundings of track and army camp.

For Kriss, the 1980 athletics season was one of consolidation. He continued to represent Gutersloh, when in Germany, and also competed in the various service championships. When *Athletics Weekly* published the new top fifty in November 1980, Kriss, his name now spelled correctly, had risen to number 32 in the British rankings, with a time of 48 seconds. He was one place ahead of Daley Thompson, but a long way behind the number one, David Jenkins, who had recorded 45.29 that season.

After his leap forward the year before, Kriss had now reached another plateau. He was to remain there for two more seasons, being unable to break the 48 second barrier in either 1981 or 1982. It was as if success was on hold.

Kriss ran and enjoyed competing. In army circles and at his club he was still a consistent winner, but he was given no reason to suppose that greater things lay ahead.

In 1982 he had slipped to number 40 in the British ranking, 2.5 seconds behind the leader. The reason for this can be found in Kriss's own priorities. From the point of view of his army career, Kriss had decided that his future was in physical training and he applied to be sent on an advance course. The course was not only designed to enable him to take greater responsibility in the gym, but was also a selection test for entry to the elite Physical Training Corps. To be accepted on the course, Kriss also had to take the written and practical exams required for promotion from lance-corporal. These proved to be no problem and Kriss began his advanced course in September 1980.

Normally an assistant instructor who completes the advance course returns to his unit for a year before being called back to the next stage. Kriss did so well that he was immediately invited to stay on at Aldershot and take the junior and senior probationary courses.

It was a significant decision, both for Kriss and for the army. At the time it was noticed, Kriss says, that although many of the assistant instructors were black, very few were progressing and getting into the PT Corps. Kriss had even been told unofficially, when he had completed his first course and become an assistant, that he should not set his sights too high; very few black people became members of the corps. It was an example, says Kriss, of racism but also of tradition. Units, corps, regiments in the army are often hide-bound by their traditions. If they have not had a black member, or rarely admit black people, then it runs counter to that unit's tradition to admit one.

'But what is racism?' Kriss wonders. 'Is it racism to be called a coon or a black bastard when on parade? I remember on one of my advanced PT courses being out on a stretcher run and being racially abused all the time by one of the instructors. Was this racism, or was this designed to test me under pressure?' In this particular instance Kriss believes racism was at the root of the abuse.

The same instructor later set Kriss and some of his colleagues a test. It involved drawing up a series of planned moves in a particular sport. It was one of Kriss's specialities. He coached his colleagues and wrote their plans for them. When the time came for the marks to be given out, everyone got an A grade, except Kriss, who got a C. Kriss suspected racist motives, but also wondered whether he was being tested, the army thinking that out in the real world as an instructor he would have to be prepared to take racial abuse.

Kriss left Aldershot in July 1981 as a sergeant, again with the unofficial word in his ear: 'Well done, but don't expect too much. The Corps has never had a black officer.'

This made Kriss quite determined. He was going to be the

first black officer. In the event, his athletics career took precedence over pursuing that particular goal, though Kriss is in no doubt that had he set his mind on it he would now be an officer. Again the question is raised in his mind. Was he being warned of army racism, or did the army deliberately set him a challenge because it wanted him as an officer? Perhaps the truth lies in between. Kriss would have become an officer, and the army wanted him as an officer, but because of a subtle and unspoken racism in the service it was going to take someone of his outstanding potential to break through the barrier. It could be argued that had Kriss been white, there would have been no doubt about him gaining a commission. Many years later, as Kriss was deciding to leave the army, he was asked to stay on, being told there was every chance he would become an officer. By that time, for many reasons, Kriss had decided he did not want to stay on in the army. And he certainly did not want to stay to become a token gesture.

The courses at Aldershot had clashed with much of the 1981 athletics season and Kriss did not compete in the army championships that year. He was, however, selected to run for the army against the other services and in the 400 metres beat the new army champion. Kriss was at peak all-round physical fitness, but he was not giving sufficient time to the specialist training which a top-line athlete needs. Consequently, while his performances on the track were consistently good, they were not improving.

Nevertheless the athletics club at Gutersloh was keen for their key runner to return to Germany. Club officials wrote to the army asking that Sergeant Akabusi be given a local posting. The army agreed and Kriss was given an attachment with the First Battalion, The Gloucester Regiment, serving in Munster. What the Army Physical Training Corps records did not show, however, was that Kriss's new unit was due back in the United Kingdom in September. So instead of joining them in Germany in August, after his six weeks' leave, he joined them instead at Tidworth on 7 September. He was responsible for the physical fitness of a thousand men, a fully fledged infantry battalion.

Kriss found that life with The Gloucesters was more formal than any he had known before. Colleagues were addressed by their proper ranks and titles, where Kriss had been used to using more familiar names. He also had to become accustomed to the day-to-day terminology of an infantry regiment. Instead of squadrons there were companies, for instance, and staff sergeants were known as colour sergeants. Kriss also had to become familiar with the administrative side of his work, learning how to indent, or apply, for equipment.

During 1981 Kriss had a break from army life when he returned to Nigeria for a second three-week visit. This time he was accompanied by Monika as his fiancée. Monika was fascinated by what she saw, but never felt at ease with Kriss's family. The culture gap was huge and unbridgeable. Being white and young and unmarried in a totally foreign environment, she was also, she realized later, in some potential danger. Like many of the countries of the world, Nigeria is a nation of contrasts. Lagos is like most modern urban centres, with its airport, office buildings and freeways. The country has known times of great prosperity brought about by the oil industry. However, away from the cities life continues much as it has for generations. It is a common pattern repeated throughout Europe and Asia as well as Africa that the twentieth century tends to concentrate in the cities, while out in the countryside living conditions, as Monika found, can still be very basic. Electricity was limited to the output of a single generator which provided light in the evening. There was no piped water and the brick-built house where she slept had lizards running around. The food was hot, spicey chicken or goat with rice.

'Kriss's father had many wives and also worked away from the village. When he visited I realized he was a man of position and authority. Everyone in the compound would obey him. He had a second wife living in the compound who had other children.

'I think Kriss's mother thought that she could change me

into a Nigerian wife. She soon found out that this was not going to happen. She would tell me off if I argued with Kriss, and said that I should concur with the wishes of my man. We also had problems in that, not only was I white, but I was also very thin. She tried to feed me on rich food and I said no. She would say that I ought to be fat, in that to be fat implied one had wealth. She was embarrassed by the fact that I was so skinny. And I really was. The way I dressed was a problem for her, and looking back I think I was wrong. If I ever went back I would try and conform more by wearing longer dresses and not wearing shorts. I would sit in a bikini and sunbathe. She got very upset, but at the time I did not want to give in.

'In the end Kriss and I fell out with his mother over me. Relatives came to visit and his mother thought I was wearing inappropriate clothing. Kriss stood up for me. Since then I haven't been back and I know I wouldn't be welcome there.'

Riba believes that the tension that exists between Monika and his mother is less to do with the fact that Monika is white and more with the characters of the two strong willed personalities. Outwardly Clara criticizes Monika's build. She thinks it is too thin for Monika to be a good wife and mother. To his mother, Riba says, Monika looks too much like a boy.

Kriss spent six good months with The Gloucesters but found the regiment made no special allowances for his athletics. Sergeant Instructor Akabusi was, to them, first and foremost a soldier. And while he had his specific job to do in the gymnasium, he also had his military responsibilities. On exercises he was detailed to be the commanding officer's bodyguard. He was therefore on call any time the C.O. needed him. His duties, in times of war, would have been to check locations with the military police and cover and protect the C.O. as he moved about. In peacetime these duties had to be rehearsed. Whenever there was an exercise requiring the presence of the C.O. Kriss had to be available. Consequently his athletics training programme suffered. Regular practice became increasingly difficult.

'It became apparent that I was not going to do my athletics properly. I spoke to the chairman of the Army Athletics Association. As a result I was posted to the First Battalion, The Prince of Wales' Own Regiment. They were stationed just a few miles away at Bulford on Salisbury Plain and I joined them in March 1982.'

This attachment was described later by the army magazine *Soldier* as the next vital link in the chain. 'His athletics-minded commanding officer gave him the go-ahead to do his Basic and Combat fitness training test statistics in the morning so that he could spend the afternoons looking after the battalion athletics team and his own training regime.'

On many occasions in later years Kriss was to express publicly how much he appreciated the latitude given him by the army to concentrate on his athletics. The army was not to know in 1982 how far the sergeant instructor's career was destined to go. As Kriss's achievements on the international athletics scene grew, the army enjoyed a significant public relations spin-off.

Back in 1982 the army could only trust in his potential. To give Kriss the opportunity to concentrate again on his sport was also good man management. Having trained a specialist regular soldier, there is no benefit to the army, or to the individual concerned, to allow him to stagnate during peacetime. Military exercises are all very well to keep regular soldiers in peak readiness if they have no other special non-military talents. Such exercises can be counter-productive if all they do is impede a key individual's personal development. That person, as long as he retains his combat fitness and is available as a soldier in times of war, is better off, in the meantime, pursuing his own interest.

In an interview in *Athletics Today* published in January 1991, Kriss told Mel Watman, 'At 24, when a lot of people may have decided to hang up their boots, I carried on. I was fortunate in that I was in the Army, and the Army gave me a lot of backing at that time in my career, whereas a lot of guys of 24 who haven't broken 48 seconds for 400 metres have to start worrying about their wife and kids.'

In Kriss's case, not only was he given the chance to persist with his athletics, he also got married—though it was a marriage which almost did not take place. Spending so much time in England had meant that Kriss and Monika had been seeing less and less of each other. They had flown back and forth between their two countries, buying cheap weekend off-peak tickets when leave, holidays and finances permitted, but were not able to see each other more than once every three or four weeks. In England Monika would stay with Steve and Joycelyn, or unofficially in camp. The regular disco-ing weekends were over.

Monika was by now living an independent life away from her parents' home. She had a flat of her own and was teaching dance and physical fitness. She had thought of moving to join Kriss, but her life was going well in Germany and all her friends were warning her that whatever she did she should not move to England. She was also concerned about her parents and younger brother. She was concerned that if she left Germany, her mother's health would decline. Kriss found this difficult to understand, as he did not fully appreciate the seriousness of her problem.

Eventually, at the end of the winter of 1982, Kriss decided their relationship did not have a future. Their most recent time apart had been longer than usual and Kriss had met someone else. She had just left her Swedish boyfriend and she and Kriss had also met at a discotheque. He came back from her house one day and telephoned Monika to break off the engagement.

'Sorry, it's history. We've had a great time together but things have moved on.'

Monika made an instant decision. Kriss could not, or would not, talk freely on the telephone. She had to see him face to face. She put the receiver down, jumped in her car and drove to the airport. Within hours she was in England.

The next day, Kriss was in his room at the sergeants' mess when there was a knock on the door. To his astonishment, there was Monika standing in front of him. She dropped her bag.

'I had to come to see you,' she said. 'We can't finish.'

'I don't even know how she found her way,' Kriss remembers. 'She had never before been to the sergeants' mess. Women were not allowed in. It really touched me, but I was adamant it was history. She began to talk to me. It was crazy trying to explain to her that it was over.'

In the course of the phone call and the journey and the meeting with Kriss, Monika says she realized just how much Kriss meant to her.

'Up until then I was always putting him on ice. Deferring a final commitment. I didn't want to let go of my lifestyle. But at the same time I wanted him to be there for me.'

Maybe, too, she would have suggested coming to live in England sooner had it not been for the anxieties she had for her family. She now decided she had responsibilities to herself and to her own future happiness as well as that of her parents and family.

They talked for a while and then Kriss had to go back to his duties.

'I came back later to find Monika sitting on my bed. She was wearing a turquoise tee-shirt with glittering dots. I looked at her. Such a nice girl, and I thought, "She really loves me." She had come so far to see me. And I wondered, would I ever be happy if she was with someone else. The other girl was fun, but this girl loves me and would do anything for me. My heart melted. "OK," I said. "We'll give it a try." And she said, "So we'll get married?" and I replied, "Well, yes, OK, why not?"'

It was hardly the romantic proposal of the century, but the result was that Kriss and Monika were married in the registry office in Salisbury on 2 April 1982. The wedding was planned quickly and Kriss rapidly completed all the necessary formalities with the registrar and the army. Kriss had to have an official interview to inform the officer commanding of his decision, and then had to visit the pay office to discuss such practical arrangements as married quarters and taking appropriate leave.

Steve Longworth describes being summoned rather than invited to the wedding, and then being amazed to discover that

Kriss had made all the arrangements including booking him and Joycelyn into a hotel. They were given such little notice that Steve had to arrange special leave from his department to attend.

At the short civil ceremony, Steve and Joycelyn were the witnesses. Monika's parents came and two other friends. Because of illness, Riba had gone to Nigeria and was unable to attend.

Monika's parents had given their blessing to their daughter and new son-in-law, but were disappointed that the wedding had not been held in Germany, where the ceremony would have been familiar and comprehensible to them. Kriss and Monika married in England because for a German woman to marry a British soldier in Germany involved going through a time-consuming legal process. They married in a registry office because, Monika claims, they were turned away by the church they approached. The clergyman quizzed them about their reasons for a church wedding. 'Did they attend church?' he asked. Monika is convinced, looking back, that behind all the questions lay the clergyman's reluctance to marry a mixed race couple. Having been turned away by one church, Monika refused to approach another.

When Kriss and Monika had first met it was Kriss who had been keen to get married. Monika had favoured waiting. Two years later, Kriss was the one who was more cautious. In the end, perhaps, it was the idea of security which Monika would bring to his life that won Kriss over. 'I didn't really think about the seriousness and sanctity of marriage, or the finality of being married. It didn't cross my mind. Before I knew it I was a married man.'

Monika gave up her flat and her job in Germany and moved to England to an army house. Once her decision had been taken she was not worried about living in a foreign country. She had travelled extensively around Europe with friends and sports teams, and knew she could make a home in most places.

Nevertheless the reality of making a home in married quarters at Bulford Camp in Wiltshire came as a shock. It was cold, and Kriss and Monika had very little money. It was an army settlement and all the other families living around were connected with the service. Apart from a German next-door neighbour, all the other women Monika met were 'typical English army wives'. She found she had little in common with them. Most of them had children and she did not. She was also surprised at the way a husband's rank made a difference to the way friendships formed.

To begin with Monika did not even understand the ranking system and when she learned the differences she could not comprehend why an officer's wife should be treated in any different way from a lance-corporal's. In the course of time, however, she realized that to the wives themselves these things did matter.

As for any newly married army couple, the army provided basic furniture and kitchen items for 4 Darwin Close. Before long the newly married couple found they could afford to buy a television, and Monika had some items of her own to contribute to the household which she brought over to England in a van.

After a short while Monika enrolled at local ballet and dance classes and her command of English rapidly improved. Within a short time she was able to start teaching classes in her new country. She was quickly in demand and introduced the new fitness programme 'aerobics' to the area. She ran children's movement and dance classes, and within a short time was taking fifteen classes of various kinds every week.

Monika says she was at the time always out and always busy. 'I was never sitting waiting for my husband to come home, if anything it was the other way round. In a new country there was so much to learn.' That summer she watched Kriss run at a number of army meetings and was pleased when he won, but she never, ever considered that one day his athletics would be his life.

In his time in the army, Kriss never had to fire a shot in battle. In his years of service, the cold war in Europe never resulted in the NATO and Warsaw Pact forces exchanging fire in anger. Nor was Kriss ever called upon to do a tour of duty in

Northern Ireland. The nearest he ever got to being called upon to put his professional training as a soldier into practice on the battlefield was at the time of the Falklands War in 1982, shortly after he and Monika were married.

They had just returned from honeymooon when, as Kriss remembers, one Friday the whole battalion, 'was called up on the square at Bulford. We were told we would be confined to camp that weekend on a high state of alert to go to the Falklands. I phoned Monika and told her that I could be sent to the Falklands on Monday. On the Saturday morning I was out running in the camp when the thought struck me, why am I training? The whole weekend I was thinking about it. Monika didn't want me to go. I even wondered about leaving camp and going to Germany. I told Monika I had to go. That Sunday I went to the shop and bought a little pad to write to Monika on. I looked around and thought, this could be the last time I see England.

'What really bugged me was that although I was prepared to go, and knew it was my duty to go, some of the guardsmen at the camp were really happy, really excited. They'd been training for fifteen years and at last were going to put everything they had learned into practice. They read the *Sun* and were into Argy-bashing. It wasn't so much that they were anti-Argy but that at last they would have live targets. I thought these guys must be crazy.

'On the Monday we got called up on the battalion square. I was ready to go. I think I might even have prayed. Then the colonel got up and said, "I've got some bad news for you." My heart sank, this was it, we were off. I would be away from Monika for weeks or months and might even never come back. But then he said, "You are not going to the Falklands." He explained that we were considered too young to go, and the Scots Guards would go instead. The feeling of relief was enormous. I phoned up Monika. And for the next couple of days, the world looked so different. All those silly things that get on your nerves no longer seemed important. I looked at the countryside and at plants with new eyes. I went down to the track in Southampton to train and it was incredible. I really felt emotional for England and all the things dear to me and familiar.

'That was the nearest I ever came to active service, but I then knew what the army was about. Until then I hadn't really appreciated that the army was about going to war. From then I knew that I would have to get out of the army. But the problem was the money was too good and the opportunities to do sport were so good. But I knew I didn't want to go to war and convinced myself that the Falklands thing was just a one-off and would never be repeated in my time. Little did I think that the Gulf War would happen a few years later, but by that time I was leaving the military.'

Spared from being parted by the Falkland Campaign, Monika and Kriss settled down to married life. Monika kept in regular contact with her parents in Germany, but often the news was not good. Not having had a constant or loving relationship with his mother, Kriss found it hard to understand how Monika felt about hers. There were times when Monika would be telephoned and asked to come home immediately as her mother was very ill, and Kriss would not appreciate the seriousness of the situation.

'Don't worry about her so much,' he would tell Monika. 'She's a grown woman.'

'But she's my mother,' Monika would reply, 'I must go.'

Kriss found it difficult to understand the attachment and love of daughter for mother; Monika says she now appreciates why he found it so difficult to understand. 'He had never felt that attachment himself.'

When her mother died, it was a time of both sadness and relief. Despite Monika's anxieties, it was only on the day of his mother-in-law's death that Kriss fully appreciated how seriously ill she had been. Even then he was detached from many of the family's emotions. Admittedly he was not a blood relation and had not known his mother-in-law all his life, as Monika and her brothers had done, yet he was very fond of her. The detachment from the family grief and trauma which accompanied her death was perhaps more to do with the way he had learned, in childhood, to protect himself from becoming emotionally involved and damaged by events outside himself. As a child, moved from one place of care to another, he had too often experienced the angry sorrow of finding that people to whom he had become attached were snatched away just as he had grown to love and trust them.

It was only following her mother's death that Monika felt sufficiently relieved of her family responsibilities to be able to concentrate on her own life. For a while she and Kriss looked after Mark, her eleven-year-old brother. He came to live with them in England. Monika and Kriss, who had not yet had a family of their own, were plunged into proxi-parenthood, with little experience of what was expected or involved. Mark had many troubling memories of his mother's decline. Monika had been emotionally hardened by the experience, which had also given her a determination not to repeat her parents' mistakes in her own life. She decided that whatever difficulties she and Kriss might face in their life they should never be suppressed or drowned, but faced and talked through.

On the lighter side, it was in 1983 that the Akabusi household acquired an extra member, Dillinger. He was a Doberman and became a loyal companion to Kriss on his training runs over the hills and downs. The loneliness of the long distance runner was no more. Where Kriss ran, so did his dog. Kriss, with the Doberman snapping playfully at his heels, became a familiar sight. As Kriss ran he would carry a stick and throw it for Dillinger to retrieve. It was a game which one day went wrong: Dillinger saw a man carrying a bicycle pump, mistook him for Kriss, and began to attack him. It was a playful rather than a vicious attack, but the victim was not to know the difference.

7

National and International

For the sender, John Le Masurier, the honorary secretary of the British Amateur Athletic Board team selection committee, it was just one of a pile of duplicated letters he signed on 29 May 1983. To Kriss, the recipient, getting the letter was one of the proudest moments of his life to date. He remembered the words of an army athletics colleague four years earlier, 'When you get one of these you know you've arrived.'

> Dear Kriss,
>
> I have pleasure in informing you that you have been selected to represent Great Britain and Northern Ireland in the match, GB & NI v USSR to be held at Alexander Stadium, Perry Park, Birmingham on Sunday 5th June 1983, in the following events: 400 metres and 400 metres relay squad. If for any reason you are unable to compete please contact me immediately.
>
> Yours sincerely,
>
> John Le Masurier

Nine months earlier, Kriss had finished the 1982 season well and truly stuck on his latest plateau. He had made no advances to boast of the entire summer. His time for the 400 metres had not shifted from 48 seconds for three seasons. He had regained his army and inter-services titles and not run badly, but he realized he was not in the first division of track athletes. His army duties no longer disrupted his training and he was in excellent physical shape, but he could not lift himself up from the lower echelons of the British Top Fifty. He had even thought of changing events and made an attempt at running 400 metres over hurdles. He ran and stuttered around the track. It was meeting a new athletics mentor, to take him on to the next stage in his career, which proved the turning-point.

Kriss knew of Mike Smith by reputation and had met him once when he had visited Aldershot. He knew that the South-ampton-based coach had encouraged and developed the talents of numerous athletes. As he was now based in Britain, Kriss wanted to make contact with a British coach and join a training squad of good runners. The first problem was finding the squad. Kriss knew roughly when they went out training, but where was a different matter. Mike believed in building up the general strength of his athletes and sent them out on tough out-of-season runs around the Hampshire countryside. For a number of weekends Kriss drove around the Southampton area looking for likely cross-country courses where he might find the squad. In the end, one Sunday morning, Kriss caught up with Mike Smith at the sports centre in Southampton.

Mike had heard of Kriss on the athletics grape-vine—that there was a 'chap in the army who was not a bad 400 metres runner and wanted to train with us'. It is Mike's unvarying policy never to seek out potential athletes and invite them to join him, but to let them find him. It is his way of sorting out who is really determined. So Kriss had to come to him, and when they met Mike made no special fuss. He agreed that Kriss could join as an ordinary member of his training group and, before long, Kriss was out running across the South Downs. After a few weeks of tough training, Kriss developed an injury. Mike remembers it as a knee to hamstring injury, 'typical of an athlete who isn't doing exceptionally well'. He dropped out of the group for a while, rejoining it for the winter training programme of 1982-83.

'It was very quickly obvious with Kriss that he had athletic ability. And he also had determination. I knew he had run for the army and that he had not broken 48 seconds. That is good 400 metres running but not the sort of time that would lead me to think we've got a real find here. He was, at that immediate time, the sort of athlete who, if he was chasing and trying hard, I was delighted to have. But I didn't think to myself he was going to make it. Strangely enough, for a man in the army PT Corps he was not tremendously co-ordinated. From everything I knew of him I knew he was quite talented but by 1983 he was already 24 years old. That is not old age in athletics, but it didn't make me think of Kriss that here was real talent coming through. He was just another member of the training group. A nice bloke, prepared to work, and I was pleased to have him.

'Having said that, when he started training in early 1983 and got going, I began to think there was a talent there. By early May in 1983 I became aware he was going to run quite fast.'

Until he joined Mike Smith, Kriss's specialist training schedule had been shaped by his club in Germany. There they concentrated on technique but not fitness and strength. The programme Kriss followed with Mike Smith built up a new layer of strength. And Kriss had the talent to make the most of that additional power.

Much of the out-of-season training Mike Smith encouraged involved hill-running over varying distances and at varying speeds. Once the squad took to the track, training sessions might include six 300 metre runs in succession with breaks of four minutes' rest in between, or eight 200 metre runs punctuated by short rest periods. Indoors, Kriss and the team would spend up to two hours at a time on an intensive programme of drills and circuits, designed to build up the necessary extra power. The work was familiar to Kriss from his army experience. Mike's philosophy was that it was little use having good running or hurdling skills if the athlete did not have the fitness to be able to produce good performances over and over again.

In 1983 the United Kingdom Championships were due to be held at the end of May in Edinburgh. Until the winter of that year it had not occurred to Kriss that it would be worth his while taking part in such a leading event. When the suggestion had been made to him the year before by an army colleague, he dismissed it. 'That's where the good guys run,' he said. 'But how,' came the reply, 'are you going to be one of the good guys if you don't compete against them?'

Towards the end of the winter of 1983 Kriss asked Mike Smith what he thought about him entering the main national athletics event. Mike Smith had no hesitation. Kriss had recorded the qualifying times, and of course he should send away for an entry form and apply to take part.

As one of Britain's top forty, Kriss had no problems in entering and at the end of May he set off in his Ford Capri 2.8 injection car from the south of England for the Meadowbank Stadium in Edinburgh. Accompanied by an army colleague, Tony Lester, Kriss drove from Salisbury to the Scottish capital in six hours. At one point on the journey he touched 120 m.p.h.

Kriss and Tony stayed in army accommodation and on the evening before the race Kriss was running up and down the corridor feeling full of confidence. He felt both light and powerful. He told Tony, 'I'm in great shape. I feel terrific. I can't wait for tomorrow.'

When the next day arrived Kriss drew lane 8 in the heat. It was the outside lane, and all those he considered to be the better runners were on his inside.

'I left my blocks and before I knew it I was coming home along the home straight. Nobody had overtaken me. I hadn't realized I was in that sort of shape. I crossed the line, 47.07.'

It was Kriss Akabusi's personal best time, an improvement of almost a whole second on his previous best. He had had an idea that the winter's training schedule might pay good dividends when he had run his only race of the season, three weeks earlier in Germany, in 47.5 seconds. But the race had been hand-timed and Kriss had not felt that he had run particularly fast in the race. His new personal best in the UK Championship heat not only confirmed the 47.5 seconds but also confirmed that Kriss had at last lifted himself off his performance plateau. He decided to dismiss any idea he might have entertained about becoming a hurdler.

The final was held the day after the heat. When the runners lined up for the 400 metres, all the talk was of Kriss Akabusi and another outsider, Alan Slack, a former long jumper, who between them had recorded the best qualifying times in the heats. Neither had appeared on any of the experts' lists of potential champions, and there they were stepping forward as two of the country's top 400 metres runners.

Just over 46 seconds after the starting-gun had sounded, the two little known runners crossed the finishing line in first and second place. Kriss, trailing by only 0.05 of a second, ran yet another personal best—46.72 seconds. He had been caught on the line by Alan Slack. He won a watch. But the greatest prize was to come. He was asked if he would be available to run for Great Britain the coming Sunday in Birmingham. Kriss was incredulous.

'Are you being serious?' he asked Frank Dick, the national chief coach.

'I'm always serious, son,' came the no-nonsense reply.

The race had also been televised, and Monika had been watching at home in Bulford and had taken photographs of the screen as Kriss appeared.

Driving back home, Kriss was ecstatic. He had gone to Edinburgh to get experience running at a top national level and was returning home about to start his international career. 'Am I really good enough to run for Britain?' he wondered aloud to some of his fellow athletes. He was told not to be ridiculous, he had proved himself as runner-up in the national championships. He powered down the M6 motorway in his jet-black Capri, laughing and joking as he went. He was on cloud nine when the sight of a police car in his rear view mirror brought him back to reality. Kriss slowed down to 70 m.p.h. The police car overtook and pulled him in. He had been spotted doing 126 m.p.h. It earned him a £60 fine.

News of Kriss's achievements spread rapidly in army circles. When he applied for leave to compete for Great Britain the next weekend, it was enthusiastically granted. He was told to take the Friday afternoon off and get to Birmingham in good time to prepare.

What Kriss now remembers is not the 400 metres race he ran but the occasion. He admits to having been awestruck as he rubbed shoulders with the athletes who were his heroes. He came fifth out of six in his event, beating a Russian junior. The result was not important. It was the atmosphere of the whole day and the pride of having achieved international recognition which mattered. He was invited to dinner as one of the competing athletes by the Lord Mayor, and afterwards went on to the official disco at the Birmingham Holiday Inn.

Two weeks later, Kriss was running for his country again: this time in Lappeenranta in Finland in a three-cornered international event, Great Britain and Northern Ireland versus Finland and Switzerland. This time Kriss beat his UK Championship rival Alan Slack. Then on 1 July Kriss was in an England vest, running in the 4 x 400 metres relay against Poland, Austria and Belgium. A week after that he was flying out to Oslo, where he ran 46.74 seconds in the 400 metres, coming second to Claude Moseley. Kriss's athletics career was now on track.

By this time Kriss was well established on the European international circuit and accustomed to airports and aeroplanes. In August his regiment moved to Berlin and Monika returned to Germany to set up home in new army quarters. Kriss continued with his sporting and army commitments, flying between Germany, Britain and other European cities.

In the second week of August he was back in Finland. Not

this time for an ordinary international competition but to take part in the inaugural World Championships, a prestigious athletics meeting which has grown in stature to become second only in importance to the Olympic Games. Kriss was one of the six runners chosen to travel to Helsinki from which the 4 x 400 metres squad would be selected. His status as an athlete was rapidly improving, one measure of which was that he received his first offer of commercial sponsorship from Adidas, the sports kit manufacturers.

Kriss was awestruck by the whole event. It was organized on a massive scale. He had flown out to Helsinki with all the British athletics stars and was given a room in the athletics village.

The games produced for Kriss both delight and disappointment. He ran with the British squad in two of the heats and the team won a place in the final. However, the British team manager, Nick Whitehead, decided to drop Kriss from the final, believing Ainsley Bennett, Garry Cook, Todd Bennett and Phil Brown represented his strongest field. As Kriss watched from the stands, the four finalists grabbed third place.

Although the rules allowed for team substitutions it did not allow for more than four runners to step up onto the podium to receive medals. Despite having done much of the hard groundwork to enable Britain to win the bronze medals, Kriss did not receive one himself. He accepted the situation bravely, saying that he had no complaints and the games had been a great experience. As compensation, Nick Whitehead promised to try to get him a medal. Eventually Kriss received one.

Mike Smith does not criticize the team management for dropping Kriss. 'They have got things wrong in the past,' he says, 'but in this particular instance they were probably right. Kriss was obviously strong and obviously useful, but he wasn't that strong and that useful. He was there to ease it out for the other runners. In all honesty he was absolutely delighted to run in the heats.'

Kriss's season ended in Oslo on 23 August when he beat Phil Brown, then Britian's number one 400 metres runner. This new personal best time of 46.10 seconds placed him third in the year's British ranking. In twelve months Kriss had improved his personal best time over the distance by almost 2 seconds and lifted himself 37 places in the official list of the country's top 400 metre runners.

The record of Kriss's 1983 season successes reads: First, Army and Combined Services 400 metres; Second, UK Championships 400 metres; First, 400 metres versus Finland and Switzerland; member of bronze-medal-winning World Championship 4 x 400 metres relay squad; First, European Cup 4 x 400 metres.

Kriss had been selected for the European Cup final on the strength of his performances at the World Championship. He ran the first leg and was in fifth position when he handed the baton to Garry Cook. He took the team to second place and Todd Bennett maintained the position. It was Phil Brown's last lap which raised the roof at Crystal Palace. The partisan crowd cheered him on and he ran a lap of 44.4 seconds, overhauling a lead of 4 metres, to win the race. The aggregate time of 3 minutes 2.28 seconds was the fastest ever run in Britain.

It was after winning the European Cup relay at Crystal Palace that Kriss knew for the first time in his own mind that he was now on course to become a serious athlete. He was still in the army and earned his living as a physical training instructor, but in his mind he was no longer a soldier who ran as a hobby. He was an athlete first, whose job happened to be in the army.

As Kriss joined his regiment in Berlin in September and joined Monika at their new home he had a remarkable season to look back on. The army's decision to allow him to concentrate on his sport had been vindicated. By his own achievements and example he had lifted the profile of army athletics, and with that the army was well satisfied. He had become well known in athletics circles and a dependable member of his national team.

In November 1983, *Athletics Weekly* not only featured a colour photograph of Kriss on the front cover, but also published a technical profile describing his training programme and trying to analyse his recent remarkable progress. It began by Kriss describing the German club approach:

'They have the right idea when it comes to injury prevention. Every club has its own physiotherapist and facilities. If after any training session you suffer from any muscular or ligamental strains, you get it seen to straight away. They are able to finance this due to the active support of local council and industrial aid. This enables them also to build more synthetic tracks and indoor halls, and provide weights and other equipment.'

At the time, Kriss's training schedule involved six sessions a week in winter and five a week in the summer. He had to drive a round trip of 100 miles to find the good facilities he needed. Each session would start with an extensive 'warm-up' and finish with a 'warm-down', and last from one-and-a-half to two hours.

'For me there is a difference between being coached and being trained. I was first coached by Hansi Bohme while serving in Germany from 1978 to 1980. Here I learnt the basic techniques of running relaxed, economically and converting the power into speed. I saw him four times weekly. From 1980 to 1982 I was self-coached and trained, working from schedules given to me by my German coach. From 1982 I was trained by Mike Smith of Southampton and Eastleigh. He worked out schedules for Todd Bennett and myself that tuned my body to make the most of my potential and relaxed, economical style, drilled into me by my German coach. The result was the two-second improvement from the previous season. Both coaching and training are as important as each other. You can train as hard as you like but if your style is ragged, due to lack of coaching, you've got to be at a disadvantage. Likewise, you can have the sweetest style out, but if you don't get the right training it has got to be detrimental.'

He told *Athletics Weekly* that he enjoyed all phases of training and constantly looked forward to the next phase, adding that he was more suited to speed endurance than sheer speed sessions. Mike Smith's summary of Kriss's 1983 season is honest and direct.

'From a guy who had done, in top athletics' terms, absolutely nothing before in his life, he came away at the end of the season as one of the medal-winning squad at the World Championships.

'It gave Kriss all the determination in the world. During the winter of 1983/84 he worked and worked and worked.'

The year ended with an invitation to Kriss to appear on the BBC Television 'Sports Review of the Year' programme, where at a studio in the Television Centre at Wood Lane in London he met with the nation's other leading sports personalities, including the footballers who were still his heroes. And he also received a letter from Lieutenant General Sir James Glover, President of the Army Athletics Association.

> Dear Sergeant Akabusi,
>
> The executive Committee of the Army Athletic Association at their meeting on Tuesday 8 November 1983 considered the performances achieved by Army athletes during 1983 and voted unanimously to award you the Harington Cup for outstanding service to Army Athletics in addition to jointly awarding you the Cotterill Cup for the best performance in the Army Championships Track Events.
>
> Congratulations on becoming a member of the Great Britain Athletics team and on your performance in the World Championship.I wish you every success in the future and sincerely hope that you are selected for the Olympic Games in July next year.

By the time the President of the Army Athletics Association had written to Kriss, arrangements had been made by the army to give him every facility. It was realized that to have a serving soldier as an Olympic athlete would be of considerable publicity value and prestige to the service.

In Berlin in 1983 the army had to be in a state of readiness which required all personnel to be able to respond to circumstances quickly. This involved taking part in exercises, and Kriss once found himself in the late summer of 1983 out on an exercise only hours after returning from a major international athletics meeting.

To the Army Athletics Association and the PT Corps this was not satisfactory and, through army channels, they lobbied for Kriss to be given the facilities he needed to prepare for the Olympic Games. Consequently the army athletics officials sat down with the department responsible for army postings and discussed Sergeant Akabusi. The solution arrived at was to post Kriss to Marchwood in Hampshire. He would be there, attached to the Army Physical Training School in Aldershot, with 17 Port and Maritime Regiment, Royal Corps of Transport. And he would be there not to work, but to train—near to Mike Smith, with the minimum of army duties.

8

Ashanti – and an Olympic Silver

Everybody over here see you as a wastepipe. I
would have been more excited and happy to hear
that you are a father, you have got a son or you are
expecting a child than to hear you have bought a
dog. A dog is no human being, such a things
should come last in a family. Even if you tour the
whole world without an issue you are a dead lost.
At your age is about time you think of reproducing
yourself. You are long overdue to be a father
having lived with a woman for four years now. If
you know you can't pregnant a woman then let us
know.

Kriss and Monika had been married ten months when a
relative from Nigeria wrote to Kriss admonishing him for his
failure to be the father of a son. The sentiments expressed echoed
those of Clara Akabusi. When she had met Monika, she had
made no secret of her reservations about Monika as a suitable
wife for her son. Then, after Kriss and Monika had been married
a number of months and there was no sign of a child on the way,
Clara felt her reservations had been correct.

Kriss recalls Clara writing to remind him that his father had
to date thirty children. 'I was told,' says Kriss, 'that I was wasting my blood energy time with Monika; that she might satisfy me

sexually but that is not what mattered to blacks. My mother reminded me that she never approved of my marriage and that it was shameful we did not have one child after knowing each other for five years.'

Such contacts with Nigeria were cruelly timed. Kriss and Monika were keen to have children and when Monika had consistently failed to become pregnant they had sought medical advice. In 1981 in Germany Monika had undergone an exploratory operation to find out why she was suffering from a series of lower abdominal pains. Fears that these pains might have something to do with her inability to conceive were confirmed when it was discovered that her left fallopian tube was irrevocably congested due to a series of infections. In the winter of 1982, however, Monika, now living in England, became pregnant. But after only eight weeks she was rushed, in considerable pain, to hospital in Salisbury where an ectopic pregnancy was discovered. The tiny foetus had become blocked in the right fallopian tube. During an operation it was removed and the tube cut, rendering it ineffective.

With one tube severed and the other blocked, the chances of Monika and Kriss becoming parents seemed remote. They went to Hammersmith Hospital to see the team of doctors looking into alternative methods of fertilization. They could, however, at that stage, offer little hope. When Kriss was posted to Berlin, Monika again sought advice, this time at the university clinic in Berlin. After numerous tests she was told again that one of her fallopian tubes was blocked and micro-surgery would be required to clear it. The clinic was at the same time working on an *in vitro* fertilization project and was hoping to be able to perfect the technique of producing a 'test-tube' baby. Monika was asked if she would be willing for the doctors, when performing the operation on her fallopian tube, to remove some eggs from her ovary for them to be fertilized in the laboratory. Monika agreed.

'They thought I would be a good client and talked me into it,' is her version of events.

On reflection, however, she thought it a good suggestion. If a fertilized egg could be implanted in her womb and a pregnancy followed it would be what she and Kriss were wanting. The technique was still in its early stages of development. Around the world perhaps two hundred test-tube babies had been born, in Germany less than half a dozen, and at the clinic in Berlin there had been no successes. Nevertheless, Monika was willing to be the local guinea pig.

Kriss was not so keen on the idea. Yet at the same time he did not want to say no. He went with Monika to see the doctors and was told more about the technique. He heard that the doctors would require him to produce some sperm and was embarrassed by the idea. It was a challenge to his view of masculinity. Was it right for his wife to be pregnated in this abnormal way?

On the day of the operation Monika did not feel that the *in vitro* fertilization experiment was the priority. She reminded the doctors that the primary purpose was to unblock the fallopian tube to allow her to conceive in the normal way.

Under the anaesthetic, Monika had a number of eggs removed. She does not recall the number or the other medical details—evidence, she says, that she was not taking that side of things seriously. To her, the main purpose of the operation was to enable her to become pregant naturally. While the short operation was under way, Kriss was taken to a side room at the clinic to deliver some sperm. He hated and was embarrassed by the whole procedure.

A little later a fertilized egg was implanted. Afterwards Monika had to lie still for a number of hours. When Kriss came to see her, Monika told him she was certain she was pregnant. It was her positive thinking, she believes, which enabled the implanted egg to remain in her womb and develop.

Monika went back home happy, convinced in her own mind that she was now expecting a child, but not especially aware of the medical significance of the event. She returned to her normal busy life. When the doctors at the clinic confirmed the pregnancy, they were delighted with their first success. When one of the team visited Monika at home to tell her the news officially, he was horrified to find his patient busy moving furniture. In his view, she was not only running a small risk of dislodging a priceless pregnancy, but also of destroying months of research work.

Kriss was delighted with the news, and Monika became a very special patient at the clinic as her pregnancy developed. Everything was monitored and a close check kept on every small detail. Monika returned to the hospital every week and numerous ultrasound scans were carried out. The doctors were able to tell, even before the birth, that the baby was a girl, news which Kriss was specially pleased to hear. Monika was a little disappointed: as a girl, she had always wanted a big brother, and she would have preferred to have had a boy first followed by one or more girls.

Ashanti arrived on 19 June 1984. She was born in Berlin and today is entitled to dual German and British nationality. She might have been born in Britain but for the persuasiveness of the Berlin doctors. Kriss had been posted back to England but Monika remained in Berlin. The clinic was most unwilling that their star patient should give birth in another hospital. Monika stayed with one of the doctors as her pregnancy continued. She and Kriss were apart for six weeks before the birth. Kriss returned just in time to see his firstborn daughter arrive.

Monika has the impression that Ashanti's arrival was witnessed by the whole research team. There was nothing exceptional about the birth, except for the fact that it was attended by an unusually large number of doctors.

The medical success received substantial press, radio and television coverage. Kriss stayed well out of the limelight, for once disliking the media attention intensely. Kriss's reticence stemmed from the embarrassment he felt about the original method of conception, together with the pressures he was subjected to by his Nigerian family. He was feeling the clash of cultural values.

Monika did not give general interviews and, for publicity

purposes, her name was changed. It was never made public that the father of the celebrated baby was a famous athlete. One paper bought rights to the story, using the pseudonym Marion Dillinger, but Monika was recognized from the photographs.

'It was something to remember, but not the ideal way for one's first child to be born. I remember I was never alone. Reporters kept trying to get photographs and interviews, so my telephone calls had to be monitored and visitors checked in. The press got up to all sorts of tricks. One reporter even posed as a doctor. It was unbelievable. There was no peace and no time to sit with Kriss. He would always hide when the press turned up. I was still in hospital when he had to return to England. And when I came to leave with Ashanti, we were on our own. It was sad, not nice.'

It was a sad as well as a happy time because it was during Monika's pregnancy that her mother had died at the relatively young age of 48. She was buried on Christmas Eve, the day before Monika's birthday. She had been with Monika at the time the doctor came to her house to break the news that the pregnancy had been confirmed. She had offered advice as Monika went through a bad stage of morning sickness. But she had not lived to see her grandchild. Monika had no one to lean on as she went out from the protected environment of the hospital into the outside world.

Monika and Ashanti stayed one night at the doctor's house, where they had been for the period before the birth, and then flew to England. She left Dillinger the Doberman behind with the doctor's family, so as not to subject him to six months in quarantine, and he stayed in Germany until he died at the age of six in 1989.

When she got to the airport for the flight home, Monika did not tell the airline that her baby was only five days old or they might have refused to take the risk of carrying her. Monika just wanted to get back to Kriss and away from the publicity as fast as possible. The name Ashanti was chosen even before her birth. It is the name of a West African tribe, but not a Nigerian one, so the name has not been accepted by Kriss's mother. She refers to her grandchild as Chinonyeram.

Monika and Kriss had just a few days to settle down to family life in their new home in Calshot in Hampshire before Kriss was away again, to Los Angeles in the USA for the 1984 Olympic Games. There the publicity-shy father became the high-profile athlete watched by hundreds of millions of people on television around the world. He was away for two weeks and Monika recalls a happy time getting to know her baby, taking her for walks by the sea in her pram and watching the news from Los Angeles with growing excitement. She started to exercise again and was glad no longer to be weighed down by pregnancy.

Kriss found it took some time for him to adapt to being a father. It was not until Ashanti was a year old that he felt he had developed real paternal feelings towards her. Up until then he saw Ashanti as being totally reliant on Monika, who breast-fed her and seemed to him much more closely bonded to their daughter. In the early months Kriss could not detect any signs that Ashanti recognized him and it was only at around a year old, when she could smile and laugh when he played with her, that his fatherly feelings began to grow.

It was at the start of 1984 that Kriss became, for the first time, a full-time athlete. His working week during the winter was an intensive programme of training with Mike Smith. He would practise running in difficult conditions, up hills and shingle as well as on the track at Southampton. By the spring he was prepared for the season and looking forward to his first race, to see how his performances on track had been affected by the winter's hard work. He had to convince the selectors that his 1983 season had not been a flash in the pan.

As in 1983 Kriss started the season with a meeting in Germany. At Gutersloh he recorded 47 seconds in the 400 metres on 13 May, plus a time of 10.8 seconds for the 100 metres and 1 minute 52 seconds for the 800 metres, the last timing being a personal best. The omens were good. Kriss went to the UK Championships in Cwmbran, not as the diffident newcomer who had taken his marks in Edinburgh just a year earlier, but as an established international athlete. The favourite to win the UK 400 metres was Roy Dickens, but Kriss's chances were acknowledged to be good. In the heats, Roy Dickens' position as favourite was confirmed. He ran fractionally faster than Kriss and looked the more comfortable of the two runners.

The weather for the final was dreadful and television viewers around the country watched Kriss, Roy Dickens and the other finalists line up in wind and rain. The gun went and Roy was out of his blocks and into a quick lead. By the 300 metres mark he was five or six metres clear of Kriss. But the last 100 metres were to be decisive. Kriss's strength and stamina, built up over the winter under Mike Smith, came to the fore. At the line, Kriss had run the race in 46.1 seconds, 0.1 second in front of his rival. He had run another personal best and had won his first major title. He did not know from the result, however, whether he was now the best 400 metres runner in Britain. Todd Bennett and Phil Brown had not competed; what form, Kriss wondered, would they be in that year?

He did not have long to wait to find out, as the Olympic trials were held only a week later at Crystal Palace. In a steady late-night drizzle, Kriss ran yet another personal best, running under 46 seconds for the first time. But he was only third. Todd and Phil beat him. Nevertheless the run was good enough, Kriss hoped, to earn him the third place in the 400 metres team destined for Los Angeles, and a place in the 4 x 400 metres relay. It was a moment of particular pleasure for Mike Smith, who was the coach to both Kriss and Todd.

Kriss was sure he would be on the plane for Los Angeles, but he had one remaining worry. He heard rumours that David Jenkins, who had been Britain's number one 400 metres runner, was thinking of making a return to the track to try to win an Olympic place. Kriss was told he was due to be running at a meeting in Loughborough to which he had been invited. He feared that if he raced David Jenkins and was seen to be beaten, he might lose his claim to an Olympic team place. Kriss opted to run the 200 metres; he watched from the sidelines as David Jenkins failed to clock a good enough time to be considered.

Kriss had another important meeting to complete that Olympic summer. Throughout his career he has felt a special loyalty to army athletics and, even when it involves interrupting his training schedule, he has always attempted to compete with and encourage other army athletes. He has sometimes risked injury in doing so, and a number of his late-season niggling injuries have been caused by his enthusiastic approach to competing for the army. In 1984 he led the army to its first inter-services title for twenty years. In one day he won a tight 200 metres, set a new inter-services record in the 400 metres and then, with everything hingeing on the 4 x 400 metres relay he took to the track again to clinch victory over the RAF.

When an Olympic Athlete is officially informed of his or her selection for the games, it is not just a duplicate letter which is sent out. At the beginning of July, a registered letter from Buckingham Palace addressed to Kriss arrived at his home in Calshot.

Dear Mr Akabusi,

I am delighted to inform you that you have been selected by the British Amateur Athletic Board to represent Great Britain and Northern Ireland in the following events at the Olympic Games in Los Angeles: 400 metres, 4 x 400 metres relay squad. Many congratulations. I send you my best wishes for a happy and successful visit to Los Angeles.

Philip

The letter from the Duke of Edinburgh was the first of many official good wishes Kriss was to receive. From the army's point of view, to have a serving soldier as an Olympian was not only rare but enormously prestigious. Kriss was the first British soldier to take part in an Olympic track event for twenty years, and the first member of the Physical Training Corps to run at an Olympic Games since 1948. For Kriss, the glory of competing in the Olympics was only slightly tarnished by the political controversy surrounding the Games, involving the Russian and Eastern bloc boycott and the row about the presence of the South African athlete Zola Budd.

'It was my first time in the US, the good old US of A. I was obviously totally excited.' Kriss retells his story of the Olympic Games with an enthusiasm which, even after seven years, is absolutely undiminished. 'Not only was I an Olympian but I was going to America. It had been my boyhood dream. I had read all the comics, seen it on television. And I must admit I was not disappointed. I came into L.A. airport and the Americans were louder than loud and "Hey how are you doing?" and "Gee that's neat", "You're an Olympian, wow!" They were really excited. I was getting even more excited than them. It was my first major international championships as an individual. I went in as the third string and came out the best in Europe.'

As Kriss arrived at the Olympic Games village he had no illusions about his place in the British team. He was number three. What mattered to him was that he was taking part in the greatest sporting pageant in the world. In international terms he was little more than a make-weight for the stars, people like the American Antonio McKay, the fastest man over the distance in the world. To the officials at the twenty-third Olympics he was athlete number 351.

Yet by the morning of Monday 6 August, the name Kriss Akabusi was known even to those who had not been following the games on television. He was the only British runner to have secured a place in the 400 metres semi-finals, having recorded two personal best times in the preliminary heats. Where Todd Bennett and Phil Brown could get no further than the second round, Kriss was defying the form books. Again it was his finishing strength which gave him a crucial edge, as he ran a time of 45.64 seconds in the first heat and 45.43 seconds in the second.

Kriss has a knack of being able to raise his performance to match the occasion. The Olympic Games were no exception.

'When I saw the clock at 45.43 I couldn't believe it. The British guys were going crazy. I was through to the semi-final, and that was my problem. On the day of the semi-final, instead of thinking, right, I'm going to get into the final, I was too content with what I had done. Go and enjoy yourself I thought, it's a long time before you'll be doing anything like this again. I thought I had done what I had set out to do. Consequently I ran, and it was only coming round the bend that I realized I had it in me to make the final. There were chaps ahead of me starting to die on me. I finished just a tenth of a second behind the fourth qualifier. I really messed it up. I wouldn't have had a chance in the final, but to have made it the first time as an individual would have been just incredible.'

There have been other times when Kriss has wondered if he has set his sights too low and been content to achieve too little. Perhaps it is because as a child he was never in a position to expect the best that, to avoid disappointment in life, he has sometimes held his ambitions in check. In the past he had needed people like Ian Mackenzie and Mike Smith to give him the extra confidence in his ability. Sometimes an event itself gave him the necessary boost, but at the Olympics in 1984 in the semi-finals, his third race in front of the Olympic crowd, Kriss realized only when it was too late what was then within his grasp. If he had had only a little bit more belief in what he could do, Mike Smith believes, he could have been in the final.

'He ran so well in the second round that he was really quite content that he wasn't going to get through. If he had set himself the target of getting into the final, he would have been there.'

When the British relay squad met to discuss the 4 x 400 metres race, the four men were in different moods. Kriss was keyed up with his unexpected success; Todd Bennett and Phil Brown were keen to better their individual performances; and Garry Cook arrived from his good 800 metres run. They all agreed that they had something to prove to certain British commentators who gave them little chance even of winning a place in the finals. And once they had secured a place in the final, none of the experts gave them a chance of a medal. Kriss acknowledges that on paper his squad did not stand a chance. But each of the four runners was convinced that together they could do well.

The four-lap final began with Kriss running 45.89 seconds, the fastest first leg ever run by a British athlete.

'I ran a blinder. Garry runs another blinder. Todd comes out and by the final lap the three of us can hardly bear to watch Phil. The Americans are off doing a lap of honour and we are jumping up and down, so pleased to get the silver.'

Their collective time was a new British and European record of 2 minutes, 59.13 seconds. It was truly a team affort.

That moment on the rostrum when an Olympic champion receives his gold, silver or bronze medal is one to remember and savour for life. It is a brief moment of national and personal pride without comparison. Kriss and his three fellow runners were so amazed to be on the rostrum they continued laughing and joking. They had even forgotten to dress suitably for the occasion and were still there in their shorts. Kriss had the brief thought that the photograph of him improperly dressed might not go down too well in army circles. But in their joy the team had got to a silly stage of sheer delight. They threatened that, as each solemnly received a medal, the others would pull his trousers down. It was a moment of such unexpected happiness that none of the British team fully savoured the moment—and it was gone. But each had a silver medal to keep and cherish for life.

By complete contrast Riba's adult life, which had started with such promise, was going through a harrowing period. For their first fourteen years Riba and Kriss had been each other's constant companion. Then they had parted and gone their own ways. Riba had had a spell as a successful actor, but mental illness, which resulted in him spending time in a British psychiatric hospital, took its toll. Monika believes it was the way the acting business built up his hopes that he had a great future as an actor ahead of him, and then dumped him, that triggered his breakdown. He lost interest in food and went for long periods without speaking. He decided to go to Nigeria to rest and convalesce, and was there for four years. It was during this time that his older brother's athletic career had taken off.

In Nigeria, Riba was told that his mental problems were due to the spirits of his ancestors. He was being punished for the way he had structured his life, and in due course Kriss too would be punished by the ancestors for wasting his time with Monika and ignoring his birthright. His mother arranged for him to go to a Roman Catholic healing centre and also to be given treatment by a native healer.

'I don't know why she did it,' Riba now says. 'She wanted me to have that kind of experience. She thought she knew what was best for me.'

Riba recounts how for one nine-month spell of 'treatment' he was held manacled to a pole by chains attached to his wrists and ankles. It was feared, he says, that he might have damaged himself if he had not been restrained. He was fed and washed, and his mother stayed nearby and cooked him meals.

'I had a mat and could sleep on the floor. I could manoeuvre myself into a sleeping position with my arms and legs still attached to the pole. There were nine poles in the room, each one occupied. There were some very disturbed people, a lot worse than me. They would shake their poles and try and climb up them. We were in a sort of shed, with a roof, but open to the fresh air. I was moved around and eventually came to occupy each pole. That was one of the things I wanted to do while I was there, occupy each pole.'

After a while this bizarre way of life came to seem normal. Riba even felt how fortunate he was to be given regular meals. He was very sick and confused and would spend much of his time staring and looking at the other people in the room. As he was at a religious healing centre people would come and pray with him. Yet there were also times when he laughed and joked; he even talks of having had some good times.

Looking back, Riba must now feel it was a nightmare period. Some of the time he was receiving his 'treatment' he had malaria. He also contracted worms. A native healer he stayed with gave him foul-tasting potions to drink and regularly beat him.

'The native professor beat me a lot. I still have the scars on my back. I think I was flogged to beat the spirits out. It was frightening. I didn't know if this man was the insane one or me. My mother saw him flogging me. She thought it was good for me. I was even flogged about the head and the face.

'He used an instrument with three ropes tied together and knots at the end. He had a great fetish about flogging me round the head. It wasn't a punishment, but treatment. I might have started muttering something in my sleep or started singing from boredom, and then I would be flogged. It hurt so much afterwards. I would lie on my bed just holding my head. In England they diagnosed schizophrenia, but my mother was a top nurse and she thought my problems were caused by spirits, so I thought "she may be right". The professor certainly cured me of malaria with his tree bark remedies.'

Another treatment Riba received was one involving his head being shaved and a concoction of chemicals placed on his scalp. The resultant burning of his skin caused scars which remain to this day. One set of scars, however, was the result of Riba being punished by the professor's wife. He had taken some fish to eat from the kitchen and was lying on his bed when she came to him and stuck a poker she had freshly taken from the fire onto his bare back and then began to beat him with it. He shouted at her in anger but refused to cry, just as he had refused to show he was being hurt when he had been flogged as a child by the Spanish lady.

Almost a year after his Olympic Games success, knowing almost nothing about his brother's plight, Kriss received a letter from Riba. Written from their mother's address, it makes sad reading.

Dear Kezie, my dear brother,

Things have not been going well for me here in
Nigeria. I am having a very rough and tough time.
Life is not treating me well. Life is extremely hard.
I have never been happy living a miserable,
disorganized low existence disturbing and frightening to think of. Every situation a complete
shambles, utterly humiliating. I have no clothes. I
have been ill though now recovered. Absolutely. I
have not seen much of our father. He shows very
little serious interest though he is well. Umanachi
is rather pessimistic, every experience is unjusti-
fied and favours against me. I wish to leave
Nigeria . . . Please help me to return to London
promptly . . . please do your finest. Help me Kezie
I am at my wits end. I have nobody else. Please. I
appear foolish and absurd. Nobody shows interest
in helping me . . . Can you buy a flight ticket for
me? . . . I will refund your money back to you when
I reach England. I want you to be proud of me. I
cannot cope with suffering . . . I seriously miss you.
My heart yearns. It saddens me. I know you are
doing well . . .

Lots of love, your brother Riba.

PS. I have no money and cannot get a ticket. Please
help me in this. It is of great importance . . . I trust
you will succeed. Please God bless you.

It would have taken a great effort for Riba to have written in
such a vein, to have pleaded with his brother for help. The letter
is a measure of his despair. In the event, Riba's father paid for a
ticket to London. He had also, Riba says, paid for many of the
cures; but when Riba told him what it had involved he appeared

surprised that he had been subjected to such rough treatment.

Riba returned to Britain hoping to find work, and for a while stayed with Kriss and Monika. He met his niece Ashanti for the first time. Kriss noticed how his brother now spoke with an African sound to his voice. He was glad to see him back but disturbed by seeing the scars.

Staying with Monika and Kriss, however, was not a long-term solution. When Kriss was away and Monika at home, tensions built up as Riba started to adapt to European ways again. Riba could not understand why Monika, who was pregnant at the time, spent so much time cleaning the house when to him it seemed spotless. Monika resented it when Riba sat in the house not offering to help.

Slowly Riba returned to an independent life and, although his acting career has not picked up, he can support himself and remains well, as long as he takes prescribed medication on a regular basis. He is a studious and thoughtful man who has lived through bad experiences and emerged scarred but with his inner strength intact. He is quiet and given to his own company. His work, as a night-time security guard, gives him long hours alone, which he copes with well. He has now begun to write poetry and has a gift for creating telling word images. He and Kriss see each other from time to time but essentially live separate lives. They are on good terms, but no longer close on a day-to-day basis, no longer reliant upon each other as they once were.

9

Temptation and Tragedy

Kriss returned home from Los Angeles as one of the British stars of the Games. Little Ashanti, having been the centre of attention at the time of her birth, was much photographed again, sharing the centre stage with her father and his silver medal. He received letters of congratulation from a brigadier and a general, and an invitation from the Prime Minister and Mr Denis Thatcher to attend a reception at Lancaster House in London.

As pleased as the army was for Sergeant Akabusi, and glad as it was that its decision to give him every support in training had paid off, Kriss detected an undercurrent. He felt as if it was being suggested to him that now he had achieved everything that had been expected of him, and more, the time had come for him to return to his proper job as a soldier. Kriss, on the other hand, looking back on what he had achieved, felt he had yet more to do as a serious athlete. He returned to work and was soon called for an interview. Kriss explained that he had plans to carry on as an athlete. The army hesitated, but agreed that he could stay on at Marchwood and train with Mike Smith; Kriss would be put in charge of the gymnasium.

This suited Kriss, but he quickly became aware that the team at the Marchwood gymnasium was going to have to cope with him being absent for long periods of time. The unit at Marchwood enjoyed the prestige of having an Olympic hero in their midst and was very accommodating. As long as Kriss made sure the battle fitness and other tests were carried out efficiently, he had a free run to organize his time-table to suit his athletics career. He also kept on good terms with the unit by turning out for the basketball team and running extra-curricular courses in the gymnasium for the local families. But in due course it became apparent that he needed assistance, as he had set himself such a busy schedule. He was now a staff sergeant, and the PT Corps decided to send him the help he needed in the form of a sergeant, Taffy Williams. (Taffy Williams himself was to achieve international sporting recognition as a weightlifter, winning a gold medal at the 1986 Commonwealth Games.)

1985 was the year Kriss was appointed England team captain. He held the position, which is usually more of an honour than a responsibility, for one match—the meeting between England and the USA held at Birmingham on 21 June.

Some cynics might argue that the appointment was an example of tokenism. It had been noticed that, although a number of the country's leading athletes were black, no black athlete had ever been appointed captain. Earlier in the summer one leading coach, John Isaacs, had openly criticised athletics officials for not bringing black athletes into the sport's governing structures. Kriss Akabusi, the likeable army sergeant, would therefore be an obvious choice as captain to meet such criticism. On the other hand, Kriss, the likeable and clubable army sergeant, might have been seen as the best man for the job, just the right man to rally team spirit.

Kriss cannot be sure of the reason for his appointment, but he is fairly certain he knows why the appointment did not last beyond the one meeting. He says it is because he took the job too seriously.

'I was in there, talking to the young guys, talking to the old guys, talking to the officials, and began to challenge some of their authority. I was asking questions, disagreeing with things. I raised the issue of travelling expenses and argued a case for the athletes to be able to claim first class rail fares. I raised other issues, but I think I must have been too vociferous. It wasn't quite the done thing and next time I didn't get appointed captain. My relationship with some of the officials had gone sour.'

According to Mike Smith, being captain can mean 'absolutely nothing', or the individual appointed can set himself up as a 'kind of shop steward'.

'Kriss took the job seriously, which was probably why he didn't last too long in the job. He has always had a slightly brittle relationship with the team management. Management in athletics is like management in any other sport. If an athlete is successful, people in management pay court to you. If you are not so successful they forget to pay court to you. Today, certain people at the top will be full of praise for Kriss, saying what a great part he has played in British athletics, but it wasn't always so, particularly when Kriss was being difficult to them.'

The meeting against the USA failed to attract some of the top American runners, notably Carl Lewis and Ed Moses, but it did attract considerable interest. All eyes were on the 400 metres race in which Kriss was taking part along with Todd Bennett and Phil Brown, three of the winning Olympic relay team. The question being asked was would the ten-year-old British record for the 400 metres held by David Jenkins be broken? In the event, Todd won the race with Kriss second, but the 44.93 seconds record held firm.

On the track that summer Kriss had a consistent but not spectacular season. He ran a 45.56 second race at Madrid to open, but did not find the steady improvement he was hoping for. Mike Smith describes it as a quiet year. Indeed, the season ended prematurely when Kriss pulled a hamstring in Berlin and opted out of the European Grand Prix finals meeting in Rome and other international meetings. Kriss feels that in 1985 he had hit another plateau. Although he followed a tough training schedule, his mind was not totally on his athletics. He had responsibilities to the army and had to maintain an overview of work at Marchwood. The main reason for his failure to improve that season Kriss attributes to his own make-up. His body is such that after an improvement in performance it needs to consolidate before the next step forward. In Kriss's words, 'it adapts and then it springs.'

For many athletes the season which follows an Olympic Games is something of an anti-climax. It is too soon to draw up detailed plans for the next Olympics, and the season is often spent marking time or attempting new personal best times and records to sustain motivation.

For Kriss, 1985 and 1986 were times of reflection. He had achieved much by way of status and recognition as an athlete, yet he had no clear idea where it was leading him. He also realized he was of an age when to stay at the top was going to become increasingly difficult. He reflected on the words of the Swedish woman who had told his fortune at the children's home. He was to achieve much but never be the best.

In material terms Kriss had more than he could ever have imagined as a child. He had money, a home, a car, prestige and status in the army, the world of sport and society at large, a beautiful wife and a much longed-for daughter. But what does it profit a person to gain the whole world and lose his or her soul? There was a gap in his life. Looking back, Kriss might say he was experiencing the truth of Christ's words, that no one can live 'by bread alone'. The deepest need of the human heart is to know God. Certainly, Kriss would now acknowledge that he was leading a very shallow life. The pleasures of worldly success were not satisfying his own inner need, and most of those who knew him at the time would agree that Kriss's life lacked depth. He had had something of a Christian upbringing, but the seed lay dormant.

Army life and the macho culture it encouraged had stamped themselves on his personality. Before marrying Monika, Kriss enjoyed the 'challenge' of luring a woman to his bed. He was proud of the fact that he could impress his male colleagues by the ease and speed with which he could persuade an attractive woman to join him for a one-night stand. Looking back, he realizes that impressing his mates—who would be watching him at a party or at a bar—was as important to him as the final denouement in the bedroom. He talks now of sometimes finding himself in bed at the end of an evening with a woman he barely knew and for whom he cared not at all. He had won the race but was not interested in the prize. He detached himself emotionally from what he was doing. One of his friends at the time recalls that, with Kriss, womanising was a sign of bravado. It could even be put down to his own insecurity. He was interested in proving himself to his peers with his conquests. He enjoyed the challenge and the boost to his ego which came with each success.

Even after marrying Monika he still enjoyed going to parties and impressing other women. As a famous international athlete he had no difficulty in attracting female company and admiration. But he knew it would be dangerous to his precious relationship with Monika to allow a flirtation to go too far. Today Kriss knows how to avoid being trapped. He knows the danger signs of when a light-hearted flirtation could lead to serious temptation. He understands how casual sex can become addictive like a drug and, like a reformed addict, he now knows how not to get trapped into returning to his old ways.

Kriss has a vivid memory of returning early one morning to his home. It was a still, quiet March morning with a low mist hanging across the Hampshire countryside. The night before he had been at an engagement which had turned into a party. Always one to be the life and soul of any such gathering, Kriss stayed on. As the evening wore on he realized he was not going to be able to get home that night, and telephoned Monika to tell her. By the time he was on his way back to his wife and daughter, dawn was approaching. He arrived home, and for a few minutes sat in the car wondering, 'What am I doing? What is life for? Is it just to be squandered with parties? Am I taking Monika and family life too much for granted? What should my priorities be?'—a string of questions for which he needed to find answers.

There was another worry too. Not only was he realizing a spiritual impoverishment in his life, he was also in danger of losing his material standing. Once a sports star has peaked, he

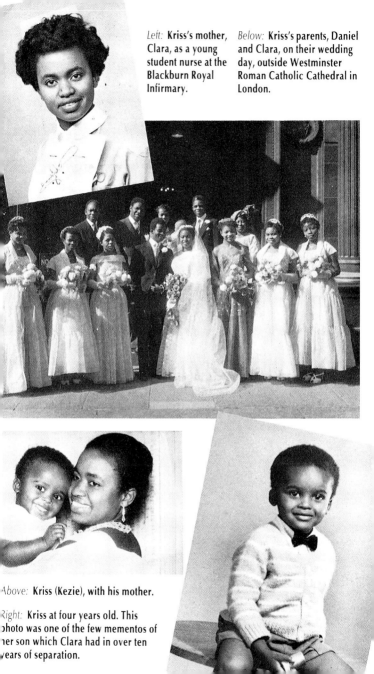

Left: **Kriss's mother, Clara, as a young student nurse at the Blackburn Royal Infirmary.**

Below: **Kriss's parents, Daniel and Clara, on their wedding day, outside Westminster Roman Catholic Cathedral in London.**

Above: **Kriss (Kezie), with his mother.**

Right: **Kriss at four years old. This photo was one of the few mementos of her son which Clara had in over ten years of separation.**

Left and below: **Kriss runs for the bronze medal at the 1983 World Championships (Helsinki). This and the Olympic silver (Los Angeles, 1984) were his first two major medals.**

Above: **The Army Physical Training Corps, 1983–4.**

Playground fun on a visit to a Southampton school, 1987–8.

Far right: **Back home in 1985: Kriss with Monika and Ashanti.**

Below: **Tod Bennett and Roger Black join Kriss in leading the pack during a sports course Kriss arranged for local children at Ringwood, 1985.**

Kriss in serious mood, on the platform at a Billy Graham meeting, speaking about his Christian faith.

Above and right: **1990** the European Championships at Split: Kriss wins the gold medal in the 400 metres hurdles, breaking David Hemery's long-standing British record, and afterwards kneels in prayer.

August 1991: The British 4 x 400 metres relay team celebrate their victory at the Tokyo Games. Left to right: John Regis, Kriss Akabusi, Roger Black, Derek Redmond.

May 1995: Kriss on TV's *This is Your Life* with daughters Ashanti (left) and Shakira (right), Monika, his father and brother.

is no longer of interest to the sponsors and the commercial world. It is not even good enough to win medals with a relay squad. The endorsements and the financial incentives to take part in the big commercial meetings are offered only to athletes who succeed as individuals.

In 1985 Kriss was on the verge of passing his 'sell by' date. He was a popular and established athlete and an integral member of the British team, yet slipped three places in the UK top fifty. Most significantly he was overtaken by Mike Smith's latest protégé, an up-and-coming youngster called Roger Black.

1986, the year of the Commonwealth Games and European Championships, was much the same, with the youngsters impressing on Kriss Akabusi that he was unlikely, at the age of twenty-eight, to win a gold medal in the 400 metres at a major event in his own right. At the European Championships he was picked only as relay reserve. He was back to where he had been three years earlier. Whereas in 1983 to be an international reserve was the realization of an ambition, by 1986 it was a blow to the pride. As a result of Todd Bennett being injured, Kriss did run; he won a gold medal but swore that never again would he allow himself to be the reserve, 'the baggageman'.

Kriss realized that his career as a 400 metres runner was on the wane. At the same time he realized he would no longer be content to remain a soldier. Despite earlier ambitions to become an officer, Kriss knew that his future did not lie with the army. It had been good to and for him, but having seen something of the attractions of the life beyond the confines of the military, Kriss knew he would not be content simply to be a soldier. Yet, at the same time, now that he had family commitments, he had to think of earning a living.

Wondering where his future lay, Kriss considered taking illegal performance-enhancing drugs. He remembers weighing the pros and cons in much the same way that he had as a youngster. He had no moral scruples, his approach was entirely pragmatic.

'Maybe I have reached my full natural potential and I will

never again beat the up-and-coming runners like Roger. Maybe the only way forward is to take drugs. But, on the other hand, where would I go to get drugs? One of my saving graces was that I didn't know. I would need to get them on the sly, but I didn't know who to ask or what to ask for. I just knew the word steroids, but had no idea about the various categories and which would have been most suitable, and I had no idea about the various stimulants. And anyway the arguments against taking drugs were too strong.

'I was already an established international athlete, if I was caught taking drugs all my achievements to date would be assumed to have been drug-assisted and I would lose all credibility. I was an Olympic silver medallist and very proud of my medal. If I had taken drugs and been caught, people would have discounted all my achievements. My whole career to date would have been smeared.

'I was in the military, and if I had been caught taking drugs, not only would my athletics career have gone down the pan but my military career as well. I had hopes of being an officer. If I was caught taking drugs I would have been given an ignominious dishonourable discharge.

'And, more important, my family. I was married and had a child and wanted more. The social pressures bore in on me and I decided to persevere without drugs. I am really thankful for that. But, in saying that, when I see people who have given in to temptation and have been caught I say, there but for the grace of God go I.'

Early in 1991, the British tabloid newspapers ran a story in which Kriss denied a suggestion that he was one of three British athletes who had taken banned drugs. The stories were written carefully, to avoid any danger of libel action against the newspapers, but Kriss was called upon to explain his association with the athlete David Jenkins, who had served a prison sentence for dealing in drugs. When the story broke, Kriss was in California following his winter training programme. When Kriss had first gone to the west coast of America to train he had met David

Jenkins who had helped him find accommodation and shown him around.

The former 400 metres British record holder was arrested in April 1988 on charges of conspiring to smuggle and distribute anabolic steroids. It was claimed that his smuggling ring controlled 70 per cent of an American black market in steroids worth $100 million. The drugs were manufactured in Mexico and Jenkins arranged for them to be illegally imported across the border. Despite well-documented medical evidence that the anabolic steroids could produce side effects including cancer of the liver and prostate, sterility, behavioural changes and an increased risk of heart disease, the drugs were much in demand. Competitors in a variety of sports used them to increase bulk and strength. The Americans were particularly worried that the drugs were becoming available in colleges and high schools.

David Jenkins mixed freely and was friendly with a number of British athletes who trained, during the winter, under the Californian sun.

'It had nothing to do with drugs,' he says. 'I kept that part of my life very much away from them. I wasn't in the business at the street dealer level. I was involved much higher up in a criminal conspiracy. In court they said I was at the top. I kept it all secret from the British guys. They didn't know about it. I was the architect of a huge criminal conspiracy and I wasn't going to blow it all by selling a few bottles or jars to one or two athletes. That is not where I was at. I was into substantial numbers. I handled the big orders and the money. Part of my motivation in keeping in touch with Kriss and the others was to keep up with the 400 metres events in which I had been involved and pass on any hints I might have.'

David Jenkins, who has a degree in chemical engineering from Edinburgh University still works in the sports medicine and vitamins business near San Diego. Today he still lives in California, dealing in legal substances, special diet concentrates and other nutritional performance enhancers which hundreds of top-class sportsmen and women take as an accepted part of training. He spent time in prison for his part in the criminal conspiracy and, despite warnings from people such as Mike Smith, Kriss was one of a handful of British athletes who kept in touch with him and visited him in jail.

Mike Smith says: 'When, after the Olympics, Kriss got permission from the army to spend some time training during the winter in California, he met David Jenkins. Daley Thompson knew him and Roger Black joined the group. When the drugs business blew up I said to both Kriss and Roger, you are rather foolish to keep up any association with the man because it is going to be guilt by association. But their attitude was that he was a friend and you don't let a friend down if he's in need.

'I don't give any credence to any suggestion that any of them were involved in drug taking. I wasn't surprised that David Jenkins had taken drugs. I was taken aback by the scale of his conspiracy, but I would be absolutely shattered if I heard that Kriss had ever taken drugs. I can be as positive as one human being can ever be about another one that Kriss never took drugs. Apart from my faith in Kriss, the simple practical fact of the matter is that he has been randomly tested on so many occasions that he would have been quite amazingly fortunate not to have been caught out if he had been taking anything. And taking drugs is not a thing which can be kept a secret. You must have a supplier, so he will know. The supplier has to have a source and he also will get to hear about who is and who is not on drugs. Then there are the other signs which colleagues will notice: moodiness, bulking up, minor muscle tears, lots of niggling injuries.'

Even today, Kriss does not moralize about drug taking at the personal level. He views it as cheating only because it involves taking artificial substances which are proscribed by law. In the nineteenth century it was considered ungentlemanly even to train, as it gave a sportsman an unfair advantage. Today, carefully planned scientific programmes of training are essential for any world-class athlete. But what is training if not physiological manipulation? Special foods and special supplements are taken, and again are essential for top-class performers.

Kriss says that if he discovered that by eating asparagus half an hour before a race he could guarantee to improve his performance on the track, he would eat it. More than that, he would keep his discovery a secret. The only clear-cut definition of cheating, Kriss maintains, which must be accepted, is that no athlete should do anything which is outside the boundaries of the law of the land or the sport.

He acknowledges that a special difficulty arises over taking artificial performance enhancers which are not outlawed, but would be if practical tests to detect their use had been devised. The twilight zone of pharmacy, which offers drugs to the less scrupulous athletes, is always trying to keep one step ahead of the official chemists. Often they succeed, but as the tests for drugs become more sophisticated and reliable, the costs of the drugs to by-pass these tests become more and more expensive.

David Jenkins believes that far fewer athletes are now taking banned drugs. He predicts that from the 1991 season, international performances will plateau and the people who will benefit from this will be athletes like Kriss Akabusi who have always been 'clean'.

In a typical season Kriss can expect to be tested for drugs at athletics meetings half a dozen times. He can also, having been given just a few hours' notice, be tested at any time during training. Not once during his career, at either a regular or random test, has there been any hint of an illegal drug in Kriss's body. Nevertheless Kriss remains anxious about testing. He knows that today, as a declared Christian, should he be caught using drugs, his disgrace would reflect not only on himself, but on his fellow-Christians—the church—as well.

'I always have that fear now that someone is going to slip me something, somebody will be really mean and put something in my drinking bottle. I know that if I got caught on drugs now, no one would believe me. And I wouldn't expect anyone to believe me. Now that I have declared myself publicly to be a Christian, I would be slaughtered by the press. My name would be dragged through the dirt. Reason tells me it is highly unlikely anyone would be so wicked as to try to set me up. Having said that, people are capable of anything. Someone might think I'm getting too good, too cocky. Someone may just want a story. If they all want a story in the press, they'll make it happen. People can be stitched up. My fear is, my paranoia is, that someone will think, yes, born-again Christian guy on drugs, what a great story. It is an unreasonable fear, but it's still there.'

Doubts about his lifestyle, and the pressure resulting from his failure to improve as a 400 metres runner, preyed on Kriss from 1985 through 1986. But it was a sad family event in 1985, which put all his questions into a much sharper focus.

Following the extraordinary circumstances surrounding Ashanti's birth, Kriss and Monika believed that they would not be able to become parents in the normal way. However, to their surprise, after a while, Monika was found to be pregnant. She had conceived normally and as the pregnancy progressed she was not anticipating any special difficulties. But when the pregnancy had reached six and a half months, it became clear to the doctors that problems had arisen. Monika went into premature labour and twin girls were stillborn. It was November 1985.

'They were just too young to live. If there had been only one, she might have survived. In all other respects they were normal, they were just too little to live.'

Kriss was not present at the birth. He was training at the time and everything happened so quickly, it was all over when he returned.

'They asked us if we wanted to see the little girls and we did. It wasn't very pleasant and it really took Kriss back. To me, at first, the birth was a relief. I had been so ill I thought I was going to die. The fluid in my womb had expanded so much, I thought I was going to explode. I couldn't sit and I couldn't lie. The pressure was such that I went into labour. I was told that sometimes this happened with twins, and the children were born with water on the brain. But they did a post-mortem and there was nothing wrong with them.

'We didn't give them names. We didn't have a funeral. They just took them away. I wanted to forget about it. It was painful enough as it was. That is my way of dealing with things. It happened when my mother died: I develop a hard protective shell. People think I'm hard. If I wasn't like I am such an experience would eat me up from inside.'

The image of his little twin daughters, looking cold, but still warm though lifeless, has never left Kriss. He often wonders about them and what they might have been like, and thinks of himself as being the father of four children.

'Up until then life was pretty good and easy and I didn't have to think about the difficult questions of life and death. Monika lost her mother but it hadn't set me thinking in quite the same way as seeing these two little children. They were so innocent. I wondered, where are they? Where have they gone? It started me facing some real issues in life.

'I saw the twins, but it all happened so very fast. I came back from training and Monika just said, "That's it, that's it. Look." She punched at her stomach. I didn't know what she was saying. I didn't understand what she was telling me. I had never realized the urgency, how severe the situation was. I thought it was just doctors being over-protective. I had taken her back to hospital in Southampton just before I went training, I told her she would be all right, said a few words of reassurance, and then left. On my way back from training I thought I would pop in to see her, as a surprise. The first thing she said was "Look," and I said, "Look at what?" and she said, "It's gone." She was still a bit dozy from the anaesthetic. I thought she was trying to say all the excess water had gone. Her stomach was still pretty big. "I've lost the children." I said, "You're joking." "No, honestly." I didn't cry, but just thought, she's lost the children. Deep down I wanted to blame somebody. How can it happen? How can you lose two children like that? The doctors are professionals, how did they let it happen? I didn't get angry. I just wanted to find someone who was responsible, whose fault it was.'

When Kriss was asked if he would like to see his two daughters, at first he declined. He thought they would be slimey and unsightly. He was assured they were fully formed. He agreed. They were brought to Kriss and Monika, wrapped up as if they were alive and sleeping.

'The biggest one, markedly bigger, looked so much like Ashanti when she was born. The little one looked so different. It was only two years later that I realized she looked so much like Shakira when she was born. They looked like two small little babies sleeping. I didn't touch them, but their skin looked cold, very fine with little goosebumps all over. Their eyes were closed. Two peaceful-looking babies. They took them away for the autopsies and then disposed of them. I hadn't seen them born or seen them die, but Monika must have been a lot closer to them and known them as two people.'

Kriss, today, will often think about his twin daughters—the memory sparked off by seeing Ashanti and her sister at play. Kriss wonders too what life would be like with four young daughters in the house. How the twins would be doing at school, what their interests would be.

For the first time since his own childhood, the protective emotional shield he had built around himself was pierced without his consent. When he married Monika, he willingly allowed her to share his inner life. The twins reached through his long-established barriers to touch Kriss where he was most vulnerable, and there was nothing he could do to protect himself. It was the first experience he had had of grief. He talks now of feeling detached from the events of their birth and how unreal it all seemed at the time, yet he has not been able to blot out the memory. He cannot deny what happened and how, six years later, the twins live on in his mind, his memory, his emotions and, as Kriss now believes, in heaven. Today, Monika says, Kriss can sometimes still get very sad about the twins—he may return home having been thinking about them, or had his memories revived by seeing a mother with twins.

In 1985 Kriss's thoughts were in a turmoil for which he was unprepared. Old insecurities had surfaced and his outward, extrovert self no longer provided him with an adequate defence. He realized that life at the top, for all its status and glory, was essentially shallow and insubstantial. His brief glimpse of his dead twin daughters was also a glimpse of his own mortality. Was this all that life was about? These two little girls had completed their short journey through life and there they were, without feelings or consciousness. Kriss knew that he was enjoying a longer journey, but would the end be the same—a meeting with a secret called death? He was afraid. What would it feel like to die? Most forms of living pain he could imagine, and many he had experienced himself, but death was something he knew nothing about.

Throughout that winter of 1986, questions kept returning to his mind. He was still living the high profile, hyper-active life of the top sports star, but the moments of contemplation increased in number. He did not brood for long periods on the inner mysteries of life, it was just that he became increasingly aware of needs, spiritual needs, he had seldom recognized before. He found he was questioning his lifestyle and values. He still enjoyed money, glamour, status, parties and the temptations of fast living, but they provided less and less satisfaction.

In July 1986 Kriss travelled to Edinburgh, the scene of his first major success three years before, for the Commonwealth Games. Nothing now was new; the novelty of the crowd and the television hype had, for Kriss, evaporated. The incredulous beginner had become the hardened professional, for although the sport was still nominally amateur, those at the top viewed their sport as their livelihood. If, like Kriss, they had another job, they viewed their standing in the world of athletics as their investment for the future. The Commonwealth Games were not unimportant to Kriss; and he had been working towards them, but he was curiously diffident about them and lacked his usual self-confidence. He did not feel he was running well or training well. He was not right with the world, and his troubled mind was affecting his performance on the track.

As he lay on his bed in his room in what was normally student accommodation in Edinburgh, ruminating about life, Kriss picked up the special edition of the Bible produced by the National Bible Society of Scotland and presented to all the competitors at the Games.

Kriss knew the most familiar Bible stories from his time in Sunday School and at the Roman Catholic Convent. But since deciding in his youth that he did not wish to go to church any more, and since joining the army and becoming familiar with barrack-room values, Kriss had given his religious upbringing little thought. To him 'Jesus Christ' were swear words and the Bible an unopened and an uninteresting book. Just of late he had begun to consider some religious ideas and had even scanned a Bible at home. Kriss had a Gideon Bible he had lifted from a hotel room many years before, though he admits that the few times he had looked at it he had understood very little. But in the quiet of his room in Edinburgh during the Commonwealth Games of 1986, he picked up this modern 'Good News' version and read the Bible afresh.

10

True Vision

'Hey guys, last night I met Jesus!'

Roger Black, Daley Thompson and the other athletes training on the university track at Irvine in California were used to Kriss. Always loud, cheerful, argumentative and prone to make a dramatic entrance. But his claim that morning certainly made them take notice.

'What drugs are *you* taking?' Kriss was asked mockingly. His friends thought him crazy. So he told them the story of his vivid dream. It was still fresh in his mind and confirmed by the details of the notes he had taken at the time, scribbled in his Filofax.

'My baptism by the Holy Spirit. 0300 hours, 14.4.87. I had a vision early in this morning. I had travelled a long way and was weary. I was on the side of a great expanse of water, but I could see the shore on the other side. A voice known unto me was reading a text with which I was familiar, regarding the trials and tribulations of man, and in some peculiar way about me itself. I jumped in and began swimming in the direction of the shore and the voice which I heard. I swam for a while but the shore came no nearer. It was getting increasingly harder and soon I felt as if I was swimming uphill. Something kept on telling me to turn back, but I wanted to go on. I had not come this far to turn around. All of a sudden I surmounted the hill and went over the precipice. The voice became more distinct and clear. The water less calm but active, bubbling like a whirlpool. I was being swept faster than I could swim breast-stroke by another current. The water seemed to be building into a crescendo. I was moving fast. Then in front of me appeared a gigantic configuration of Jesus himself, like a waterfall, with his arms held out wide. As I bobbed up and down approaching this I heard these words, "Come unto me all those who are heavy laden," clear as a bell. These words struck me as I entered into Jesus, Jesus's kingdom. I shouted out his name, "Jesus!" long and hard. And an amazing feeling came over me, not only did I feel a burning in my chest, but my whole torso felt tranquil and happy. I felt born again, and forgiven for my sins. I felt baptism, not of water but of the Holy Ghost. I felt compelled to write these things straight away. I say these things in the name of the Lord. Amen.'

The Filofax account, written in the small hours of the morning, is a bit stilted in style—not a polished piece of writing—yet it is an important piece of evidence. It is the contemporary record of a vision which changed Kriss's life. Psychiatrists will no doubt have explanations. Dreams often encapsulate anxieties in a visible and comprehensible form. They can also contain hidden messages about unresolved tensions. This is not a view which necessarily contradicts the Christian interpretation, that God can use dreams to communicate with people.

Kriss was quite clear in his own mind that something monumental had happened to him. His God had personally answered his prayer. After the vision he lay still on his bed, enjoying the peace of the moment. Then he wrote down an account of what had happened and the next morning, when he woke up, he checked to see it really was there in his Filofax. It was. He could barely contain his excitement as he raced down to the track to tell his training companions, 'Last night, I met Jesus.'

It was the first time that Roger Black realized how great an impact the search for meaning and faith was having on Kriss. For a while before, Kriss had kept many of his thoughts to himself. Roger knew that he was exploring spiritual matters, but until that morning on the track, when Kriss announced himself a Christian, Roger had not realized how serious the search had become.

The vision was the culmination of a real quest, which had begun even before the Edinburgh Games the previous summer. Uncertain about life and his future, Kriss had been reading, discussing and listening to a whole host of spiritual ideas. He had tried many churches and was being persistently wooed by the Mormons. They had told Kriss that they were the one true church on earth. He found the Mormon missionaries very friendly, plausible and good people. They would visit Kriss at home and explain their way of salvation; although Kriss had doubts, he was continually pulled back to their church, even when intellectually he had drifted away.

When he debated with them, they always had an answer. But when he tried to read the Book of Mormon he found it difficult to understand. Today, Kriss has an immediate empathy with the words of the Bible. The Book of Mormon, he found remote, stilted and unapproachable. And there was one crucial passage which blocked the way for Kriss. He read that black people had been cursed as a race. He asked the Mormons for an explanation, but received nothing satisfactory.

The Mormons, or members of the Church of Jesus Christ of Latter-Day Saints, are an active worldwide missionary church based in Utah in the USA. In Britain and elsewhere they are familiar for their door-to-door ministry. Clean-cut young men, travelling in pairs, visit people in their homes. Kriss first came across the Mormons one June day shortly before the Commonwealth Games in 1986. He was tinkering with his car, outside his home in Hythe in Hampshire, when he was approached by two neat young men in suits; one was American and the other Dutch. They asked him if he would mind helping them with a survey. Kriss at first said that he was very busy, but when they assured him it would take only a few minutes, he agreed. He carried on with the job in hand, sitting inside the car in the driver's seat with the door open and the two young men standing alongside.

One of the questions was this: 'Do you ever think about the meaning of life?'

Kriss replied enthusiastically, 'Of course.' At that time he was in the throes of his period of self-examination. He went on to explain some of his ideas. Then it struck him that he was being rather inhospitable leaving the two visitors standing outside, so he invited them in for a drink. They declined the tea and coffee offered but were glad of some grapefruit juice.

Seated in Kriss's and Monika's living-room they asked their next question: 'Do you believe in God?'

'Sure,' said Kriss. 'I believe there's a God. I believe in something. I'm not sure I can define what that is, but yes, I believe in a God.'

'Do you ever wonder about creation?'

Kriss recalled the times when, as a boy, he would look up at the stars and wonder how they were made. He was only too willing to talk, and in the two visitors he had ready listeners.

At the end of the conversation, the two young men thanked Kriss for his help and asked him if he would mind if they returned at some time to speak with him further. Kriss said he had no objection, but warned them he was very busy. They suggested a date and Kriss agreed.

A few days later, they returned and resumed the conversation. They asked Monika if she would like to join in, but she was unwilling. They told Kriss that they were from the Church of Jesus Christ of Latter-Day Saints, but Kriss at that time knew nothing about the Mormons, except that two American pop singers he had heard were members of the church. When told about the Book of Mormon, which with the Bible forms the basis of the church's scriptures, it was information entirely new to him. They outlined the Mormon way to salvation, and on their third visit the two missionaries asked Kriss if he would like to come to where they held their services.

'They were held in a hall, not a purpose-built church. What I liked about the people I met was that they were all very friendly and that the person out at the front was not wearing a gown or any special clothes. There were about forty or fifty in the congregation. They sang pretty traditional songs, not that I knew them, but they were hymns accompanied by a piano. Times I had been to church before and nobody had sung. They all did. They prayed openly. They didn't appear to be ritualistic like the Church of England or Roman Catholic services I had been to. The service was, though, a bit more formal than the congregation I now go to. The meetings were long but never boring. They had a family meeting for an hour and then a priesthood meeting.'

Monika never went with Kriss to the Mormon service and was becoming worried about what she saw as a growing commitment. She knew a little about the church, having met the Mormons in Germany, and advised Kriss not to become mixed up with them. Kriss denied he was getting too involved. He just said that he was curious and wanted to find out more about them. Steve and Joycelyn Longworth were also concerned for Kriss as he became increasingly involved in what they saw as a heretical sect.

For Christians, the Mormon claims are certainly way beyond the accepted boundaries of Christian interpretation. They are based on the claim that in 1827, their founder Joseph Smith received inscribed gold plates on which were written a new scripture for the world. He translated the plates into the Book of Mormon. It is claimed to be the account of the truths made known to the ancient inhabitants of America by the risen Christ.

Kriss began to go to the Mormon meeting on a regular basis, and Monika accepted that on Sundays he went to church from 10 a.m. to 1 p.m. For as long as the church made no other demands on Kriss's life she was prepared to leave it at that. The Mormons, however, realized that in Kriss they had a potentially first-rate recruit. He was a well-known and popular athlete and, more than this, to have a leading black member would give the church excellent publicity and open up new opportunities to proselytise within the black community.

When the Mormons stepped up their conversion pressure Monika became concerned.

'It got really bad,' she recalls. 'As soon as these people realized Kriss was showing an interest, they would turn up very regularly and far too often. They knew I wasn't religious, but

there they were, in my house, on the floor, praying with Kriss.
We were in an open-plan house. There was nothing I could do.
They turned up on Sunday afternoons; the times when we
wanted to be on our own, they'd arrive. Sometimes Kriss wasn't
there. They wanted to talk to me. They even got me Mormon
books in German. I prayed with them once or twice but never
down on my knees with them. All that was pretty bad and I got
Kriss to tell them to make appointments before turning up.

'One day they said to Kriss, you are now almost a Mormon
and every Mormon gives a tenth of his income to the church, as a
tithe. They gave him a figure of what they wanted. That did it for
me. I really turned against them. I decided they would no longer
come to my house and if Kriss wanted to see them he would have
to go to the Mormon church. They really made me feel uncomfortable.'

Kriss accepted Monika's ultimatum, appreciating that his
home was Monika's home as well.

It was while Kriss was attempting to learn more about Mor-
monism, that his interest in Christianity had also been rekindled
by finding the Good News Bible beside his bed in his room in
Edinburgh. For the first time he found the Bible exciting to read.
He describes himself as having been spiritually hungry and eager
to devour every idea. He was guided through the Gospel story by
the reading plan in the Bible, and shown how different events
fitted in with each other. Kriss read how St Paul's letters fitted in
to the stories of the Acts of the Apostles, and for the first time the
early Christians appeared to Kriss to be real people. But, most
significantly, the character of Jesus came alive and leapt off the
page as Kriss read.

'Man, this was alive! I read the whole thing while I was up
there in Edinburgh. I couldn't put the Bible down. I would go
training with the guys, do my stuff, and then race back to read
more of the Bible. I was reading the Bible for four hours a day.
That really got me interested.'

The Bible was a counterbalance to the Mormons, it deflected
his interest away from their teaching, but nevertheless he

continued to attend the Mormon services. He would argue with the Mormons from the basis of the Bible. He would continually ask, why? Why believe in this or that Mormon doctrine, when the Bible had a different message? The Mormons reaction was that they had in Kriss a man eager for the truth, one who had the potential for becoming a really good Mormon. They were pleased he had read the Bible but insisted he also read the Book of Mormon with equal enthusiasm. He was given a copy.

Yet the more he argued and read, the more he came back to the one stumbling-block, the Mormon doctrine on race. To Kriss it was nothing short of racism. He gathered that because of the curse, black people had been excluded from certain offices in the priesthood of the church. He also gathered that many believing Mormons thought that only white people could be beautiful. The Mormons pointed out that the Bible had a similar reference in the story of the mark of Cain. But that, Kriss argued, was not said to be a black skin; it could have been any mark.

Monika was particularly pleased that Kriss had found for himself a weakness in the relentless Mormon propaganda. The Mormons, however, were anxious not to lose their potentially valuable recruit. They introduced Kriss to black Mormons and used every means they could to meet his objections. The arguments became increasingly contentious, but because Kriss found the Mormons as individuals so friendly he kept going back to their meetings.

What especially impressed Kriss about them was that because they believed in something their whole lives had been changed. Not only had they given up drink, tobacco, even tea and coffee, they lived good honest lives and were welcoming and friendly. They went out knocking on doors to share their faith and were generous in providing for each other when in need. One Mormon member would come round to Kriss's house and help him with some of the practical household chores. He continued to do this, even when Kriss had been denouncing his faith. They would always, Kriss says, go the extra mile. He liked them and found them better people than many of the Christians he has known since.

Kriss's religious quest took him up many avenues and into a number of cul-de-sacs. For three weeks he attended a spiritualist church. Again, as with the Mormons, he liked the informality of the service. No one was dressed in robes and there was no feeling of 'them and us'. They started with hymn singing and then had a speaker, a different one each week. He recognized one very respectable member of the local community in the church.

'One speaker,' Kriss recalls, 'told the congregation that he could see an old man with a dog walking down the aisle towards him. All of a sudden someone said, "Yes, that's Harry." "Yes, that's right," said the speaker, and started to relate what Harry was telling him.'

'If this is what they do,' Kriss thought to himself, 'I'll see if they can find out anything about me.' But he was disappointed. Not one of the speakers, in the three weeks he went, spoke to him or about him. He concluded that people must have been planted in the congregation. The experience left him cold. He was prepared to believe in ghosts but not in the invisible ghosts he was being told appeared in the church.

When Kriss was driving around the Hythe area, just across the water from Southampton, out shopping or going up to Marchwood, he would keep an eye open for likely churches to try. His search extended generally to the Solent area. He heard that the United Reformed Church was the successor to the Congregationalists he had known as a youngster and went to one of their services, but the people there were far too old. He found no signs of love within the church. People came to their pews, worshipped as individuals, listened to the preacher and left. Whatever it was that Kriss had enjoyed as a child was no longer there. He also went to the Baptists and the Methodists, and again found most people older than himself and all of them white. Interspersed with his sampling of the local church life, Kriss went to the Mormons.

His search for a church where he felt doctrinally, spiritually and socially at ease continued from July to December. On one occasion he found a church to try as a result of a conversation he fell into at a formal reception for European Games medal winners hosted by the then Prime Minister, Margaret Thatcher. There Kriss met a man who was a leading member of one of the country's black churches. Kriss explained to him that he believed in God, yet was finding it hard to discover a congregation where he could settle down and learn more about faith. As a result of the conversation Kriss was given the name of a church within reach of his home.

'It was just after Christmas and I went along to the church and sat in pew and listened to the preacher giving a sermon on the new year.

' "What are you going to do in 1987?"

' "I'm going to praise the Lord," said one woman from the congregation. "And I'm going to thank the Lord in 1987."

'Everybody started praising the Lord. I had never been to such an active church before. I had certainly never been to a pentecostal church. They were singing and shouting "Alleluia" and "Praise the Lord". There were young people there and old people and I remember a big white woman shouting "Glory to God", and I remember looking at her and thinking, "She's into the black trip." I didn't know white people did this sort of thing as well.

'Then the preacher started talking about how God had created man by blowing into his nostrils. God's breath was the breath of life for this man. And the Holy Spirit is life for man today. I thought, great. It was the first time I had heard a preacher expound on the word. Take the Bible verse by verse and explain. Every other sermon I had heard might have started with a few words of scripture but then went on to talk of some social or topical issue. This excited me. This image of how God took a piece of clay and breathed life into it. "If you're walking around without the Holy Spirit, without the breath of life, you're just a piece of clay." And everyone shouted "Alleluia".

'I went back to Monika and told her, it was great. They were friendly and I thought this must be the place to go. It was quite a way to travel but it really appealed. At the end of the service I spoke to the pastor.'

Kriss told him he was looking for the true church. This was important to Kriss, as the Mormons had impressed on him that he had to find the true church for himself. One of the elders had said he could search for two years, looking for the perfect church on this earth, but would still come back to the Mormons. The Mormons gave Kriss a checklist of things to look for, in order to judge any new church he came across.

On the Wednesday following his first visit to the church, Kriss went to see the pastor. He had strong views on the Mormons which he was quick to share with Kriss. He said it was a right wing church, very conservative, and members did not like black people. Kriss told him about his doubts about the Mormons, particularly over their attitude towards black people. He told the pastor how much he had enjoyed his sermon and the atmosphere of his church. The conversation was going well, until the pastor turned to the subject of sin.

'Before we know God we are all sinners,' he said. 'But God calls us to be holy. He calls us to be sinless. I haven't committed a sin since I was ...' But Kriss did not let him finish the sentence.

'You must be joking!' Kriss exclaimed.

'No,' the pastor insisted, 'I'm sinless.'

Looking back, Kriss feels he might have misunderstood what the pastor was trying to say, but the way it came across to him put him right off the church. The claim seemed too preposterous, that since Jesus had come into this man's life he had never sinned.

Kriss knew as he looked at his life that there was no way he could ever hope to approach the sinless state of Christ. He might have put behind him some of the extravagances of former years, but he knew he could never go through life without giving way to temptation in one form or another, even if it was only speeding in his car.

Kriss left the meeting thinking it was not the church for him.

It was crazy to suppose that anyone could be sinless. He never went there again.

In March 1987 Kriss went to California, without Monika, to train and prepare for the coming season. Still unable to sever his connections, he looked for a Mormon church. He was given an address and set out on foot to find it. It seemed to Kriss that he walked for miles, and when he eventually found the church he discovered he had walked in a huge circle and come back to where he had started. The Mormon church was only a few hundred yards from where he was staying. The analogy did not escape Kriss. Maybe, in his search for the one true church he had also walked in a huge circle, gone to a whole host of different places of worship, only to end up where he had started, with the Church of Jesus Christ of Latter-Day Saints.

It was a sign, Kriss thought: the Mormons must be the one and only church and the problem he had about its attitude to black people was something which would sort itself out. He went to the church for a few weeks, even though the congregation was exclusively white, because he didn't know where else to go. Everyone was welcoming and Kriss was befriended by some of the members of the youth group. He was invited to people's homes and to special study groups. He was even taken to the temple in Los Angeles.

Yet the battle for Kriss's mind—for his soul—was still being waged. As the Mormons presented their case, so did the Christian church. Driving along the huge urban freeways, Kriss would tune into a local Christian radio station, KWVE, 'Springs of Living Water'. One morning he heard a talk about the Mormons, warning listeners of some of the errors in their scriptures. And later, on the same wavelength, he heard about Calvary Chapel in Costa Mesa, Orange County and its Pastor, Chuck Smith. Kriss liked what he heard and wrote down the address.

Kriss decided to pay the chapel a visit, and what he saw amazed him. It was no small chapel but a huge building capable of holding thousands of worshippers, within a complex of buildings which were all part of the same ministry. On the Sunday Kriss went, he arrived for the third service of the day and found himself, he estimates, as one of a congregation of 3,000. They represented all ages and all types. There were black people amongst the worshippers, although they were in a minority.

Kriss felt they were people he could relate to. He enjoyed the service, met some of the congregation and decided to return that evening. Kriss was impressed not only by the lively atmosphere at the chapel but by the way Pastor Chuck Smith explained the Bible. Kriss found it so intellectually stimulating, he says, 'It blew my little brain!'

Kriss felt he had come home, but wanted some reassurance that the Christian message he had now discovered was the one he could rely on. He felt he knew that Jesus had accepted him as he was, despite all his imperfections, but wanted a sign that all was truly well and that his quest was over. He prayed that Jesus might reveal himself, so that he would know the right way to go. In his prayer, Kriss said that all he wanted to do was follow Jesus—and that night he had his vivid dream.

After that, Kriss was sure he was saved and that, if he died then and there, Jesus would claim him. From that day he never returned to the Mormon fold.

If there was such a thing on earth as a perfect church, Kriss reasoned, it was not for him; he, as a sinner, would quickly spoil it by joining.

He found he was happy to go to Calvary Chapel and, as he puts it, be fed the word. He liked the fact that Calvary Chapel was non-denominational, although in one sense it is now its own denomination. He liked the fact that Pastor Chuck did not dress in elaborate robes to conduct the services and that there was no ritual to worship.

'I was reading the Bible, listening to the radio, going to hear Pastor Chuck, it was real living.'

Kriss was on a religious high. Everything he heard and read fell into place. The jigsaw puzzle of ideas which had been churning about in his head was beginning to make a discernible picture. He leaped at every new idea with an undisguised enthusiasm.

In a profile in the magazine *21st Century Christian*, Kriss describes the change in himself which resulted from his conversion experience.

'I was searching for something, but I didn't know what it was. I wouldn't say I was a male chauvinist pig, but I was a man's man. I liked to think I was rough-toughy, scared of no one. For a man to say that he hasn't got all the answers isn't macho. You've got to put your trust in Jesus, but a man says, "I don't need anybody. I can do it on my own."'

In embracing Christianity, Kriss says, he was shedding the old image and taking on a new one. 'I stopped having to prove that I was as good as everyone else.'

During the time that Kriss was in America he kept in touch with Monika by telephone and told her of his new discoveries, but it was not until they met again that she really saw the change in Kriss.

'I knew that despite having every material benefit anyone could reasonably want,' Monika recalls, 'Kriss was not entirely happy. There was something missing in his life. Now he feels he has got Jesus, he is happy.'

But Monika adds, 'Funnily enough I haven't got Jesus and I'm just as happy about that!'

11

Over the Hurdles

Coinciding with the major change in Kriss Akabusi's personal life, another transformation was taking place. 1986 was the last year that he competed solely as a 400 metres runner on the flat. To almost anyone else, his career record of Olympic, Commonwealth and European medal successes would have been sufficient indications of achievement. Kriss, however, felt that he still had not proved himself on the track; a graceful retirement into relative obscurity was not an option. Indeed, as he left his period of soul searching and personal dissatisfaction, when success on the track and the glory that went with it were his motivations, he moved to a new phase in which success on the track was again all important, but for very different reasons. Not only did he realize that his brief running career to date would not have provided the means of financial security for Monika and the family for life, he also had a new motive to succeed. As a Christian he could run for Jesus and glorify God by using his God-given talents to the full. Yet that summer Britain was well represented in his chosen event. With Derek Redmond, the new British record holder, improving fast and Roger Black emerging as a superb natural talent on the international scene Kriss had little chance of maintaining his position as a top individual runner in the 400 metres event.

Roger Black, a young medical student, had burst onto the international scene in a spectacular manner, winning gold medals in the 400 metres at the European Junior Games in 1985, the Commonwealth Games in 1986 and the European Games in the same season. A less selfless man than Kriss might have taken exception to this upstart overtaking him in his event after he had been working so hard and so long to get where he was.

However, Kriss's reaction was quite the opposite. He took Roger under his wing. He guided him past the pitfalls of international athletics, in much the way he had sheltered Riba in times gone by. Roger is eight years younger than Kriss and, being white and middle-class, comes from a totally different background, yet he and Kriss have become close friends and training partners.

They first met when Roger, as a young student, joined Mike Smith's training group in Southampton in 1985. He saw Kriss in the gymnasium. The awestruck student spoke briefly to his Olympic hero for the first time. The first lengthy conversation they had was when Kriss offered to drive Roger to an indoor meeting at which they were both running. Kriss was the big star and Roger the nobody, but Kriss found the young runner somewhere to stay and generally made sure he knew what to do.

As the months passed and they met more frequently in training Kriss became very excited as he watched Roger's talent blossom. He both encouraged and protected him. He introduced him to Adidas, the major sponsors. By the time Roger beat Kriss on the track at the Commonwealth Games their friendship had grown, and Kriss felt no rancour at having lost his crown to the newcomer. Kriss had expected to be beaten and was genuinely pleased with Roger's victory. By the winter, when the two of them were training together in California, the partnership had been sealed.

Roger describes his friendship with Kriss as unlike any other friendship he enjoys. From having a 'big brother, little brother' relationship, they are now equals. On the track they are no longer rivals and they can help and advise each other without any tension or jealousy. It is an easy friendship built on trust.

They talk incessantly about everything under the sun. One moment it can be a technical matter relating to their training programme, the next moment, news about a mutual friend. Or it might be one asking the other for some business advice. More often than not the subject is religion, with Kriss the enthusiast and Roger the interested agnostic. Kriss, however, listens carefully. They respect each other's opinions and they have never had a quarrel.

Roger has witnessed the immense change which has come over his friend since Kriss became a Christian. He has seen a more sensitive, less bombastic, character emerge. Beneath his loud exterior and public image, Roger has seen the deep-thinking side of Kriss. He has witnessed his whole attitude to life alter, particularly Kriss's orientation to money and success. Roger is the first to testify that becoming a Christian was the best thing that ever happened to his friend. He has seen Kriss turn from a man with little purpose to a man who knows where he is going.

For Roger, his friendship with Kriss, he says, has personally brought him nothing but good. 'I am good for him,' he says, 'and Kriss is good for me.' As Roger puts it, some athletes need drugs, but he has his own performance enhancer—Kriss Akabusi.

At the end of the 1986 season Kriss took a deliberate decision to switch from the 400 metres on the flat to the same distance over hurdles. To stay at the top in sport he needed to maintain a high profile as an individual performer. He was already becoming a sports personality with his radio and television appearances; in particular, his jokey competitive style went down well on the BBC Television quiz 'A Question of Sport'. But he needed to maintain a high profile as a performer on the track. To put it in Mike Smith's words, 'Winning a gold medal in a relay doesn't butter many parsnips. The endorsements and the real money come from being an individual winner.'

So Kriss systematically reviewed the British scene, noting that in the 400 metres hurdles he would have no outstanding rivals. As he watched the event take place at the European Games in Stuttgart in 1986, from his position as relay team reserve, he noted that no Briton progressed further than the first round. Admittedly, on the international front, the

American Ed Moses dominated the event, but initially Kriss set his sights on becoming Britain's number one.

In the United Kingdom the event had not progressed in almost twenty years. The British record of 48.12 seconds, set by David Hemery at the Olympic Games in Mexico in 1968 (a year in which a new British record had been set on no fewer than five different occasions), was still unbroken.

One top coach felt that one of the reasons that the 400 metres hurdles was not an event at which British athletes had excelled since the days of David Hemery was that too many other coaches saw it as essentially a 400 metres race with hurdles added, whereas it was a completely different event, demanding a whole new approach. Another reason why the event was in the doldrums in Britain could have been the old truism that success breeds success. While Britain boasted the top middle distance runners in the world there were youngsters eager to try to emulate their heroes. The 400 metres hurdles was a less glamorous event to attempt because there were no heroes to follow.

'I made the decision to switch to the hurdles,' Kriss recalls, 'after the European Championships in Stuttgart. I looked around and realized that unless I made a move these would be my last championships. Never again would I run in front of a huge crowd and enjoy the atmosphere and glamour of a major championship. My rivals for the 400 metres places were young. I could see the next squad coming up and I was out of it. But watching the British guys in the hurdles I knew I could make the World Championship team. Earlier in my career, when I had hit the plateau of 48 seconds, I knew that if ever I needed to extend my career the hurdles would give me the opportunity.'

Kriss had it in him, he thought, to become one of a new generation of hurdling heroes, but first he decided he needed an intensive course in the techniques of hurdling. From the little he had done in the past, he knew he needed to perfect his style and learn about the detailed technicalities of the event. He talked to Mike Smith and discussed the problem, then approached Peter Warden, the 400 metres hurdles national coach. But to visit him regularly for training involved a 500-mile round trip to Manchester. Thinking this was a crazy waste of time and effort, Mike Smith at Team Solent put Kriss in touch with another coach, Mike Whittingham, who lived a great deal nearer and, at the time, worked in Reading in Berkshire. Mike Smith himself was experienced in coaching hurdlers but felt Kriss needed special individual attention which demanded time and commitment he could not at that stage spare.

Mike Whittingham and Kriss had first met six years earlier at a training session in France. Mike himself was a British international athlete and Kriss was there as a member of his German Club. They had met occasionally since, as Kriss's career developed and Mike approached his retirement from the track. When Mike Smith suggested the two get together to look at Kriss's potential as a hurdler, a good partnership formed. Kriss had been unhappy working on his own and was keen to learn from a specialist hurdler on a one-to-one basis. Mike Whittingham had trained with David Hemery, raced Ed Moses, and been a Commonwealth Games finalist at the 400 metres hurdles. Initially Kriss continued to train with Mike Smith as well, to maintain his strength and general stamina as an athlete, visiting Mike Whittingham for the specialist coaching.

'On day one, when he came to see me,' Mike Whittingham recalls, 'Kriss knew exactly what he wanted. He asked me some very honest questions and I was honest with him. He said he wanted to be the best in Britain at the 400 metres that year: could he do it, and what time would he run? I said that potentially he could run something fantastic.'

It was Mike Whittingham's experienced opinion that Kriss had the potential and the latent talent to break the 48-second barrier which had eluded all British athletes, even David Hemery. He also said that Kriss should have a long-term plan aimed at reaching a peak by the European Championships in 1990, by which time he would have had three years learning the event and learning how to hurdle.

But to start with Mike told him bluntly he would have to be

treated as a novice and be prepared for a great deal of hard work. Kriss agreed.

'Kriss is admired particularly by club athletes as a worker,' says Mike. 'Unlike Roger Black, who was a Porsche from the word go, Kriss has achieved what he has achieved by dint of hard work. He has lifted himself from being a good club athlete to being an international runner by sheer effort. That is why he is an inspiration to many youngsters.' And that is why Mike Whittingham felt confident that Kriss could become a top hurdler.

So, at the age of twenty-seven, Kriss embarked on learning a new skill. To begin with he was put through a variety of drills which mimic the hurdle action. These include lead leg drills, trail leg drills, alternate leg drills, and a constant repetition of the movements which make up the hurdling action. There was also the stride pattern to learn. Thirteen, fourteen, fifteen strides between each of the hurdles, depending on the state of the race and the experience and fitness of the hurdler.

Some of the drills Mike expected him to learn, Kriss found very difficult. The first barriers he hurdled were low, 2 foot 6 inches, and spaced to suit Kriss's stride. Because Kriss was a complete beginner, Mike was able to teach him to hurdle on both legs. Sometimes the left leg would lead and sometimes the right. As a result, his instincts never developed to favour one side. This was very useful later on when evolving stride tactics for major races.

At his twice-weekly sessions with Mike Whittingham Kriss spent half his time honing the technique and the other half learning how to hurdle even when tired. In a race, maintaining the ability to judge and surmount the very last hurdle is all-important. Flat runners without the experience of being able to judge strides and distances at speed, when tired, often hesitate and stall when keeping up the rhythm is essential.

After a while, Mike Whittingham and Mike Smith realized that there was a danger that Kriss could be worked too hard. Their two programmes had to be integrated to avoid giving Kriss two exceptionally hard sessions back-to-back. They telephoned each other to coordinate their work. Yet, as time passed, Kriss felt the coaching of Mike Whittingham was more important to him. As a result of his years with Mike Smith he had learned enough about general training theory to be able to devise much of his own programme; what he was now looking for was specialist advice in his new event. He was also enjoying the challenge of the new work more than the routine grind of the old training. He was immensely grateful to Mike Smith for the progress he had made in the past, but felt it was Mike Whittingham who could best take him on to the next stage in his career. He talked about this in an interview published in *Athletics Today* in January 1991.

'I siphon information from people, and after a while I began to know and understand Mike Smith's philosophy on training to the extent now that I know when I should be doing what physically. By 1986 it got to a stage where Mike and myself would have a lot of discussions as to what I thought I should be doing and each year Mike's input has become less and less. Basically he has coached himself out of a job.

'Last year (1990) I saw relatively little of Mike Smith physically but still had a lot of discussions with him on the telephone. I think from here onwards that even that will cease, because I do know what I want to do and there's no point asking all the time... But technically over the hurdles I still need an expert eye and that's why Mike Whittingham is so vital to me. I don't want to denigrate Mike Smith's work, because he's still very important. I work on his philosophy and I was round to talk to him the other day about what I was thinking of doing. I always feel upset when people say, "Oh, so Mike Smith's no longer your coach, then," because it sounds as though I have chopped him out of my life. It's not that. I've evolved; I've moved on and I don't need him in that capacity. I wouldn't fool him and he wouldn't want me to fool him.'

Kriss made an amicable break with Mike Smith, unlike Roger Black who also decided to go to Mike Whittingham for coaching and, for various reasons, did not leave Mike Smith on the best of terms. Kriss was saddened by this, as he felt caught between his loyalties to two good friends.

Even the most experienced athlete still needs a coach, in the same way that a top singer relies on a teacher. For the singer the teacher is an extra pair of ears, for the athlete the coach is an invaluable extra pair of eyes. Athletes, coaches say, are notoriously bad at advising themselves. They tend to overwork themselves, practising their strengths and ignoring their weaknesses. The obsession which can make a champion can also kill a champion.

Kriss, from his army physical training background, probably knew as much as, if not more than, Mike Whittingham about the general training of the body for speed and endurance, but he relied on him for his hurdling expertise and, after leaving Mike Smith, for his objective assessment of his progress. The coach suggests the fine tuning.

To a top-class athlete a coach, however, often becomes more than a technical adviser. He becomes something between a man-manager and a nanny. He is the person in whom the athlete will confide and on whom the athlete may well rely to make other aspects of life run smoothly.

The business or contractual relationship between an athlete and a coach in Britain is one which harks back to the days when the sport was truly amateur. There are professional coaches, paid for by the governing body, the Amateur Athletics Association, but people like Mike Smith and Mike Whittingham have a far more informal arrangement. They are experts, but amateur, in that they do what they do for love of the sport and not for any reward. When a top coach and a top athlete form a partnership, the coach can be paid by the athlete for his or her services. But no coach in Britain receives a major reward. Often the sum received does little more than cover expenses. So why do coaches give so generously of their time and expertise?

Mike Whittingham, who has a full-time job as a local government director of leisure services puts it this way: 'I have always been interested in athletics and even though I never fulfilled all my ambitions as an athlete I know a lot about my event. When someone like Kriss comes along and approaches you, you miss a great chance, a great opportunity, if you turn him down. The motivation has been to get someone like that to world class. The bottom line is, I enjoy it. As I have a full-time job I now choose who I want to coach.'

Top athletes today can earn large sums of money for running. Strictly speaking, the money they earn goes into a trust fund for the duration of the athlete's career, so that he or she can retain amateur status. But money can be drawn from the fund by the athlete, and athletes negotiate with the impresarios of the sport for the fees which they believe they can command.

When a major sponsored meeting is to be held, the sponsors deal with the athletes through the Amateur Athletics Association. Appearance fees, or subventions, are arranged; these are supposed to reflect the athlete's standing in his or her event. Kriss has always been prepared to ask for what he feels he is worth and, as a result, has had a number of disagreements with Andy Norman of the AAA. Kriss describes Andy Norman as the 'Mr Fix-it of British athletics'. In theory, as the promotions officer with the AAA, he has it in his power to make or break an athlete's career.

In August 1989, the *Sunday Times* 'Insight' team produced a profile of Andy Norman and an examination of his methods. He was described as 'promoter, agent, fixer, paymaster and national selector', with a hand on every big lever of power; a ubiquitous figure at all big meetings and in the bars and lounges of the hotels where athletes, coaches and promoters do their deals. 'Reputed to have a phenomenal memory, he rarely writes anything down and fixes appearances and fee with little more than a nod.'

The *Sunday Times* claimed that out of the AAA's £5 million income for the year, drawn from television, sponsorship and other promotions, Andy Norman effectively controlled the £400,000 subvention budget.

'It is a role he obviously relishes and which he pursues with a characteristic bluntness. "When did you last run a good race?" he has been heard to ask a reigning Olympic champion without batting an eyelid.

'But it is also a role that has led him into many conflicts, and caused athletes to speak of being "frightened" of him and his ability to make or break their seasons, even their careers.

'Sponsors of athletics meetings want to be sure the stars of the day are competing at their events. They need people to come to the event and to attract television and media coverage. The big names in the sport need to be paid substantial sums of money to appear, thousands of pounds. The sponsors, together with Andy Norman, make a judgment as to what an individual athlete's standing and commercial pulling power might be, and offer the athlete a fee accordingly. Andy Norman works on the principle that if you offer peanuts you get monkeys, and that everyone has their price. If a big enough offer is made anyone, however big their reputation, will make an appearance.'

Kriss has often felt he has been undervalued and has expressed a personal view that the best way to reward top athletes would be to offer prize money. He shares a feeling common amongst black athletes that their white colleagues are deemed to be better "box office" material. There is also a feeling that athletes who overvalue themselves might be overlooked next time appearance monies are offered. Troublesome athletes are not welcomed by the sport's organizers or commercial sponsors. And athletes are expected to know their place.

However, as Mike Smith observes, having known Kriss throughout his international career, 'Kriss did not know his place within the scheme of things. And he was quite happy to tell the officials when offers were made to him which he found unacceptable that they were unacceptable. At one time there was a very firm scale and you were on that scale and nobody argued. But it became too costly and so the authorities cut back.'

A subvention will be calculated on the basis of the athlete's performance record and general popularity, but what sums are offered to whom is a closely guarded secret.

'There is almost a Mafia-style situation, where no one lets on what athletes might be getting. You learn it by accident,' says Mike Smith.

The situation has lead to a number of public rows. In 1989 there was the controversy over whether Steve Ovett had been offered money to race against Sebastian Coe. In a less-publicised incident relating to the same race, the runner Adrian Passey decided to pull out because of tiredness. Andy Norman had other ideas.

Quoted in the *Sunday Times* Adrian Passey says, 'He told me I had to run, otherwise I wouldn't be invited to run in any other races this year.' And the 'Insight' team report continued, 'Passey still refused, but is worried Norman will carry out his threat: "Being an athlete you just don't want to cross Andy Norman. He is the one who gives you all the chances in athletics. He is the figurehead who can literally manipulate your career." Kriss Akabusi, who won the 400 metres hurdles title at the recent Europa Cup final, says that Norman has frequently pulled him out of races because "I didn't do exactly as I was told. I've been held out of so many meetings, it's ridiculous."'

There is another matter which concerns Kriss and many of his colleagues, separate from the financial issues connected with Andy Norman. On one occasion during the 1990 season, Roger Black heard that Kriss had been offered less money than himself to compete in the same meeting, largely, the two friends suspected on the grounds of colour. Roger offered to pull out of the meeting, but Kriss persuaded him not to.

Kriss is philosophical about racism in sport. He says he has experienced it in all walks of life, and ever since he was a small child he has learnt to deal with it. He talks of being in a country where black people are in the minority and he has come to accept that racism or prejudice will inevitably exist in society. Athletics being part of that society, the same prejudices will come through. Sometimes racism is subtle, sometimes it is more overt. It is almost always very hard to pin down. No one says openly if a person is discriminated against, that it is on the grounds of colour. Other, often quite plausible excuses will be offered.

For a long while there were many black athletes but no superstars. With the advent of such people as Daley Thompson, black athletes now get star billing. There could be a danger of a backlash. Kriss is well aware that if black athletes start to dominate the sport, the promoters could be on the look-out for a 'great white hope' as a commercial commodity.

'Maybe,' says Kriss, 'society wants to have the great white hope. Maybe, in commercial terms, the white hero sells more of the goods he endorses, or at least the advertising agencies think so. I have heard it said in the sport that there is only room for one black star at a time. You can't have too many of them.

'I don't want to denigrate my sport. Athletics is no different from any other section of society. Discrimination is there in all parts of society, so I wouldn't want to single out my sport at all.'

The sprinter Linford Christie, in his autobiography, listed a shameful catalogue of cases of harassment and racial discrimination. Although none of these cases involved the world of athletics, they do illustrate the problems faced by many young black people in British society. He recalled the day he was driving a new car he had been given by a sponsor. He was stopped four times by the police. 'It seemed to be accepted policy to stop a black man driving a new car.'

On another occasion he was arrested for being in possession of a stolen car, even though he had been loaned it legally by a sponsor. The charge was dropped the next day. And in yet another incident he was stopped by two policemen on his way home from training and asked, 'What's a nigger like you doing in an England tracksuit?'

Kriss too has experienced the problem of being stopped by the police when driving a new car. He was flagged down a number of times on one journey, taking a new car back from Germany to his home in Hampshire.

In the winter of 1987, Kriss did not know whether his

gamble to switch events was going to pay off. If it failed, Kriss would have been forced to say goodbye to the world of top-class athletics and four-figure payments for racing.

When Kriss went to California for his late winter training schedule, he met and worked with the world's, then, unbeatable hurdler, Ed Moses. Kriss realized he was still a long way from emulating the world record holder's perfect pattern of 13 strides between hurdles, but he was assured by the master that he had the potential, as long as he learned how to relax in the run.

In California, as an ungainly beginner, Kriss decided to have his first proper race at a college meeting. By that time he was, he says, a Christian, having had the vision—though he gave a false time to the organizers to be able to qualify. He had to as he had never run a hurdles race before and literally had no track record. Perhaps there was a message from the Almighty in what happened next. He started well, but found that with the extra adrenalin of the race, as he was trying to run his planned fourteen strides between each hurdle, he was chopping the last stride and running in fits and starts. Nevertheless, by the time he got to the fifth hurdle he was up by five metres.

'I went out looking really good, the American commentator was singing my praises, "Akabusi this . . . going over the hurdles, going well, Akabusi taking the . . . tremendous race . . . ooooh." Smack, I hit the ground! The eighth hurdle just grew ten inches. It tackled me as I went across. I bit the dust, fell flat on my face and I saw the guys go off in the distance. I had been trying so hard, I had been forgetting all the things Mike had told me to think about. I looked up and saw Monika and waved. Roger was also there, videoing everything. At that stage I could quite easily have said, this is not for me. But it was two weeks before I was due back in England and I knew I had to show what I had learned to the guys back home. So I carried on. But it was back to the drawing-board.'

What few people realized at the time was that while Kriss was hoping to impress his public with his new skill, he was suffering from a very painful injury. In fact he completed a whole season suffering from a hernia. He rested when he could, and was given cortisone injections to ease the pain, but by the end of the summer of 1987 he was advised to undergo a repair operation. It is a measure of Kriss's courage that he persisted. He has the ability to distance his mind from his body in such a way that he can perform when most people would have succumbed to pain.

He entered a race at Granada in Spain on 16 May, in which he ran the 400 metres hurdles in 50.16 seconds, as preparation for the UK Championships. A few days earlier, he had surprised the participants and spectators at an open meeting in Reading, when, needing some experience in British conditions he turned up to run. It was not the sort of meeting which would normally attract an international name. He ran 51.9 seconds and, in his own words, 'made a real mess of half the hurdles'. But there were only two runners in the race and he won it easily.

Before going to Derby to run on 24 May, Kriss had had a week away from the training circuit because of his injury. With this worry at the front of his mind, in a state of relative unpreparedness, Kriss took to the track for his major British debut. His coach knew he was a novice, with much to learn, that his technique was clumsy and he ran the risk of making himself a laughing-stock. But Kriss had survived other potential embarrassments—the Olympic silver medalist and former international team captain had been watched by school children at Crystal Palace as he struggled with novice hurdlers' basic drills—so he was mentally prepared for the occasion. Even if he did not do well, even if he made a complete fool of himself, he knew the experience was essential to learning the skills of his new event.

This is John Rodda's account of the race from *The Guardian*: 'For competitiveness it was the 400 metres hurdles which set the meeting alight. Kriss Akabusi plunged into his new career like a wallowing rhino and came home sharing a UK Championship record of 49.56 seconds with Max Robertson. For Akabusi, a gold medal winner in the European 4 x 400 metres relay, this was his third attempt at the event: in the first he failed to finish.

'Yesterday he arrived at the first obstacle too early and did a hooked hop. He took a long jump at the sixth, seemed indecisive at the seventh, started to catch Robertson at the ninth and lost his stride again and smacked the tenth. The pair leaned across the line together and a dead heat was declared: the referee declined to ask them to run the race again.

'With so much improvement in technique and strength to be achieved, Akabusi must realistically be looking towards something in the lower 48s before the end of the summer.'

John Rodda might have under-estimated the sum total of Kriss's racing experience but his forecast was pretty accurate.

The press, on the one hand, enjoyed pointing out Kriss's inelegance over the hurdles, but on the other began to sense that the 400 metres hurdles was about to undergo a renaissance. When Kriss and Max Robertson tied for the UK title, only six Britons had ever run faster and four of them were winners of Olympic or European medals.

The world of athletics was intrigued by Kriss's attempt to change events and marvelled at how he had reached the top spot in Britain so quickly. Initially, the leading British hurdlers had been sceptical. They had watched his untidy attempts at their event in the early months of the winter and doubted he would ever make the grade. But Kriss had a mission. His record throughout the 1987 season was one of consistent improvement, culminating in a personal best of 48.64 seconds in the semi-final at the World Championships in Rome, where British fans cheered him on, waving a banner saying, 'Good Luck Rookie'.

Just before the final, Sebastian Coe came up to Kriss to wish him well: 'You could make history today,' he said. Kriss began to wonder if a medal was really within his grasp. In the final he ran just a tenth of a second slower than his new personal best to gain seventh place. Considering how new he was to the event, Kriss was more than pleased with his performance.

The final itself was dominated by the struggle between Ed

Moses and the two claimants for his position as the world's leading hurdler. At the line, Moses beat Danny Harris and Harald Schmid by the narrowest of measurable margins, 0.02 of a second. Kriss was one and a quarter seconds, around ten metres, behind.

Nevertheless, at the end of his first season he was the best at his event in Britain and number seven in the world. He also won a silver in the relay at the World Championships, helping the team to a new European record of 2 minutes, 58.86 seconds.

'The moment I tied with Max Robertson at the UK Championships, I knew I had made the right decision. I may have looked untidy and people laughed at me, talking about my hop, skip and jump approach to winning races. But I was winning some and doing well where it mattered.'

Kriss observed at the end of the summer that, whereas the year before in one major championship the 400 metres hurdles was the only race without a British finalist, this year it was no longer the forgotten event. Much of that was due to his own grit and personality with the unselfish help and encouragement of Ed Moses, the man who had dominated his speciality in international athletics for a decade.

Moses went for 122 races without defeat, collecting two Olympic and two World Championship Gold medals on the way. The second World Championship win involved beating Kriss, but later Ed Moses was full of praise for the up-and-coming runner. He predicted that Kriss had a great future ahead and would be the first Briton to record a better time than 48 seconds. To do this, however, Kriss had to return to the hard slog of learning his craft under Mike Whittingham and this could not start at the end of the 1987 season until Kriss had successfully undergone the hernia operation he had been postponing all summer.

Kriss had found that learning the new hurdle techniques had put unexpected strains on his body. He had been pushing himself on completing a heavy program of circuit-training, and he sustained a hernia, or muscle split, in his lower abdomen. It caused him considerable pain, but Kriss's attitude is that if he bothered to take notice of every twinge of pain he would never have time to achieve anything. He is accustomed to ignoring it.

'I got to the stage where I was in the middle of the season and I wasn't going to stop for anything. If I had enough cortisone, I wouldn't feel it for ten days and so I could get on with running.'

12

A Life-Changing Faith

On the Northam Road leading out of Southampton, just before
the Television South studios and the bridge, a church stands on
the left. Architecturally it appears to be nothing special, a standard nineteenth-century building, once used by the Church of
England and known as St Augustine's. Today it is home to an
active independent congregation, the Southampton Christian
Fellowship. Its pastor is Paul Finn.

Newcomers are made welcome and Sunday services are
lively, with perhaps eighty people, from right across the age-
range, gathering to worship. This is Kriss Akabusi's church
when he is in England. It is a far cry from the Calvary Chapel,
with its vast auditorium of a building and its multi-million dollar
ministry. Yet, at the St Augustine's Centre, Kriss feels comfortable after his long search. The congregation knows him as a
fellow Christian and he takes a full part in church life. No
special fuss is made of him because of his name as an international athlete. Sometimes he comes with his two little girls, and
he finds the church has an easy family atmosphere.

Paul Finn would describe the Fellowship as simply a gathering of Christians. Doctrinally, however, they can be more closely
identified as belonging to the evangelical pentecostal tradition,
putting a strong emphasis on the study and authority of the
Bible. The church is an autonomous gathering but is affiliated
to the wider movement of the Assemblies of God.

In its short welcoming leaflet, the congregation describes
itself as a group of ordinary people from across the city who
meet together weekly to share friendship, love and fellowship

in supporting and caring for each other in practical and spiritual ways.

'Although we are all very different people and from a variety of backgrounds, we have one thing in life that joins us together, knowing Jesus Christ. Jesus said: "I have come that you might have life and have it to the full," and, "If anyone is in Christ he is a new creation, the old has gone, the new has come."

'We have found new life in Jesus that has brought a peace and happiness into our everyday living. We would love to share this new life with you. Do you need friendship? Do you need healing? Do you have problems you cannot solve? Do you have needs to be met? You can find all your needs in Jesus Christ, because He loves and cares for you.'

In America Kriss had enjoyed worshipping as one of the crowd.

'No one knew me as Kriss Akabusi. Back in Britain I knew that finding a church where I could do this was going to be harder. Also I didn't want to get tied down to a denomination. I am a Christian, not a Baptist or a Methodist.'

Kriss found the church just by driving past and noticing the sign. What attracted him was that the sign made no reference to any denomination, it just said it was a Christian Fellowship. Eager to find the right church to attend in Britain, having found Calvary Chapel in California, he went along one Sunday morning in May 1987. The congregation was at the time meeting in a temporary room upstairs, and Kriss was given the usual friendly greeting. No one recognized him, except Paul Finn's son, who thought his face looked familiar, but said nothing until later. No pressure was put on Kriss to join. He was simply asked for his name and address and sent a short letter and leaflet a few days later.

The service, however, made a considerable impression.

'It was Bedlam in there. I could not believe it. There was dancing and clapping and hands in the air and alleluias. To begin with, even I was a bit intimidated by their sheer uninhibited worship. It was far more exciting even than the black church.

Some people were speaking in tongues. I didn't know what was going on. I thought to myself, what is happening here? But in a perverse sort of way I enjoyed it. Everybody was friendly and at that church you couldn't sit at the back and just watch.'

Kriss told Monika about his discovery and persuaded her to come to the church the next week. She did not enjoy the experience. It was far too strange. Even though Kriss felt drawn to the Fellowship he did not return for a number of weeks. His busy summer schedule prevented him from making any regular commitment until later in the year, but he kept in touch with Paul Finn and a friendship grew.

By that time Paul knew who Kriss was; he recalled having seen him on television. Monika watched Kriss's commitment to the church grow but has returned to attend a service herself only occasionally. One of the reasons Kriss was attracted to the church was that, after his first visit, Paul Finn had taken the trouble to write to him. It was a simple letter telling Kriss about the church and inviting him to return. Yet the personal touch was much appreciated.

When Paul Finn had his first serious conversations with Kriss about his faith he found that although Kriss was still a 'novice' Christian, he was clear about his beliefs. He was well informed, having been reading the Bible by himself, but in some matters, Paul considered, he was still young in the faith. Despite his dramatic vision and the personal encounter with Christ in his dream, Kriss still had many unanswered questions in his mind. The Mormon challenge to find the one true church still disturbed him. The doctrine of the Trinity, Kriss found confusing.

'He had met with God in a remarkable way and had come to a personal faith,' Paul remembers. 'Something had happened in his life, without doubt. I think he felt comfortable with us as a family of Christians because we are not a denomination. Neither do we think we have a monopoly on the truth. We seek to work out the love of Christ in a practical way, supporting, sharing and encouraging one another.'

As a pentecostal church, the Southampton Christian

Fellowship believes very strongly in the baptism of the Holy Spirit. One outward sign of this is speaking in tongues. In the Bible, in the Acts of the Apostles chapter 2, Christ's disciples are described as being filled with the Holy Spirit so that they begin to talk 'in other languages (tongues), as the Spirit enabled them to speak.' To someone unfamiliar with the sound of speaking in tongues today, it might seem as if the person is praising God in a curious gibberish. Sometimes people sing in tongues or pray out loud. Very often the sound is heard just in the worshipper's head and is a private form of communication with God. There are Christians who have the gift of interpretation and can discern a message in the outpouring of sound, even when it apparently has no linguistic form or shape. There have been claims that a few people have spoken in a foreign language unknown to themselves. Certainly, on the Day of Pentecost, as told in the Bible, the disciples spoke to the crowds in a variety of languages and everyone understood what was being said.

Paul Finn gave Kriss a leaflet about the gifts of the spirit and talked to him about speaking in tongues. It was a whole new and confusing area for Kriss. He felt that he had been baptised in the spirit when he had had his vision, yet he did not speak in tongues. He wondered, did he first have to be baptised in water? Was he a complete Christian as yet? Was it not sufficient to believe? He felt that speaking in tongues was a sort of spiritual barometer. Displaying the ability was a way of allowing other Christians to measure how far a convert had advanced in the faith.

At the Fellowship Kriss heard many of the congregation speaking in tongues and wondered whether he ought to be able to as well. In the end, Paul Finn satisfied Kriss with his answers and Christian counselling. Kriss became a regular member of the church. Although today he might have some reservations, he is generally in line with the Fellowship's understanding of faith, and he finds the church a friendly place where he is known as himself and not as the athletics star. It is a place, he says, where he can get on with the business of being a Christian.

Echoing Paul Finn's words he explains, 'We don't say we are

perfect or have all the answers. What we do know is that we love Jesus, who is the most important influence in our lives.'

Returning to America in the winter of 1988 Kriss found that worship at Calvary Chapel was subdued and staid in comparison with the services at the St Augustine's Centre in Southampton. He did not wish to sever his links with Pastor Chuck, as he found his preaching helpful, but he thought he would like to find another, livelier, place of worship as well. In one sense Kriss was homesick for the more human-scale atmosphere of South-ampton as he sat as one of the many in the huge Calvary Chapel. He discovered there were disadvantages as well as advantages to be had from being one of 3,000. Kriss even had a tape with him of some of his favourite songs from the Southampton Fellowship, which he played in the car. So, during his winter training period in 1988, Kriss evolved a pattern of Sunday worship which took him to Calvary Chapel in the evening and out looking for a more exciting Christian experience in the morning.

One day he drove past a church which declared itself, in big bold red letters to be the Life Church, Spirit Led. It was on an upper floor of a modern office building.

'I went to check it out and it was like Southampton. Those guys were leaping about, bouncing off the walls. They were great, but by now I was getting a little more critical of ser-mons. The worship was great but the presentation of the word wasn't so thorough as I had come to expect. The guy was very flash and had all the actions. But it was too flamboyant.'

Although Kriss went to the church a number of times, it didn't become his main place of worship. But something did happen at the church which was to be an important milestone in the development of his faith.

To have found both churches suited him well at that stage in his spiritual journey. He was still trying to sort out in his mind the questions concerning baptism, both by water and the Spirit, and it was through the two churches in California that he was able to resolve the problem.

One Saturday, the day before Kriss went to the Spirit-led

church for the first time, Pastor Chuck arranged for a service of baptism. It was to be held, not in the church at a font, but in the Pacific Ocean. He invited any member of his congregation who felt called by God to be baptised to join him on the beach. Kriss heard the invitation.

'I want to be baptised, I thought, I want to go for it. It was 10 o'clock on a Saturday morning. I joined a crowd on a beautiful expanse of beach. They were all singing and praising and holding their hands in the air. It was the day for me to say publicly that I was a Christian.

'It was a tremendous service and we all lined up on the beach. There were various pastors, including Pastor Chuck, standing in the water at the head of each line. I wanted to be baptised by Pastor Chuck, but he had the longest queue. But then I thought to myself, this is between me and the Lord, it doesn't matter who I get baptised by. I took my turn and remember walking into the water. It was cold at first, but it didn't matter.

'When I reached the pastor he asked me why I wanted to be baptised and I told him about my whole experience. He said I had a very interesting life. He asked me my name. He said that today I would be burying my old life and gaining a new life in Christ. He said that he baptised me in the name of the Father, the Son and the Holy Spirit and then pulled me briefly under the water. I walked out of the water feeling on cloud nine. There was a crazy guy standing on the beach who said, "Welcome, brother!" in a loud voice and slapped my hand. "Right on!" I said. I felt really happy.'

It was a profound but also an informal occasion, with everyone dressed in beachwear and Pastor Chuck in a T-shirt on which was written 'number one'. The baptism was captured on video by Mike Whittingham, who was in the USA helping Kriss with his training, and was watching the proceedings from the cliffs above the beach.

'I was staying with Kriss at the time and we were having a lot of discussions about religion and philosophy. The lovely thing about Kriss is that he is so open and he shared all his ideas and thoughts with me as a friend.'

The next morning, being a Sunday, Kriss decided that before he went to the usual service at Calvary Chapel he would visit the Life Church. The sermon was on Pentecost and speaking in tongues. Kriss, at that time, was very sceptical about the whole notion. He had been praying for the gift of tongues and nothing had happened to him. He heard people around him singing and praying in tongues and concluded that they must have been making it all up, deliberately babbling away in a nonsense language.

That Pentecost morning the preacher at the Life Church put a challenge to the hundred or so people in the congregation. If anyone there present wished to be given the gift of tongues, he or she was to come forward. To begin with Kriss stayed firmly in his seat. Then a couple of the congregation moved to the front of the church. The preacher reissued his challenge. There is someone else without the gift, he said, who should come forward.

'I felt as if he was talking to me. So I got up. I went to the front and spoke to the preacher. He asked me my name and then said he would lay hands on me. While he was doing this he said that he would pray for me and that at the same time I should also pray. We all started praying that I might receive the gifts of the Holy Spirit. And I well remember that this church overlooked the motorway and there were massive windows. As we were praying I could see the cars going past. And the pastor said to me, "Kriss, take your eyes off the world and turn your eyes to Jesus. Just think about Jesus, talk to Jesus."

'After that rebuke, as it were, I did start thinking about Jesus and thanking him. I thought of the baptism the day before and thanked him for that. I thanked him for having saved me and for becoming one of his people, when all of a sudden I started babbling. Just incomprehensible, nonsensical babbling. What I remember is that I was babbling away and yet in my mind I was still talking sense, thanking Jesus. And then I realized what was happening and the pastor and the congregation were shouting, "Praise the Lord, the Holy Spirit has fallen on this brother!"

'I also got excited because I knew I wasn't doing something I was controlling myself. I went on speaking in tongues for ten or fifteen minutes. Then someone put his arm round me and said, "Listen Kriss, Satan is going to try and rob you of your gift. He is going to tell you that it didn't really happen, that you made it all up. You know that you spoke in tongues today. It is a gift God has given you to talk to him."

'I drove home after the service. Monika wasn't there and I tried speaking in tongues again. Later I went to hear Pastor Chuck and that night I began to have doubts. Did I really speak in tongues? Was my babbling genuine? It didn't sound like the tongues I had heard at the Southampton Christian Fellowship. They sounded like a language. My sounds were incoherent. I thought I must have been making it up: I wanted so much to speak in tongues, had I just made it up?

'But when I began to speak in tongues again I found my mouth and tongue making unusual, weird shapes. No sound was coming, but it was if I was mouthing another language which didn't have the rhythms and patterns I was used to. As I analysed the shapes I realized there was no way I could be making them up. Whether I was speaking with the tongues of men or of angels, I don't know. It was certainly a language I didn't know. But God could understand. And as I don't now understand what it is I am saying, I don't speak in tongues as much as I could do, but I have the confidence to know that God understands what it is that I am saying and it is coming from my heart.

'I speak in tongues now, to say things which words cannot express. It happens when I am distraught, or if I really want to pray for something but I am lost for words and don't know what to say. I don't pray in tongues out loud. At a service I may mouth the words coming to me, but mainly tongues are reserved for those special times when I want to communicate with God but words fail me. I might pray in tongues at a prayer group. But I feel constrained in public. It is far more important in public to say a few understandable words.

'I remember going to Southampton for the first time and thinking, these guys are crazy. I didn't comprehend what was going on. I wouldn't want to put a newcomer off by doing something he didn't understand. When I speak in tongues it is now between me and God.'

Having received the gift of tongues Kriss did not, however, become a regular member of the Life Church. To him, Pastor Chuck provided the more substantial diet which enabled him to understand the Bible in greater depth.

Both Kriss's American and British spiritual homes are places which emphasize the belief that Christ will fulfil his promise to return, soon. Kriss has come to believe strongly that the world is entering the last days. He sees in biblical prophecy a blue-print for the return of Christ. He therefore believes he has to live his life as if Christ could arrive tomorrow. Pastor Chuck reinforces the belief through his sermons and radio programmes. At the time of the Gulf War he drew on the Old Testament Book of Isaiah to preach that the news from the Middle East could be the fulfilment of Isaiah's prophecies concerning the destruction of Babylon. He equated Iraq with Babylon of old and spoke of the armies from a far country coming to destroy the land. He then linked the prophecies of the Old Testament with those of the New, and spoke of the 'tribulation' Jesus predicted and the 'rapture' (the literal interpretation of the words of St Paul that, at the end, Christians will be taken up into heaven in a moment of time). It is a time keenly anticipated by many Christians, especially within the pentecostal, fundamentalist tradition. In America there is even talk of the rapture happening in such a way that Christians will be lifted from their cars on the freeways, causing traffic chaos.

Kriss is happy to argue endlessly about such matters. His first grounding as a Christian from his two churches was scriptural and very literal in its interpretation. He would be taken through the Bible and shown texts to support this understanding. He is currently studying at a Christian university in California which, while tending to be conservative in its theology, also introduces students to biblical criticism. He is now wrestling with the question of whether the Bible as we have it today is entirely without error. Could there be inaccuracies in the text because of the difficulties of translation? What in the Bible is history, what is fable, legend, poetry, prophecy, parable, and so on?

Kriss's faith is real and living and he does not doubt that he has a direct relationship with Jesus, yet there are many doctrinal issues to be sorted out. He tends towards a conservative interpretation and feels insecure if he departs from it too much, fearing that to question a traditional dogma might be seen to be undermining his core faith. At the same time, he is intellectually curious and committed to searching for truth; he hates to leave a question until it is answered to his complete satisfaction.

Many of these questions are not thrashed out in church circles but with his friends. From 1987 he made no secret of his faith, and made contact with the group 'Christians in Sport'. Some of his fellow athletes refer to Kriss and other active Christians in athletics as the God Squad, but there is a genuine respect for his position and his friends have noticed how, in gaining a faith, Kriss has changed markedly for the better. He still debates and argues furiously. These days conversation on the training track amongst the athletes, when Kriss is around, is far more likely to be about religion than any other topic.

Kriss is not the only member of the British track and field team who is open about his Christian faith. His 400 metres relay colleague Derek Redmond, the triple jumper Jonathan Edwards, long jumper Barrington Williams, Diana Edwards in the 800 metres and Judy Simpson in the heptathlon are all known as Christians by their team mates.

In the film *Chariots of Fire*, the great debate revolved around the issue of whether it was right for a Christian to compete on a Sunday. There is no consensus view on this amongst today's Christian athletes and Kriss himself has no qualms about running on 'the Sabbath', the day of rest. When asked about competing on a Sunday during the 1988 Olympic Games, Kriss consulted with Paul Finn and then put his view this way: 'I am a Christian and I have my rest in Jesus Christ. As far as I'm concerned, the law of the Sabbath was given as part of the old covenant to the Jews.'

Before each race Kriss says a short prayer. He doesn't ask to win, but just that he will run to the glory of God—though he often thinks, 'Lord, it would be nice if I could win as well.' His coach Mike Whittingham is sometimes concerned that Kriss's enthusiasm for his faith might have a detrimental effect on his performance on the track.

'Whatever he does, he can get fanatical and obsessive. When he starts studying and getting into new academic and theological ideas, it could have an influence on his training. I tell him he has the rest of his life to study but only one chance to go to another World Championships or Olympics. He is only as good as his last race and if he doesn't run the right time to qualify he will not only be out of the World Championships final, but out of the British team as well. He knows this but needs an outsider to remind him and nag him from time to time.'

Kriss believes that his faith has enhanced his athletics, and his record over the last four years would tend to support that view. He described the way his faith affected his running in the interview with *21st Century Christian* in September 1988.

'I go into competitions now and I've got no worries at all. I've just got to get onto the blocks and Jesus does the rest.

'It sounds stupid to a lay person, but it's not me that's winning... now I'm running better than I have ever done in my career.'

At his first 400 metres hurdles final at the World Championships, Mike Whittingham was nervous but Kriss was confident.

'I'd prayed about it before the race and God said, "You can't do it, but just go out there and start." '

Kriss felt a greater calmness before that race than before any other he could remember, and he successfully completed the race.

He also told the magazine about how he had severely pulled a right hamstring when training after the Commonwealth and before the European Games in 1986. This was when he had started to read the Bible avidly and explore questions of faith. With only three weeks to go before the European heats of the 4 x 400 metres relay, running flat-out was impossible and Kriss looked destined to watch the Games as a spectator.

The day of the heats dawned and Kriss was named as a member of the four-man team. Only Mike Smith knew of the painful injury. Kriss knew that if his injury forced him to pull up during the race, the whole team would lose.

'So I prayed and read through the Bible. I read about putting your faith in the Lord; if you have the faith of a mustard seed you can move mountains. I said to myself when I warmed up, "You're all right. The Lord is with you."

'I got to 120 metres and started to worry about my leg. The niggling pain came right back but I told myself to have faith. I carried on running. I made it and won a gold medal. That day I knew that putting your trust in the Lord is the greatest thing in the world.'

Roger Black in particular has noticed the difference in the new Kriss.

'While there is part of Kriss which is very excitable, he is a deep thinker. When he is in public, he's a performer. The real Kriss is much quieter, even introverted to some extent. The best thing for Kriss about finding Christianity was that it gave him a purpose. No longer did he need to show off. After a period when his ideas had been in turmoil he found peace in his own mind. He had peace in himself. His relationship with Monika became stronger, he gave her more time. Monika might not see it that way, thinking that his Christianity has taken him away from her, but it's not true. Before becoming a Christian he was a terrible sexist—I'm the man, you're the woman. He's now overcoming this. He has given more time to other people. He has become a much better person.

'The change in Kriss in the last four years is enormous. He has changed in every way, including his politics. Once he was very right wing, now he is much more of a middle-of-the-road democrat with a social awareness. They say a leopard never changes his spots, and Kriss is very aware of that charge, but he is not the same person he was four years ago. I have been happy to see him finding a new joy in other people, finding his mind stimulated by reading and by becoming more philosophical.

'Five years ago he had no direction in his life. He was finding success on the athletics field but was fundamentally insecure and was covering this up by being an incredible showman with people, showing off, full of macho bravado, and materialistic. Now he has found a peace in himself.'

To illustrate the point, Roger tells the story of a conversation he and Kriss once had. They were discussing earnings, and Roger was saying how he would be satisfied with a good income, but had no need for great wealth. On £50,000 a year, he said, it would be possible to be very comfortable and have total freedom, so who needed more? Kriss took the opposite tack. He was at the time mixing with people who talked about hundreds of thousands of pounds. He scoffed at the notion of £50,000 a year, and said it was nothing, and they should be thinking about turning their talents into substantial sums of money. Roger said he was crazy. With that attitude it was impossible ever to be satisfied.

Today Roger says, Kriss would no longer take such a view. His values have been completely changed. If he once looked to money for the security he never had as a child, he now looks to his faith. Money is still important for the family, but if he was on his own, Roger thinks, money would cease to be a major factor in his life.

Although Kriss and Roger have remained close colleagues and friends since Kriss's conversion, Roger is aware that there is now part of Kriss's life in which he can have no involvement.

They discuss theology and moral issues freely, but Roger does not appreciate Kriss's emotional involvement in his faith. He does not have the personal experience of finding and believing in a supernatural power who is at one and the same time Lord, forgiver and friend.

Roger was brought up to go to church and became a chorister and server, but vividly remembers one day when he was about fourteen and he was sitting in the church in his robes. He began to wonder what he was doing there. He looked at the people praying and realized he did not come to church to pray. He just came to see his friends. He was faced with a moral problem which he solved by leaving church that day and never returning.

'Christianity dropped out of my thinking and my life until Kriss brought it back in. I would find it hard to be a total believer like Kriss. Kriss needed to change his life. He badly needed to find something. He would have been lost. When I weigh up the pros and cons of Christianity for Kriss, I would always argue for the pros, even though his Christianity has caused a lot of problems. He doesn't try to convert me. He knows that people come to Christ when the time is right for them to do so.

'He never judges people because of their faith or lack of faith and is becoming more moderate. But if someone wants to be converted, Kriss is in there like a shot. His ability to explain and argue his point of view has markedly improved. I have had some personal difficulties in the last few years, and I have turned to Kriss as a friend, and his judgments have been primarily Christian. His advice has been primarily Christian and on the whole it has been the right advice. And I usually take it. Four years, ago if I had gone to Kriss in the same circumstances I would have been given totally different advice.'

Roger does not dismiss any of Kriss's ideas, but still keeps an open mind himself. They differ on the value of other faiths. Kriss tells Roger that Christianity is the only way. Roger replies, but what about the good people from other traditions, are they destined for hell?

It is a question which worries Kriss. It is exceedingly painful when related to his non-Christian friends and his family. In its most brutal form the question is exceedingly painful. What is Monika's eternal destiny, he asks himself, if she does not become a Christian?

13

Tensions

'I think he has fallen for one big fairy tale.'

Monika makes no secret of her view. Despite many lengthy discussions she has not been converted to Christianity or shared Kriss's experience of faith. Too often it is assumed that a conversion, that finding Jesus, is the happy-ever-after end to a search for faith. Often it is just the beginning of the struggle. Jesus said that to follow him involved taking up a cross, in other words carrying through life the instrument of torture and pain.

It is not an unusual experience for a new and enthusiastic Christian to find that a loving husband or wife does not share in, let alone understand, the joy of being born again. It is not unknown for the wives of newly converted Christian husbands to feel as if the church has become as demanding as a mistress. Even if the discovery of Christ brings a transformation in character, the wife can be forgiven for thinking that the changes are too good to last. Church leaders can underestimate the marital tensions which can result from the discovery by one partner of a faith.

Monika is pleased for Kriss in a number of respects. She too has noticed that he has become a more sensitive husband and father. She too has noticed that he has gained a new purpose in life, one which will continue after his inevitable retirement from the track. She has noted too his new interest in study and learning which she is pleased to encourage. She resents, however, the demands many Christians put on Kriss. She has warned Kriss that they take advantage of his enthusiasm and willingness to please, and that he should not accept every invitation he receives from churches. Time must be put aside for the family.

She has noticed that Kriss has become more vulnerable—a virtue, some Christians might claim; but Monika would hate to see Kriss hurt. She dreads the idea that Kriss might become a professional Christian himself one day, a minister or preacher, and she would have to be involved in something to which she cannot give herself wholeheartedly. Monika also finds that she has lost some of her confidence in her husband's judgment. If, she reasons, he can fall for the more improbable parts of the Christian faith, and even almost fall for the Mormons, how reliable might his judgment be in other areas of life? Has he become too gullible and naive?

Monika does not recall when Kriss first expressed an interest in religion. This may be, she says, not because Kriss did not tell her, but because she did not rate it an important enough piece of information to remember. She does, however, recollect the day the Mormons arrived. She thought it typical of Kriss to invite them in, when she would have told them firmly, 'No thank you.' And she also remembers how pleased she was when Kriss split from the Mormons over the issue of race.

She then watched Kriss becoming an increasingly enthusiastic Christian and admits she would not be surprised if one day he lost his interest in Christianity too and developed an enthusiasm for something else.

Monika thought she saw the first sign of this when, in the winter of 1990, Kriss returned from the college where he is studying philosophy and theology and admitted that he had had a hard day and there were certain ideas pertaining to his faith which he could not figure out.

Monika's reaction was one of hope, 'Maybe one day he'll come home and say he has packed it up and he is not a Christian any more and he can't believe in religion.' But then she reflected on the positive effect Christianity had had on him. He was now an easier person to live with. Would that all go? Would she want Kriss to give up his faith? At present Monika's answer is a finely balanced yes, even though she realizes she cannot have both sides of Kriss together and that it is possible he would not remain a reformed non-believer. 'I want Kriss to give up his faith—but I don't want him to change as a person. Saying this, I do realize I want both to have my cake and eat it.'

Kriss attributes his change in character, his increased thoughtfulness and consideration for the feelings of others, directly to his faith. Monika feels the changes might have happened without requiring a commitment to a religion.

Of the particular literalistic pentecostal form of conservative Christian theology which Kriss has embraced, Monika says, 'For me it is something I cannot follow and I cannot believe in. This of course creates a lot of problems for us now. I am a non-Christian because, much as I have tried to look into things and read and tried to pray with Kriss, I just haven't got there. It is sad, because he has got this side of his life which I cannot be part of and which we cannot share. We both, and I in particular, find this very, very disturbing. It is very hard to live with.

'One way of solving this problem would be if I were to become a Christian. For Kriss, that is all he could possibly want. I think I could also live with the situation more easily if Kriss were to become a more liberal Christian. At the moment he is deeply into it. People in his church have sometimes said to me, "Monika you just have to be patient, he's still a baby in the church. He will grow and he will mature." Hopefully then he will become more liberal and then I think it will be easier for me to accept that side.'

There are signs of change, although up until now, since he has been a Christian, everything that Kriss has done and decided has been influenced by his new-found faith. Even decisions in the home have been related back to his understanding of the Christian gospel. Kriss has an unquestioning belief in the powers of good and in the powers of evil. The darker forces of Satan are an everyday reality to him. He will interpret temptations as being the devil personally testing him, and attribute success to the personal intervention of his Lord and Saviour.

There have been times when the relationship between Kriss

and Monika has been tested by Kriss taking a decision affecting his home or business life which Monika has not agreed with. On one occasion, Kriss decided he could not work with a particular individual because he was not a Christian. Monika found the decision very hard to understand, as the man in question she felt was good, decent and honest. Roger Black too found that a business venture he and Kriss were due to develop could not proceed because of Kriss's attitude to doing business with non-believers. Monika compares Kriss's tendency to categorize people according to their beliefs with racism. She feels that Christians view non-Christians as 'not being as good as they are. That I find very hard because I feel that although I am not a Christian, I am no worse than they are and I don't want to be turned away by a Christian because I am a non-Christian. It is wrong to have that kind of attitude in the world we are living in.'

'Obviously,' she adds, 'I am now in one category and Christians in another. Very often I say something and he looks at me through his "Christian glasses" and he will say I do not understand what I am saying as it is the devil speaking through me. And I say, "No, this is how I feel, this is reality." He also gets terribly misused by people to do things under the Christian cover. He doesn't see this. He sees this through his "Christian glasses" and feels that God wants him to do something, to appear, to speak to a group. Very often these people just want to be entertained and feel they have met a celebrity. They use the cover of being fellow Christians to get Kriss to do what they want. They know they will get a good entertainer. They will get it for nothing, and Kriss will even pay to get to their function, often driving a long way and spending time away from the family. If he thinks it is God wanting him to do something he will do it, and his family will come second. Although this is changing and I do sometimes hear him saying to someone on the phone that he needs time with his family. It is getting better. He is calming down.

'Our problem is not that he is a Christian but that he is so fanatical about it. I am waiting and hoping that he will calm down.'

Pastor Paul Finn has talked at length to Kriss about his relationship with Monika. He believes it is very important that Kriss does not rush ahead with his new-found faith and leave Monika behind. He stresses that Kriss's first priority is his own family, to care for them and to be sympathetic and understanding. Paul Finn has also talked to Monika, but never felt that it is his position to force his views on her.

'We have prayed for her. But we have never wanted to put pressure on her to make her think that she has to conform to where Kriss is at. Monika has to come to a point where she believes of her own accord, where she comes to faith because she wants to and not because of Kriss. That is very, very important.

'Whichever Christian church Kriss had come to and felt at home in, Kriss would not have been any different. He loves God with all his heart and he makes it clear that God is more important to him than his athletics, and yet through his athletics he wants to serve God. That enthusiasm is all part of Kriss. He hasn't become all hyped up because of his faith, that's his character.'

It was in the winter of 1990 that Kriss enrolled at Azusa Pacific University. Three days a week he left the family apartment in Fountain Valley on the outskirts of Los Angeles for a three-quarters-of-an-hour drive inland to the foothills of the mountains. Because Kriss had no formal qualifications and because he was unable to keep to the normal academic terms, the university has allowed him to take a special course of theology and philosophy by way of testing his aptitude and introducing him to academic discipline.

The system of teaching is very different from that found at a British university. Students do not have the same liberty to set their own time-tables. Students at Azusa must turn up for set classes, and in many a roll call is taken. Classes of up to thirty or forty pupils a time, though sometimes as few as ten, are taught by a method which combines the formality of a lecture with the give-and-take of a seminar.

As well as classes on such subjects as biblical criticism, the history of western philosophy, the lives of leading Christian thinkers, Kriss has to attend compulsory classes to study the written English language. At the end of a day in which classes have normally followed one after the other in a steady and demanding stream, Kriss has assignments to take home. He works on them conscientiously.

Each morning at the university is punctuated by an assembly, when all students gather for a short act of worship. Kriss has been surprised by a number of aspects of university life. First, that even at a Christian university his faith has been put to the test. He has had to face the difficulties and mysteries of faith head-on. Second, that many of his fellow students are not so eager to learn. They are young and take life for granted. They fail to complete assignments and often do not concentrate in class. And thirdly, Kriss has found it difficult to acclimatise to life out of uniform. All students, including himself, can wear what they wish, a choice Kriss has never had to make before at work.

Ultimately Kriss will have taken a special version of the university's BA liberal arts course by accumulating 60 units over two and a half years. At the end of that course he hopes to continue with a programme of full-time study. This may or may not be in the same area; Kriss might switch to a course which is more orientated towards the social sciences and politics. If he does not, in the end, look for a full-time role within the church, he may decide to go into politics. He would be interested not so much in becoming a party politician as in being a lobbyist, who would campaign for a particular cause. This would not preclude him from preaching and teaching, and Kriss feels at the moment in Britain there is a shortage of clear explanation of what the Bible means.

Kriss readily acknowledges that he wasted his time at school. He now has an eager mind, thirsting for knowledge. At the end of his athletics career he feels an academic qualification could enable him to pursue a number of careers. He might become an evangelist, or a teacher, if he does not choose politics. Much will depend on his academic success, his vocation and Monika's feelings at the time.

Mike Whittingham knows Kriss and Monika better than most and describes theirs as an 'intriguing' relationship. 'It is lovely and yet sad at the same time. In a way I wish Kriss was not quite so fanatical, as Monika would then find it a lot easier to live with and, who knows, he might have converted her or she might have been willing to accept his faith more. But now she has gone to the other extreme. She appears to me not only to have rejected Christianity but to have totally ruled it out. Perhaps it is just their different characters finding the opposite way to deal with the same issues. I do worry about them sometimes and hope it will not lead to a split. But I don't think it will.'

Mike's optimism that the marriage will survive is perhaps based on the experience of what has happened so far. From the start, their marriage was one of opposites, both in terms of race and nationality. That it is now a partnership between two people of different religions will not necessarily introduce tensions which they have not experienced already.

A case could also be made for suggesting that Kriss and Monika are not as far apart in their view of Christianity as they might think. They are both approaching the same destination, but, because they have contrasting temperaments, they feel they are not journeying together.

Many of the divisions in Christendom appear to be caused by a language barrier. Spiritual ideas, questions of faith, religious experience and the concept of God cannot be adequately expressed using words alone. Yet words are the prime means of communication between people. So to express religious ideas, special words have to be used.

These special words are usually used metaphorically, or according to an agreed formula, and as long as they are used between people who have shared the spiritual experience to which the words refer, then the special words can be used safely. However, if someone uses an expression to describe a religious experience, and the listener has not shared that experience, the words can be strange or even meaningless. Indeed, the words can be a barrier to understanding because if they create in the listener's mind an image contrary to that which the user intends, misunderstanding inevitably follows.

To give an example. A Christian can tell another Christian that he or she has been born again and that expression conveys a whole range of meaning relating to a shared experience. If the expression is used in the hearing of a non-Christian, who has no personal understanding of the life-transforming experience of being born again, it is a meaningless phrase—how on earth can a person return to his or her mother's womb and enter the world as a baby again?

Another example might be the use of the expression 'the lamb of God'. To a Christian this phrase can be full of meaning about the sacrifice of Christ at Calvary. But unless someone is conversant with the background to the expression and the ancient Jewish practice of offering lambs as sacrifices, the phrase is incomprehensible.

In the case of Kriss and Monika, it is arguably the language barrier which stands between them. Evangelical Christianity has a whole host of expressions which only the initiated recognize: 'outreach', 'to be saved', 'sins washed away by the blood of Christ', 'to share', 'to be blessed', 'principalities and powers'. Many of the expressions are metaphors borrowed from the Bible or Christian tradition. Even the idea of Satan, some would argue, is a kind of metaphor. It is easier for the human mind to cope with the concept of evil, and its very real presence in the world and in the human make-up, if it is personalised.

So if Kriss says to Monika that he has had a difficult day 'being tempted by Satan', he knows what he means, but Monika may not. She will understand the meaning of temptation, but she may be diverted from what Kriss is trying to say by her distrust of the use of the personalised 'Satan' to describe the source of that temptation.

What Kriss may well discover from his work at Azusa is that the Christian faith is so rich in metaphor and poetry and allegory that he need not confine himself to the narrow range of expressions used by the particular conservative tradition he has encountered. He may discover too that what he feels and what he has experienced of faith need not be undermined by adopting a wider range of language and that he might, in due course, hit on the right words to convey to Monika some of what he feels. These words will probably be ones which are more suited to Monika's temperament and social background, words to which she can relate and with which she will feel comfortable.

Kriss realizes that what he now believes in, and the form in which he expresses it, is a product, not so much of his own experience and research as of his contacts with teachers and churches of the conservative tradition. He describes himself as a theological conservative and hopes that at the end of his studies he will remain one. All the elements of doctrine he now subscribes to, fit together, for him, as a whole. He is worried that a serious challenge to any area of doctrine might undermine the whole. He feels he is on safe ground as a conservative.

'But I am well aware that I am going to be challenged and I already have been challenged. For example, for some reason I believed, and probably on balance still believe, that the world is ten thousand years old. I take that from the literal interpretation of time-scales in the Old Testament. Now I have gone into class and a professor has suggested that maybe the world is at least 150,000 years old and could be millions of years old. This threw my ideas on the age of the earth into total disarray. But why should this matter? No one really knows the age of the earth.

'I have had my experience of Jesus—shouldn't this be enough to sustain faith? But experience alone is subjective. Nobody else can thrive on my subjective experience. Therefore if I'm going to be telling everybody else about Jesus, I need to give them some objective facts that they can grasp, from which their subjective experience will follow.

'Now at the root of my belief at the moment is that the Bible is the inerrant word of God. I understand the arguments that it was written down by men and translated over the years, but if I start questioning the biblical accounts of events, such as the creation and when it took place, then I have to question my acceptance of the Bible being without error. Those are problems I am going to have to come to terms with.

'Maybe in the end I shall come to accept parts of the Bible as poetry or allegory, containing truth but not being literally true. Maybe that's a conclusion I shall come to at the end of my study. Perhaps in years to come I shall be able to look back and say, 'when I was a child I thought as a child, but now I am a man I think as a man.' As we grow older, childish things are disproved, but that is not to say they were not true and real then. As I grow I expect I will come to think differently, but I pray not to lose the fundamentals. I cannot just rely on my subjective experience.

'I do not doubt my experience. From that day onward I had the assurance that I could go to heaven when I die. But people of all faiths have experiences and some are delusions. My experience by itself is not enough to convey to another person who God is. We need the foundation of the word. It is not just enough for me to say I met Jesus Christ. I want to know more and more about him, so that I can tell others about him.'

Kriss calls himself a Christian and Monika does not, but they appear to have much in common as people, parents and friends. And it is said that people should be judged by their lives and attitudes, not by their labels. Monika may never make a public declaration of faith which will take her from outside to within the Christian fold, as Kriss now understands it. But that is not to say she will not become a Christian, or even that she is not one now, even though she does not subscribe to certain dogma or formulae of faith. What she is, is at least something only God can judge.

In the meantime, Kriss worries about Monika's destiny and that of his two daughters. Monika does not prevent Kriss from taking Ashanti and Shakira to church. Kriss knows that Monika does not reinforce the church's teaching at home. Neither does she undermine it. The girls say prayers at bedtime and just as both girls are learning to be bilingual in English and German, so they are learning two approaches to faith. When they are old enough, they will decide matters for themselves. Perhaps they will find for themselves a path to faith that both parents can recognize.

Shakira, who was born in 1987, and Ashanti have known from the earliest age what it is like to identify with two languages, cultures and religious perspectives. Already they are equally at home in English and German. Soon they will have to come to understand the special problems which can emerge from having parents of different races. One of the reasons why Kriss and Monika spend time in America, and may even decide to live in America permanently, is that children of mixed race are far more accepted there. Ashanti has already been on the receiving end of taunts because of her colour. And Monika is aware of the looks she has been given by people in the street in Britain, which imply disapproval of her marriage to a man of a different race. In Germany the children can be something of a curiosity, which can be trying, if not insulting. Monika recalls times when she and the girls have been at a swimming-pool and strangers have come up to Shakira and felt her hair as a novelty.

The girls have a problem which is shared by many children of well-known parents: that of coping with being conspicuous. Kriss expects to pay the price of success in being recognized wherever he goes and being treated by many people as public property. He is glad to meet people and be friendly, but finds it increasingly difficult to do ordinary things like shopping with the family. He will be stared at by passers-by and pointed out.

Ashanti and Shakira also have a price to pay. On one occasion, Kriss went to see Ashanti in a gymnastics display. He arrived as quietly as he could but was recognized. People started talking to him and one man made such a bid for his attention that Kriss completely missed his daughter's performance. The girls have learned that they have to share their father with a wider public, and Ashanti is having to learn how to distinguish between genuine schoolfriends and those who just want to know her because of her father. She is sensitive and quickly detects a false friendship. Ashanti now asks for her mother to take her to school, as when she turns up with her father they find themselves the centre of attraction.

Shakira is still too young to notice such things and Monika feels that, because she has a very different personality from her sister, Shakira might enjoy the reflected glory. Anyway, the attention may not last. Kriss and Monika are both well aware of the fickle nature of public affection. Once Kriss is no longer winning races, Ashanti's problems may well disappear.

'Now,' says Monika, 'people say "Hi! Ashanti" and come and talk to her and make a fuss of her—and they may well be the same people who, if Kriss was not her famous father, would say dismissively, "Who's this mixed race kid?".'

Ashanti gets a confused set of signals: popular because of her father, yet conspicuous because of her colour. Monika recalls the occasion when—just after Kriss had won a major gold medal on the other side of the world and Ashanti had been the centre of attention with friends and adults celebrating—Ashanti became very confused. The school had pictures of Kriss up on the wall and the whole community was proud of his achievements. The teachers were doing everything to enable her to enjoy the occasion, and yet the effect was quite the opposite. She was missing her father and becoming increasingly puzzled by questions of identity.

'She kept asking me, why am I the centre of attraction? Is it my skin? Then she burst into tears and said, "I'll tell you what I'm going to do tonight, when you are asleep. I'm going to go downstairs and get a big knife and I'm going to scrape off my whole skin and throw it on your bed and then when I bleed I'll go pink. And when that pink wears off I'll be your colour." It was that bad. She just wanted to step out.

'At first I was so lost, I didn't know how to handle the situation, but I told her that I had mixed race children because I really wanted them.'

14

A Golden Year

When a top-class hurdler like Kriss explodes off his block at the start of a 400 metre single circuit of the track, the muscles in the body are powered by the most immediately available and rapidly absorbed energy source, the phosphates in the blood. This stage lasts for little more than six or eight seconds, after which glycogen takes over as the main fuel for the muscles. This is anaerobic running, speed rather than stamina is required, and so the body is powered by its stored sources of energy and not by the oxygen from the air.

Distance runners use the aerobic system: they derive their staying power from their efficient use of the oxygen they breathe in as they run. Short distance sprinters rely almost entirely on the anaerobic system. But a top-class 400 metres runner must train to use both the anaerobic and aerobic sources of power. From around 300 metres, if he is running at anything approaching maximum intensity, he must be able to make the smooth transition from one system to the other.

A jogger completing the 400 metre circuit in two or more minutes would run aerobically. An athlete able to record a time of 50 seconds or below for the same distance would treat the circuit as a sprint and the majority of his running would, like the shorter distance sprinter's, be largely anaerobic. But there would also be a crucial aerobic element. So when Kriss trains during the pre-season build-up he aims at being able to run at an average 90 per cent intensity over the 400 metres, and in the final 70 or 80 metres still have oxygen to burn.

It is not just the availability of a fuel source in the body which enables a sportsman or woman to perform. The by-product of intense physical effort is a build-up of lactic acid in the blood. As the proportion of lactic acid increases, fatigue builds up and cramps can occur. The rate at which the lactic acid builds up depends on the way the body has been conditioned, and athletes like Kriss train to be able to cope with the pain and debilitating effects of the lactic acid build-up and still be able to perform for a short while at peak speed.

One of Kriss's training routines is to run a set number of 300 metre distances, with a carefully timed short recovery period in between. He times each run for consistency and the effect is to create a controlled build-up of lactic acid. On the fourth of five such 300 metre runs, his lactic threshold will mimic what he can expect to experience in the last quarter, or 100 metres, of a race. By running in such a condition he gets the body used to the pain and the fatiguing effects of the lactic acid level and develops the body's ability to dispose of the excess. At the end of his six runs Kriss collapses, gasping for breath, and takes ten or fifteen minutes to recover before starting his wind-down exercises.

Each time Kriss goes out on the training track, as he does three or more times a week, he knows that the two-hour session, which starts with a gentle warm-up, will end in agony. But this is the only way he can get the body used to the demands of top-class competition. A training programme is deliberately designed to simulate the different physiological stages of a race, acclimatise the body and the mind of the runner to cope with each stage, and improve ways of dealing with the demands placed on the body by each phase.

A highly conditioned athlete will, for instance, have an improved system by which lactic acid is cleared from the blood and an improved transfer mechanism of oxygen from the red blood cells to the muscle tissues, so that the body can increase the proportion of aerobic effort and thus produce less by way of lactic acid. An athlete who is not so highly conditioned might have an oxygen carrying capacity similar to that of his or her highly conditioned colleague but, if the enzyme system in the red blood cells is not as efficient at transferring that oxygen in quantity to where it is required, the athlete will have to depend far more on the anaerobic sources of power. Consequently the lactic acid in the blood will build up more rapidly and the athlete will tire more quickly. As a result of a relentless training programme the muscles become knotted and tightened and, once a week, Kriss needs to visit a physiotherapist for a vigorous massage of his leg muscles.

Although Kriss often trains alone, and has the inner discipline and self-motivation to push himself to the required limits, like many athletes he enjoys training in company. During the winter training sessions in California he joins the other top-class American hurdlers. In 1991 he shared the track with Danny Harris who, since the retirement of Ed Moses, is the man Kriss has to beat to become the world number one. They practise together with various exercises and routines over the hurdles but, when Kriss is joined by his regular training partner Roger Black, they concentrate on building up strength and speed.

Roger and Kriss are now so used to each other's ways and methods that they hardly talk about running. They know instinctively what each needs by way of pacing and leading. For one 300 metre leg, Kriss will lead Roger and for the next it will be Roger's turn to lead. The lead runner takes on the responsibility for pace setting, and the runner following down wind gets a mental rest which leads to a slight physical easing of the effort required.

Kriss keeps a meticulous record of times recorded in training sessions and compares them week by week and season by season, to see how he is developing or whether there has been any falling off in speed or stamina. Roger is much more easy going and normally keeps only a record of his training times by copying down Kriss's notes at the end of the season.

Early in his career Kriss trained hard, partly for pleasure and partly through his ambition to reach the top in national, and later world, athletics. Now he admits he trains hard as a professional. He knows he must work to stay at the top. He wants to stay at the top for as long as he can, for the financial security it will bring him and his family.

'Athletically I have fulfilled a lot of my desires, but I still think I can do more. I realize now I am in a position I have never been in before and will never be in again. I am in a position to win the World Championships and the Olympic Games. That is also a great motivation. What I now have to do, with God's help, is stay injury free and keep to my programme of training.'

When top-class hurdlers race over 400 metres, little more than a second differentiates the champions from the also-rans. At the end of the 1987 season, Kriss's personal best time over the distance was 48.64 seconds. Ed Moses, the man who had dominated the sport for so long, held the world record of 47.02 seconds. It will take you as the reader longer to read the first six words of this sentence out loud, than it would have taken Kriss to cover the distance between him and Ed Moses at the finishing line of a race in 1987. Yet it was to take Kriss three years of hard, specialist training to narrow that gap to any significant degree. By the end of 1990 he was four words, instead of six words, behind the record. But that improvement, with Ed Moses himself no longer competing, was good enough to place Kriss at the number three position in the world top fifty.

Kriss's best runs tend to be in the major competitions, when the atmosphere of the big occasion lifts his performance. However, the improvement has to be founded on hard work. To maximize performance, Kriss has not only to develop the strength and stamina required, but also to refine the hurdling technique to give him as smooth a run as possible. In the early days Kriss would knock himself on hurdles, and he even once hit a hurdle so hard it broke. Contact with an obstacle inevitably slows the athlete. So a main priority is to learn how to glide over each hurdle with the maximum ease. Kriss knows there is room for improvement.

'Over the last two years I have been running very fast on the flat. If the world's top hurdlers were to have a race on the flat, I would probably win. And I still have room left to improve my time in the 400 metres hurdles by improving my efficiency over and between the hurdles.'

Crucial to this is the development of a good stride pattern. Ed Moses, in his prime, unfailingly hit a pattern of thirteen strides between each hurdle. Crucial micro-seconds are gained by being able to keep the strides between each barrier to a minimum. In good running conditions, Kriss today aims for a pattern of thirteen strides for the first seven hurdles, but at some point in the race needs to revert to fourteen or fifteen strides to preserve energy and speed for the finish. This is why it was important for him to learn, with Mike Whittingham, the art of using either leg as lead. Kriss does not have the natural leg length to find thirteen strides easy when tired and under pressure. The last hurdles would be crossed with less ease and he would give himself more chance of hitting one of the barriers, slowing himself down, or even falling over.

A crucial decision Kriss has to take during each race is when to switch from thirteen to fourteen strides. An increase in strides involves a corresponding increase in the speed of the leg movement to be able to maintain ground speed. But, for Kriss, increasing the strides between each barrier reduces the dangers of falling at or hitting the hurdle.

However much planning goes into a race, the final stride pattern can be determined only by the hurdler as he runs, according to how he feels. Usually Kriss notices the build-up of lactic acid at hurdle eight but, if he is running well, he may not even be aware of it. He has also conditioned himself to be able to 'pick up his knees' and sprint over the last thirty or forty metres with a high lactic acid content. Finishing well is often attributable to the mental as opposed to the physical state. At the extremes of endurance the mind can overrule the body for a short, crucial time.

Over the last three years, Kriss's improved times have been matched by the change in his normal stride pattern. Three years ago his thirteen strides between hurdles would last to the fifth or sixth hurdle. In 1990, his best year, the pattern was kept up until the seventh or eighth hurdle.

Kriss began the 1988 season after a further spell of winter training in California. The pleasant climate, resembling as it does a good British summer, creates an ideal environment for British competitors. The winter saw Kriss more at ease with his inner self than he had ever been. He also had a new daughter, Shakira, who had been conceived and born with none of the problems Monika and Kriss had experienced before. Kriss trained with Roger Black and Daley Thompson and the other internationals at the University of California, Irvine track.

One familiar face missing from the scene, however, was David Jenkins, who had often been around socialising and advising the current British 400 metres specialists. As a result of his arrest and the court case in which he had been cited as the major organizer behind the trade in illegal performance-enhancing drugs, he was serving a prison sentence.

Despite warnings that they should not be seen to identify with David Jenkins, Kriss, Roger and Daley felt they could not ignore him at his time of need. He had family problems and many of his 'friends' had deserted him. Kriss, Roger and Daley, however, maintained contact and visited David in prison.

It might well have been wise for the three to have kept their distance. Three years later there were still certain tabloid newspapers trying, unsuccessfully, to link Kriss and certain other athletes with the drugs business through their association with David Jenkins.

Kriss and Roger had been in California at the time of David's arrest, and had even turned up at his house shortly after he had been taken in for questioning. But, confident that they had nothing to hide, they did not abandon David, and their visits to see him in prison were typical of their loyalty and absolute confidence that they were free from any drug scandal.

'To get to the jail to see David we had to drive out into the desert. It was a long drive. We arrived, parked the car, went through a security check and then Jenks was called. He was expecting us and was very pleased to see us. We weren't quite sure what to say, but he was all hyped up. He got us some drinks and was rushing around. This was Jenks all hyped up. We started laughing and joking and pulling his leg and calling him "jail-bird" and making some wicked jokes about being in prison. We were there an hour, hour and a half. We had a good time. We hammered him, he hammered us, making all sorts of jokes at each other's expense. But then it came time for us to leave. And that was so sad. As we walked away we could look back and see him at a large window, watching us go. He was waving and we were waving back. We got into the car and drove out of the car park and away, and still as we looked back we could see Jenks watching us go, standing at the window. That hurt me. We had had a great time laughing, and now we were going to freedom and this guy was stuck behind the glass. Next time we were quieter and talked a lot more. And it is since Jenks has been in prison that I have got to know him.'

Kriss has also had time to reflect on the nature of David Jenkins's crime. He understands how a top-line athlete, once he retires, is deprived of the stimulation of competing. He can see too how turning to crime, with all the dangers involved, can replace some of the excitement. He can envisage David Jenkins on the Mexican border, revelling in the excitement of smuggling the illegal drugs. Kriss also sees how a crime can start out as something small and yet grow into something too big to keep under control. At the start, the criminal knows that what he is doing is wrong, but as the involvement deepens, questions of morality grow less and less important to him.

The coming 1988 season was an Olympic year and Kriss had hopes of another medal. In the event, Kriss discovered that while he was competing at the very highest level and was becoming increasingly respected for his hurdling, having advanced from the novice stage, his times had plateaued out. In two years his personal best time improved by only 0.05 of a second.

However, interestingly, his performance on the flat improved. In winning the AAA Championship in Birmingham in August 1988 he recorded a new personal best of 44.93 seconds, a half-second improvement on his previous best time, that recorded at the 1984 Olympic Games in Los Angeles.

But neither the improvement on the flat nor that over the hurdles was to bring Kriss a medal. He came sixth in the 400 metres hurdles final, in 48.69 seconds, and the 4 x 400 metres relay team came a disappointing fifth.

After winning silver four years earlier, the British team was amongst the favourites. The problem in the end seemed to be that Britain had too many good 400 metres runners to choose from. The final team was not chosen until the last minute, too late for the successful high spirits and camaraderie of Los Angeles to be recreated in Seoul. Kriss's special preparations for Seoul, which had included switching his watch to South Korean time for the two weeks before flying out to the games, were in vain. For those two weeks, home routine was disrupted by Kriss going to bed at 4 in the afternoon and rising at 2 a.m.

When reviewing his results of the three seasons, 1988, 1989 and 1990, the turning-point in Kriss's new career as a hurdler appears to have come in August 1989. Up until he took to the track at Gateshead, competing in the 1989 European Cup, Kriss had only twice won a major hurdles race, and on one of those occasions it was a dead heat. Indeed, reviewing his record of the season in August 1989, although he had run consistently well, he had not once reaching the finishing tape first. His best time had been 49.04 seconds when he had come third in a race in Seville. In the four-cornered international in Birmingham in June, his time of 51.10 seconds gave him fifth place. However, from 5 August 1989 until the end of the 1990 season, he claimed fifteen outright victories in 23 hurdles races.

On the morning of 5 August 1989, Kriss was on the verge of dropping out of the European Cup race even before it had started. He had been injured for four weeks and had started training only ten days earlier. He was worried that his hamstring would be put under too much stress and was very worried that he might let the team down. As he was passing the warm-up area he saw the national coach Frank Dick.

'Things don't get any easier,' Kriss said.

'That's what makes champions out of people,' came the reply.

Afterwards, he told the magazine *Athletics Weekly* about the race while it was still fresh in his mind.

'I told myself I was going to have to dig very deep. I was also worried that even if my leg held up I might die a death in the last 100. I was worried about totally falling apart. I got into the blocks and normally I then lose that sort of nerves. But I was still fighting myself. There was a false start and I just stayed in my blocks. I got up and turned to the crowd and sort of put my arms out and shrugged my shoulders, as if saying, "What can you do?" and I smiled. They all laughed and that eased my tension. Then I thought, go and do the business. I thought Harald Schmid would win it but I didn't want to be beaten by the young Czech who had run 48.9.

'When I went to the blocks for the second time I said a little prayer. I had calmed down a bit and went out very controlled. I found myself up there alongside Schmid. The crowd was cheering, there was the realization I was up there at the front, the adrenalin was flowing and there was also the realization that I could get more points than I had been tipped to get. That was all going through my mind as I took hurdle nine. At hurdle ten I thought, "Don't fall over and make a fool of yourself." I felt relief to reach the line first and very happy.'

Kriss had astonished the crowd, the experts and the millions watching on television by winning. His time was 48.95 seconds. The next day Kriss, with Peter Crampton, Todd Bennett and Brian Whittle, astonished everyone again by unexpectedly winning the 4 x 400 metres relay and clinching victory in the competition for Britain for the first time. For Kriss it was the start of an amazing thirteen months of success.

Despite having proved himself on the track, Kriss still had a brittle relationship with the sport's organizers. On 2 September 1989, the *News of the World* ran an article quoting him at length about the way top competitors were treated financially. He first recalled the day when, as a beginner, he learned how the sport's financial transactions were made. It was in Oslo in 1983.

'I was sitting with one British athlete next to me and another opposite. An official came up and gave one of them an envelope with $700 written on the front and actually counted out $700 into the hands of the other. Then he turned to me and gave me a single $20 note and said, "Your time will come."

'When I told other athletes of about my standard what I had got, they laughed at me. I didn't trust people from that day and I have had a fear of being exploited ever since.

'I have tried to be militant and stand up for myself, but I don't believe it has been very good for my career in the end.

'I don't think I have had the races I deserved, especially in Europe, and that appears to be the case even today. I can't count the times I have been told I wasn't worth the money I've been asking and I just ignored the advice everyone gave me not to cross the powers that be. I had a row with someone who wanted to pay me $100 before one meeting abroad. I said I wouldn't run unless I got $300. So he gave it to me in notes and snapped: "You'll never run in Europe again."

'I rang one official the other day and asked if I was being blocked from races. It was denied. You couldn't blame me for asking, though. I always believed that, if I was good enough, I'd get races. Well, I was number six in the world in the Olympics and have now beaten the best in Europe. I was injured in the early part of the season but wanted to run in Brussels, West Berlin and Koblenz. I was told there was no room for me in Brussels and no 400 metres hurdles at the other two meetings. How do you think I felt, watching those very races on television and reading the results in the sports columns?'

A month after the European Cup, Kriss was in Barcelona for the World Cup. Despite the far keener competition from the Americans, great things were expected of Kriss, who had by now reached a new level of celebrity status. He was not just well-known in the world of athletics, but a national favourite, with all the transitory glory that goes with the position. In the event he came third, confirming his status as one of the very best, but not yet the best, in the world. Five days later, at a meeting in Jerez, he ran his personal best time to date of 48.59 seconds—the first improvement in his own best performance for two years.

To all intents and purposes, Kriss was now a full-time athlete. Despite the residual pretence to the contrary in the athletics world, he was also a professional. He had been a member of the army since he was sixteen and the army had given him most of the encouragement and support he had needed. However, by 1989 he had to decide whether his long-term future lay with the army or in a civilian pursuit. He suggested to the army that they should give him twenty months to concentrate on winning the European Games, after which he would undertake to return to full-time military duties. The suggestion was not accepted.

Decision time came when the army arranged a posting for him as a physical training instructor to fill in the time between the Commonwealth Games and the start of his training in America, which was to be the build-up for the 1990 season and the European Championships.

Kriss felt strongly that the seven-week posting would interrupt his preparatory work. So he decided that he would have to leave the army. Leaving the service had been in his mind since 1982, but now he felt he was strongly enough established in the world of athletics not to need the financial security the army offered, particularly if remaining in the army threatened to impede his progress on the track.

In November 1989, Kriss offered to buy himself out of the army, which would have released him from all military commitments. The day of his final release was set for 13 December. However, the army authorities reconsidered Kriss's case. It was realized that, for the sake of a year's pay, they stood to lose a considerable amount of good publicity for the army. If Kriss were to win the European and Commonwealth Gold medals as plain Mr Akabusi, their past investment in him as a public standard bearer for the army would be lost.

So Kriss had a phone-call making him an offer. If he would

consider staying on the army payroll for one more year he would be given complete freedom to train and compete as an athlete. Kriss gladly accepted. In the event, it was money well spent for the army. In September 1990 the army placed a full-page recruitment advertisement in *The Voice*, the newspaper of Britain's black community, featuring a large picture of a victorious Kriss. Kriss reached all the targets he had set himself, and the army enjoyed the reflected glory.

Warrant Officer (second class), Quarter Master Sergeant Instructor, or WO2 (QMSI) for short, Kriss Akabusi officially returned to civilian life on 19 November 1990. The secretary of the Army Athletics Association described him as an inspiration to all army athletes. *Soldier*, the official army magazine, said that Kriss had repaid the service for all its help to him to become a top athlete by becoming the army's most famous sporting son.

'As the medal tally mounted, so did his media profile, and with it his acknowledgement of the debt he owed the army.'

And *Soldier* also noted how at the end of 1990 Kriss had turned down an international meeting to compete in his last army championships and that 'his list of ten Army 400 metres titles is unlikely to be bettered.'

Free to concentrate on the goals he and Mike Whittingham had set four years earlier, and with his mind clear, Kriss embarked on the 1990 athletics programme. At the age of 31, it was to be the year in which everything was to come right.

After winning two races 'down under', Kriss went to the Commonwealth Games in Auckland, New Zealand. He was undoubtedly the outstanding 400 metres hurdler in the field, and won his heat and the final with ease. His winning time of 48.89 seconds was more than 2.5 seconds faster than the next Englishman, and 0.36 seconds (or 3 metres) faster than the Kenyan who came second. He led from the halfway stage of the race to win, his victory marred only by the delay in receiving the medal. The ceremony was held up while an inquiry took place into the disqualification of the Nigerian, Henry Amike.

Monika had watched the race in the early hours of the

morning, as it was transmitted live by satellite from the other side of the world. She knew that Kriss had not been as confident about the race as the experts. It was after all one of, if not the most important hurdles race he had run to date. He was also a long way from home, and even an experienced top-class international sportsman can feel the loneliness of separation.

From New Zealand, with just a short break in Britain, Kriss set out for California, for his now customary winter training schedule. There could be no let-up in the training programme. A body can become accustomed to the stresses of competition, and can even be induced to improve its efficiency, but once the training schedule slackens performance quickly takes a dive. The European Games in Split was the focus of Kriss's attention and he was one of the favourites for the gold medal.

Through the summer Kriss was training, travelling and competing on the international circuit: Granada, New York, Malmo, Lahti, Monte Carlo, Zurich. He did not neglect his British commitments, however, and in June he won the 400 metres hurdles for his country in two major international meetings, and on 3 June at Cardiff he won the UK Championships.

In some ways the UK Championships gave Kriss more to worry about than almost any of the other pre-Split meetings. To a young athlete, winning the UK title can be the springboard to greater things, but to an established athlete the Championships can be a distraction. Nevertheless, Kriss felt a loyalty to his country and to the up-and-coming athletes who would be there, and so was willing to take part. He recognized the dangers that he might not be sufficiently motivated and lose a race, or that he might exert himself in an unplanned finish and sustain an injury. As it happened, Kriss won but in an unimpressive time.

Much of his training was now at such a high standard that he and Mike Whittingham had persuaded one of the few athletes in the world at Kriss's level to share in the schedule. Thus it was that Kriss and Danny Harris trained together for a number of crucial weeks that summer. Danny Harris was marginally better than Kriss, and is at present the world's number one. However, he lacked a disciplined programme and benefitted from the joint sessions as much as Kriss.

As an American, Danny Harris was not a rival in the summer of 1990. However, even without the Americans, the European Games bring together one of the greatest collections of top-class athletes outside the Olympic Games and World Championships. Proving himself as the number one in this company had been Kriss's main ambition for four years. He knew that in 1990 he would no longer be a novice hurdler, his technique would be almost as good as it would ever be, and his strength and speed should also be at a peak.

For the first time since Kriss became a top-class competitor, Monika was able to accompany him to Split. She left the two girls with her father in Germany and travelled to Yugoslavia. Kriss was given accommodation as a competitor and Monika had to stay in a different hotel, but they saw each other when they could and Monika was in the crowd to see Kriss on the track.

On 28 August Kriss won his semi-final in 48.84 seconds, just 0.5 seconds slower than the personal best he had recorded two weeks earlier in Zurich. The next day was the day of the final. This is how Kriss remembers it:

'I had had four years' hard work and each year my technique had got better and better, and here I was favourite to win. I had prayed as usual that morning and read from the Bible. I got down to the track and everybody was patting me on the back and saying, Kriss, this is going to be easy for you. You're in great shape, we've seen the way you ran the heats and semi-final. You're Commonwealth Champion, just go out there and do it. I'm thinking to myself, "Oh, no, pressure!"

'I remember the gun going and me charging out of the blocks, going so fast. Getting down the back straight and thinking, Kriss you've got to settle down. You've got a long way to go. Don't overdo this thing. I pick up my knees, get down to the bend, I am still within breathing distance of these other people. And I remember thinking, "See ya." Running as fast as I can round that bend into the home straight. I feel that I'm up, mustn't mess it up. Got to cross these two hurdles. Got to hurdle ten, knowing all I had to do was clear it to win. Cross the line and I'm so pleased to have got it over and done with. I leap with joy and the crowd shouts at me to look at the time. I don't immediately, but when I do I see that not only have I broken the British record, but I am the first Briton ever to go under 48 seconds. I go crazy! Loopy! Ecstatic! I had made history.

'I wanted to tell everyone, look what's happened. But they all knew I had broken the record minutes before I'd realized. All that work had come to fruition.'

Kriss had won a place amongst the top ten 400 metres hurdlers of all time.

He had much to be thankful for that evening, when he and Monika met for a quiet celebratory dinner. Despite their differences over questions of faith, the two have retained such a close bond and friendship that they could share in the triumph, knowing that each of them had contributed as much as the other to the victory. Without Monika, Kriss would have been a totally different person from the man he is today. And such a different person that it is unlikely that he would have had the self-discipline and security to have reached the top in his sport.

That evening too a message arrived by fax from David Hemery, whose twenty-year-old record Kriss had just beaten.

'Brilliant run Kriss, I'm delighted with your time and win. Congratulations.'

It was late when Kriss said goodnight to Monika and returned to his quarters. He was sharing a room with Roger Black, and he crept in quietly, knowing that his friend and training partner had his big race the next day. He undressed as silently as he could and was about to get into bed when Roger spoke: 'I've been awake all the time.'

He and Kriss began to talk. Roger was delighted for Kriss, but Kriss felt that his own celebrations could only really begin when Roger too had won a gold. They had often talked about the possibility of being joint medal winners at Split, and they were on the verge of fulfilling every ambition.

The next day Roger also won his gold in the 400 metres, and not only that—two days later both Roger and Kriss had yet more reason to celebrate. They each received a second European gold medal following their victory with the British 4 x 400 metres relay squad, in a new European record time of 2 minutes 58.22 seconds.

The pictures of Kriss winning his individual medal and going wild with excitement and joy were flashed around Europe. They appeared on the front pages of dozens of newspapers.

One of the most important images, however, was of Kriss in a slightly calmer mood, when, in the midst of the huge stadium in front of the thousands who were watching, he sank to his knees and bowed his head in prayer.

It would have been a simple prayer of thanks. A moment to recall the difficult days when only his own perseverance and strength sustained him. A moment to recall the long agonizing mental process of looking for and finding a real purpose in life. A moment to recall the hours of hard, painful physical training, when it would have been so easy to give up. A moment when the words of the prophet Isaiah would have had a special significance.

'They that wait upon the Lord shall renew their strength; they shall mount up with wings as eagles; they shall run and not be weary; they shall walk and not faint.'

15

And Faster Yet

'If this is a joke, it's a very good one,' was Kriss's reaction to the voice on the telephone claiming that she was speaking from the Prime Minister's office at 10 Downing Street in London.

When the caller to his Californian home asked if he would accept the Prime Minister's recommendation that he should be invited to receive an honour from the Queen, Kriss was quite sure he was the victim of a leg-pull.

Only when he finally received, via the family home in England, the news of the written confirmation of the call, did Kriss accept that he was indeed to receive one of Britain's prestigious honours for his services to athletics. And so, slotted into his busy 1991 schedule, was a visit to Buckingham Palace to receive his MBE. Kriss was to become a member of the Order of the British Empire.

The day of the investiture was an unforgettable one, but not just for the usual reasons. Kriss dressed immaculately for the occasion, as did Monika, Ashanti and Shakira. However, they nearly failed to keep the appointment. Fifteen minutes before they were due to arrive at the palace, they were still stuck in their car in a hotel car park unable to get the barrier open. But fortunately they made it in time.

When Kriss stepped forward to be given his insignia, the Queen asked him about his plans now that he had left the army, and said how much she enjoyed watching him run. He was impressed that, out of the many dozens of people she was due to meet that day, she had taken sufficient interest and care to find out about him as an individual.

Only the two girls were slightly disappointed. They had expected to see the Queen as she might have appeared in a fairy-story book, with a crown and robes. Instead she was dressed neatly, but unspectacularly, in green.

'Where's the Queen?' one of them asked her mother. Monika pointed her out. 'But that's just a lady, that's not the Queen,' came the reply.

An honour is usually bestowed on a sportsman at the end of a distinguished career. Kriss, however, had no immediate plans to retire, although when the 1991 athletics season started many of the sport's followers and some of Kriss's friends wondered if he had 'gone off the boil'. After the previous triumphant year which had culminated in two prestigious gold medals, Kriss's early races were disappointing. In Granada on 27 May he came a poor fifth in a time of 50.15 seconds. There was little improvement when he competed for a second time in Spain. He came fourth, although in an improved time of 49.39 seconds.

A few weeks earlier when his coach Mike Whittingham had joined Kriss in California he had expressed his concern. Kriss had set himself a punishing winter schedule, rising early to travel to his university lectures, going to bed late as he conscientiously completed his assignments and yet still pushing himself to complete a full international athlete's training programme. Kriss was, Mike observed, trying to burn the candle at both ends. He began to feel some niggling injuries and Mike also wondered if after his successes of 1990 Kriss had lost some of his motivation.

However, when term finished early and Kriss was satisfied that he had fulfilled all that was required of him by the university, he was able to concentrate again on preparing for the season which was to culminate in the Tokyo World Championships.

When he returned to Europe in May and began racing, neither Kriss nor Mike were too concerned about the slow start. Kriss often began a season slowly. Even so, his slow times in 1991 appeared particularly sluggish compared to the times of his international rivals. The Americans were fresh and running well, while Kriss was only beginning to get into his stride.

If Kriss had any fears about having passed his peak, they were gradually dispelled as the season unfolded. Over the course of the first seven races his times progressively improved. From the European Cup, which he won in 48.39 seconds, through to his last race before taking the flight to Tokyo, he never once failed to break the 49-second barrier. He twice ran 48.37 seconds and recorded seven victories.

He met his toughest opposition prior to Tokyo when he recorded 48.37 seconds at the IAAF-Mobil Grand Prix meeting in Monte Carlo. There he came third to his two main rivals, Samuel Matete of Zambia and Danny Harris of the USA, beating the fourth of the quartet of leading 400 metres hurdlers, the American Kevin Young. It was a decisive victory by Samuel Matete in 47.87 seconds. Danny, Kriss and Kevin were almost half a second behind, in a close finish for the position of runner-up. And then in Kriss's next race in Malmo, Kevin Young beat him into second place. Kriss blamed his defeat in Monte Carlo on technical mistakes at the eighth and tenth flights. If he could eliminate them he felt he stood a good chance at Tokyo.

There might have been a fascinating curtain raiser in Zurich for the World Championships, but for a dispute between race organizers which left Kriss and Roger Black, amongst others, without an invitation to compete at this key meeting. The dispute was nothing to do with the two British athletes, they just happened to be represented by the same agent as the Kenyan Richard Chelimo, whose appearance at Zurich was the contentious issue. The race turned out to be a very fast one and Kriss might well have recorded his season's best time had he been there.

While Kriss can appear to be a man of single-minded determination, this can be a mask to hide other concerns. Over the years he has been able to develop the professionalism which enables him to perform at or near his peak potential when other things are troubling him. He sees this ability as an off-shoot of his faith: he feels he can put other matters into the hands of God, while he concentrates on the immediate task before him.

In 1991 Kriss was anxious for his brother. It had not been a good summer for Riba, and Kriss was not sure what to do for the best. As it happened, Riba's condition improved once the right balance of medication had been restored and the summer proved to be a creative time for him. Riba explored further the world of poetry and found the ability to express himself with a developing precision and ease.

One poem had a feline theme and is a poignant expression of some of his deeper feelings:

> *Immediate musical genius exposed surreptitiously.*
> *Where does it come from, what can it be?*
> *O Lord let me live judiciously.*
> *Never was a lone cat more lonely than me.*

Kriss left for Tokyo a week before the start of the World Championships to begin the final stage of preparation. He was joined by Mike Whittingham and, as ever, his team mate and training partner, Roger Black. He had spent most of August isolated from family and friends, totally wrapped up in the world of the track. Tokyo was hot, sapping and humid and Kriss needed all of that week to acclimatize to the conditions. Top athletes need both physical power and speed, and the right mental attitude to cope with the stress of the big occasion. Kriss knew from his training, that, as the oldest man on the track, he might not have the physical edge over his rivals, but from his vast experience at the top he certainly had the psychological advantage. Many of his fellow athletes had arrived in Tokyo days earlier, but Kriss felt it was a mistake to turn up too early—a decision which, with hindsight, can be seen to have been fully vindicated. When Kriss joined his British team mates he was buzzing with anticipation, but found many of his fellow athletes rather flat, as if they had been hanging around waiting for too long.

The first heat was a straightforward run. Kriss won in a time consistent with his season. Come the semi-finals on the Sunday, the pressure was building up. Britain's athletes were having a disastrous time. Much had been expected of them, but through a series of injuries, bad performances, bad luck and bad judgement, from the British point of view the Games started disastrously. Only Linford Christie had lived up to expectations, yet in a blisteringly fast 100 metres final, his astonishing time of 9.92 seconds could only win him fourth place. Kriss knew that one slip could cost him a place in the final, and bring further disappointment to the athletics fans at home.

Having watched Harris, Graham, Adkins and Wallenlind qualify in the first semi-final, Kriss settled on his marks. Danny Harris's winning time was faster than anything Kriss had run that season before coming to Tokyo. Kriss, however, always rises to the occasion. The starting gun sounded and 47.91 seconds later Kriss crossed the line in the lead, in a new personal best and British record time. He had even beaten the Zambian Samuel Matete. The most important thing Kriss had achieved, however, was to prove to his opponents that he was one of the main contenders for a medal.

Almost twenty-four hours later Kriss was on the track again, preparing his blocks, composing his mind for the explosion of energy to come and asking, in silent prayer, that whatever he achieved it would be to the glory of God. He had slept well and had that morning told Roger Black, with whom, as always, he was sharing a room, that he felt sure he had a medal within his grasp, 'perhaps even the big one'.

Even as he warmed up for the final, Kriss was made aware of his team responsibilities. As he tried to concentrate on his preparations, people would come up to him, wish him well, give him the latest news of a British failure and say, 'it's up to you'. Roger tends to think of athletes as individualists, concentrating on their event to the exclusion of their compatriots. In many ways this is true. But Kriss, through his many years spent as one of a group, is keenly aware of the team identity.

Wearing number 407, he took his place in lane four, and waited with the other seven hurdlers for the 'off'. He had said very little to his fellow runners on their way to the start, save for a few words of banter with Danny Harris, the cool, big, suave American with whom Kriss had shared training sessions in the Californian sun. And then, to his surprise, he noticed Danny sink to his knees in prayer. 'It was an open formal prayer,' Kriss recalls, 'while, if I had been praying at that point, I would have said just a few words to God in my head. I had never seen Danny pray like that before, but Danny was a worried man. He was physically ready for the race, but not mentally. He had a lot of problems on his mind.'

As they took to their blocks, Kriss felt very matter-of-fact. He knew he had raced all his rivals before and had their measure. Danny was in the staggered lane just behind, Winthrop Graham and Samuel Matete ahead. He had beaten them all in the past and Matete only the day before.

It was a clean start. 'I set off running what I thought was a good pace and was totally surprised. I had done my first hurdle and the second hurdle without looking at any one else and coming into the bend saw Matete and Graham out there, three or four metres ahead. I couldn't believe it. *Don't panic. They must be going fast because Danny hasn't passed me yet*. And then Danny made a move. At hurdle eight we were together and the other two were still in front, but not too far ahead. We were all there in the frame. At hurdle nine, those guys who were so far up got closer and closer. I began to think, *I'm going to do it*. That was the worst thing. I stopped concentrating fully on the hurdles. A stride must have shortened. My right foot crashed into the tenth barrier. My momentum was lost. My strength was gone. I thought, *keep running, keep running*, and crossed the line just two-tenths of a second behind the winner. I certainly know I could have got the silver. But I'm so pleased just to have got the medal.'

The Zambian, Matete, and the Jamaican, Graham, were the gold and silver medal winners. Danny Harris had failed to find the extra power he needed. Kevin Young, the rising American star, had also been unable to keep up with the leaders. Only Kriss kept in in touch with the pacemakers. But for leaping at the final barrier a fraction too eagerly, he might indeed have won second place. But it is unlikely that he would have displaced Samuel Matete as the new world champion.

Kriss, however, was far from disgraced. His bronze medal was Britain's first of the entire Games. His time in the final was yet again a new personal and British record—47.86 seconds. He had won the medal he had, realistically, hoped to win. He had expected to be beaten by Danny Harris, but had defeated him convincingly.

After the jubilation of winning a medal at the 400 metres hurdles came the inevitable deflation which follows victory. The body is so highly charged on the natural body chemicals of speed and achievement that the journey back to normality can be a a rough ride. Kriss recognized this curious stage which follows a major race and bided his time until it passed. It often helps to have more work to do, and at Tokyo this was the case, as Kriss was a key member of the 4 x 400 metres relay team.

The squad knew they had a chance of winning the gold medal. Indeed, they were sure that only the Americans stood between them and the top step of the winners' podium.

It is normal practice for the fastest runner in a relay team to take the last leg. As silver medallist at 400 metres, Roger Black was undoubtedly the man. In the semi-finals, however, because the team had not been under extreme pressure, Kriss had taken responsibility for the last lap. Afterwards he and Roger had discussed the possibility of him doing the same in the final, with Roger taking the first leg to gain a lead over the Americans and put them under unaccustomed pressure. It was also important, the team thought, to be up with the Americans from the start and avoid the danger of being hemmed in by the pack—the teams vying for the bronze medal—over the last crucial metres of the race.

On the morning of the race, the last day of the championships, Kriss woke with a feeling of total confidence that this was the right plan. 'I looked across at Roger and said, "Roger, I can do it." "Do what?" he said. "Beat Mr Pettigrew."

'As I was saying it, I could hardly believe I was saying it. The American last leg was being run by the young man who had just beaten Roger to the gold medal in the 400 metres.'

Roger Black, however, agreed. It seemed sense for him to run the first leg and for Kriss, rather than the less experienced John Regis, to run the final lap. They discussed the plan further with Frank Dick, the national coach. The collective decision was agreed. The team would run from the front—never give the Americans an inch—so that Kriss could be alongside the American gold medallist for the final assault.

'We kept the plan a secret until the last minute. When the Americans saw what we were doing they couldn't believe it. What are these guys playing at? But nevertheless they weren't too worried. They felt they were man-for-man better than us. They were complacent.

'I felt a sense of destiny. That all had been predetermined. That I could win. I knew Pettigrew was fast, but he was inexperienced running under pressure in a huge cauldron of a stadium. We had something to prove. He just felt he had to turn up, run 400 metres and collect another gold medal. He would have written me off as just a hurdler. He wouldn't have known that when you get to the World Championships, all the runners there are good and some are hungry.'

For the British team the race went to plan. Black took an early lead. Redmond and Regis kept ahead of the rest of the field, but very close to the Americans, setting up a thrilling last lap for Kriss Akabusi.

He followed the American round the track. He was almost breathing down his neck. Then, in the final straight, he judged his moment to perfection. He pulled past the young American and took the lead. Then, realising his legs could fold on him any second, he pushed for the line. Spectators in the stadium watched as Pettigrew responded to Kriss's challenge. Millions watching at home will never forget the excitement of the last two seconds of the race as Kriss appeared to be losing the initiative. Had Kriss made his challenge too early to sustain? And no moment could have been more satisfying than that split second when Kriss knew he had beaten the American 400 metres world champion to the finish in the 4 x 400 metres relay.

The British team had defied the odds and the form guide to run the four-lap race in a new European, British and Commonwealth record time of 2 minutes 57.53 seconds. Kriss's team mates had done everything required of them to put Kriss into second place at the final baton change. All Kriss's experience had come to the fore as he pressurized the American gold medalist from behind. The planning and the risks taken had paid off. Everything had been done which could have been done to give Kriss the chance to make his bid for victory. He took his chance, took the lead—and held it just long enough to win.

'I saw John coming towards me with the baton. Fourteen stone of pure British beef charging along. I didn't feel nervous. I wasn't leaking any energy. I took the baton and exploded into action. As we went down the back straight I thought we were going too slow. I wasn't fully extended. I couldn't risk going past him too early, but I was worried what might happen if the rest of the field started catching up. I could be messed up by the pack and a bid for gold turn into a scramble for bronze. I looked up at the screen and thought to myself, *I've got to get Pettigrew to run a little faster*. I went up on his shoulder. I pretended to challenge him. He took the bait. I felt I was going well, in a good rhythm. About 120 metres from the line I elongated my stride and went into lane two on the bend. I kicked off the bend. I get just a fraction ahead. I have no doubt I'll win. I feel good. I feel a gap between us. The words keep going round my brain, "world champion, world champion, world champion". Then the energy starts draining from my legs. In the last ten metres, I am really rolling. I can hear Pettigrew coming again. I can see the baton again, hear his breathing. I get to the line, four hundredths of a second in front.

'I felt sorry for Pettigrew afterwards. He had led all the way without that extra adrenalin I had. He hadn't got my buzz. But we had won. I felt so good mentally and spiritually, but physically I had used up everything. It took me twenty seconds before I could start the celebration and the lap of honour. The stadium was packed. We were the last event. We stole the show. People love it when the underdogs win. David had beaten Goliath. Teamwork had triumphed over individualism.'

It was only on his return to Britain that Kriss realized the full impact the final relay had had on the British public. From the moment he stepped off the plane he began to hear how the final seconds of the race had had millions of viewers on the edge of their seats, willing him on. From being a well-known and recognized athlete, Kriss had become a star figure, a personality known to a far wider public than just those who follow track and field. He had acquired celebrity status.

Through the autumn of 1991 Kriss became accustomed to life in the public eye, so much so that a small incident in a London restaurant, when he was not immediately recognized, brought him up short. He found himself realizing again what life is like for the thousands of people for whom a life of privilege is only a dream.

Kriss, Monika, Roger and another fellow athlete had gone to the Ritz in London. When they went to the dining room for a meal, a waiter asked them pointedly if they had the means to pay. When the menu came they were asked again if they could pay. And when Kriss assured the waiter again that of course they could, the waiter still tried to insist that he ordered from the cheaper part of the menu. Then during the meal the waiters realised who it was they were serving. They switched tactics and became obsequiously polite, saying what an honour it was to have them in the restaurant.

'Maybe it was because we were young and we were laughing and joking and casually dressed. We also hesitated before going into the restaurant as we were in two minds as to whether we should eat then or later in the evening. One of us was black, another an Asian. Whatever the reason for their behaviour, for the way they had been so quick to make value judgments, it made me realize how I had got so used to being recognized. It brought me back to earth. I thought, *Kriss, never forget where you come from, never forget who you are.*'

Yet where does Kriss come from? He cannot identify any single place. He comes from a children's home. He is the product of army discipline. He has been shaped, both for good and ill, by what he—as a young child—felt to be parental rejection. Genetically he is Nigerian, an Ibo. The older he gets, Kriss says, the more he thinks of Nigeria and his ancestral heritage.

In the autumn of 1991 Kriss again paid a brief visit to Nigeria. He arrived in time to see his father completing the rites associated with his assumption of the title *Duro*. His paternal kinsmen felt sure that he had been brought back to them at such an auspicious time by his ancestors. Kriss witnessed the ceremonies, including the bloody slaughter of a lamb. 'They hit its head against a tree and say their incantations. It is still semiconscious and they take a blunt knife and slit its throat. It was a shocker for me.'

Yet, for the first time, he began to appreciate the history and significance of the occasion. As a Christian he could not associate himself with the meaning behind the ceremonial, but he felt that there was a not-unbridgable chasm between him and his father's family. He also briefly met his mother, now separated from his father. He found her much older than he recalled, with less vigour and spirit. 'I was shattered. She was so much quieter. She had journeyed to my father's village to see me, but invited me to return to her village, which I did and met her family. Everyone was happy to see me.'

Kriss feels he would now like his daughters, when older, to understand something of their background. At one time Kriss even thought about buying a house in Nigeria as a base, to visit from time to time. It still may be an option for the future, although Monika would find any permanent commitment to the country hard to accept. But Kriss has come to feel that his parental family, Nigeria, their culture and traditions mean much more to him now than they did twenty years ago.

After observing the initiation rituals Kriss spoke to his father about the ceremony. He was told more about the family history and it was made clear to him that the next time it all took place, he would be at the centre. 'All this is yours if you want it, when the time comes,' his father said.

Today, living a thoroughly Western life Kriss is unclear in his own mind as to how or whether he will take up his hereditary family status and duties. Returning to Nigeria has its practical problems, with both political and family considerations.

'My mother is in her sixties and I want one day to forge a relationship with her, but not one based around money. I want to get to know my family but I am worried about my half brothers. My mother panics and says that I am in danger because I am a threat to them, being the direct heir to my father's title.

'Yet I do not want to leave it another ten years before I return and am able to take the girls. Eventually I want to be buried in Nigeria, next to where my grandfather is buried and where all the Akabusis are laid to rest, in the grave by the house, which has a tree standing by it.'

In 1995 Kriss made a brief visit to Nigeria when he received a letter from his mother, pleading with him to see her before she died. The letter, posted in December 1994, took nearly ten weeks to arrive. In March Kriss had a telephone call from his father asking him to visit, and so he set off for Lagos, not knowing quite what to expect.

On arrival he was met by his father and once again Kriss made contact with his Nigerian family. Although the visit was very brief he was able to hear and learn yet more about his roots. His mother was ill, and still estranged from his father, but Kriss was able to reassure himself that she was not in immediate danger, and offered what help he could. Little did Kriss know at the time that he and his father were to meet again within six weeks, in very different circumstances.

The production team of the long-running television series 'This Is Your Life' had decided to make Kriss the subject of one of its programmes and arranged for Kriss to be surprised by Michael Aspel with the big red book at Gatwick Airport, as he returned from a family trip to California.

Monika and a number of friends were in on the secret, and Monika, in particular, had a difficult few weeks fielding telephone calls from the television team without Kriss discovering what was going on. In the event everything went well. When Kriss was let in on the secret in front of the cameras at the airport he was so speechless that all he could do was double up and roar with laughter.

In the studio he met once again with friends from the past including army colleagues, fellow athletes and the family who, at the children's home, had taken him and Riba into their special care.

Right at the end of the programme came the great surprise. The 'This Is Your Life' team had made contact with both of Kriss's parents, and while his mother was not fit to travel to London, his father did. For the great finale, he arrived on the set in his traditional dress and, for the first time, saw his two grandchildren. It was an emotional moment. Chief Daniel Akabusi was afterwards able to stay in England for a few more days and get to know his granddaughters and they him.

Kriss had been chosen as a subject for 'This Is Your Life' not only as a sports star, but also as a television and media personality. For, by 1995, he had become well established in this new career. Kriss had wanted to ensure that once his years on the track were over he would still be in a position to maintain his family and earn a good living. The transition from being solely an athlete had been well planned and had taken around four years.

Just before Christmas 1991, and two days after the relay squad had been chosen as joint winners of the BBC's 'Sports Team of the Year' award, Kriss, Monika and the family left home for their usual winter sojourn in California. Kriss returned to his winter training schedule and his studies, and the family to their now familiar American routine. After the hectic months which followed the World Championships, they could begin to live as a normal family. The girls began to see their father again every day and the pressures of constantly being in the public eye were lessened. Kriss had time to spend time with Shakira and Ashanti, to read them stories, pray with them and watch them at play.

Kriss and Monika had time and space to consider the future and to think ahead to how they would live once Kriss's career as a competitive athlete was over. For Kriss knew that his life as an athlete was coming to an end. He was one of the oldest track competitors in top international athletics and, although in excellent physical shape, he knew the time had come to plan a fitting conclusion to his career, especially with 1992 being an Olympic year.

16

A Many-Sided Diamond

When Kriss arrived in Barcelona for the Olympic Games in the summer of 1992 he was one of the old hands. The wide-eyed youngster who had been bowled over by the glamour of Los Angeles was now the mature veteran, willing to share his experience with the younger sportsmen and women in the British team.

In public Kriss's infectious good humour was much in evidence, but privately he realized that the year had not been good for him as an athlete, and that he was facing the toughest challenge of his career. In June he had won the British AAA 400 metres hurdles' title and proved once again that he was unbeatable at home, yet his time of 49.16 seconds was disappointing and he described it as a 'good session but nothing to write home about'. In the same month Kriss was to learn that all four finishers in the United States' Olympic trials in New Orleans had clocked times of under 49 seconds.

'It had been a terrible year. I had trained like a dog and was not running well at all. I had made mistakes in training and the pre-Olympic races had been disappointing. It was my last serious season. However, reviewing the opposition, I knew that I was in with a chance if all went well on the day. Prior to going to Barcelona I had trained in Monte Carlo and there, for reasons I cannot explain, I found that my mental approach changed and became more positive. I realized that I had just this one chance left and that I had to forget my early season form and concentrate single-mindedly on the Olympics. I was to learn a lot about myself in Barcelona.'

Kriss flew to Barcelona on 29 July. His last minute preparations allowed for relaxation as well as fine-tuning physique and technique. Winning a place in the final presented few problems and by the time the final came, Olympic athlete 684 Kriss Akabusi had regained his track confidence. He was certainly not prepared for what was to come, the story he was to retell many times over when in later months he visited schools up and down the country representing the Duke of Edinburgh's Award Scheme.

'It was 6 August 1992, five past seven Barcelona time, cue for the 400 metres hurdles finals. All my life I had dreamt about standing on the rostrum as Olympic champion. I had won the first heat and the semi-final and was ready to rock and roll.

'The starter shouted, "Competitors, on your marks!" and then Bang! went the gun.

'I exploded from my blocks, round the bend, high knees, looking good, feeling cool, down the back straight, out in front, when all of a sudden . . . I had barely stepped off the third hurdle and this flash came zooming past me.

'I thought to myself, *My word, you've got to keep your head together, you're obviously having a nightmare.* This hadn't happened to me since 1977 that anybody had gone past me like that. I kept on running hard, negotiating the hurdles and all of a sudden I came off number eight and realized I was up there with the leaders but there was someone way ahead of us. We were all having nightmares and when I crossed the line I looked up at the screen and saw "Kevin Young. New world record". Kevin Young, running in lane four, had blown our socks off. He had just become the fastest 400 metres hurdler in history and there was I with a bronze.

'At that moment I learnt something tremendous. I had lost but performed to the best of my ability. It's by doing your best that you find out who you are and what you are.'

Prior to the race, Kevin Young, then twenty-five, had been one of the athletes Kriss had believed that on the day he could beat. He was an American who had for many years lived in the shadow of the hurdling legend Ed Moses. When Kevin had arrived in his room at the athletes' village he had taped a sheet of paper to the wall on which he had written '46.89 seconds', the time he believed he was capable of running in an Olympic final. It was a time which would have broken a world record—established by Moses nine years earlier—by 0.13 of a second and earned him a place in history as the first man to break the 47 second mark in the event.

As it was, the time pinned on the wall was an underestimate. His finishing time was 46.78 seconds. Astonishingly he crossed the line more than seven metres ahead of the silver medallist, the Jamaican Winthrop Graham who, in turn, was 0.16 seconds ahead of Kriss Akabusi. In his usual manner Kriss had risen to the occasion and produced a personal best time of 47.82 seconds, but it was not to be good enough. His achievement, however, should not be undervalued; at the age of thirty-three he was the oldest ever medallist in the one-lap hurdles event and had succeeded in breaking his own British record.

As they stood next to each other on the medal winners' podium Kriss shook Kevin's hand exuberantly and congratulated him.

How Kevin Young had managed such a performance is something Kriss does not fully understand.

'There are times, and I have known them myself, when you have trained very hard and you go out onto the track and it all happens. It is like running on a cloud, you are floating, you are tall and everything flows right. It happens once or twice in the lifetime of a top athlete and that day in Barcelona was Kevin's day. Kevin is a really lovely guy.'

The possibility, however, will have crossed the minds of many Olympic officials and spectators that exceptional performances like that of Kevin Young could only have been produced with the help of drugs. As a matter of course, he was tested following his victory and found to be negative.

Kriss has strong views on the subject of drugs. 'I do not know how widespread drug-taking is in sport but I'm sure it goes on, however in my ten years as an international I never saw anybody at first hand taking drugs.'

As for testing, Kriss believes that the procedures can become a victim of their own success. When increasingly vigorous testing procedures catch athletes whose cheating may in the past have gone undetected, it should be something of which the sport can be proud. However, such success tends to rebound. Finding a drug-taker, rooting out a wrongdoer, is not praised, but is seen as yet more evidence of corruption in the sport.

'Testing means nothing. I think they catch who they want to catch. I'm very cynical. If you're good enough you don't get caught. Umpteen people have won medals and they have been tested and been clean, or their tests have not come through. If you are well connected, if you know the right physicians or if you are lucky, you get away with tests. Science keeps ahead of testing, so if you know the right physicists you keep ahead of testing. If you have the right people on your side you are not going to be tested or your tests are not going to come through. I'm not going to use the word "corruption", but I believe that if you know the right people you get away with things. In 1988 a lot of people got caught but only Ben Johnson got done. After Ben got caught I believe other people got caught but there was so much money involved in the event that the big people who matter, be they within the federation or outside, said "no more". They believed that because it was the Olympic Games the sport could not take any more embarrassing exposures. That is the common belief in the sport.

'I have had to keep very clean throughout my career because I know that if anything had turned up the powers that be would definitely have sacrificed me as a scapegoat. I was a big enough name for people to say that the officials were doing their job properly, but not so big as a legendary figure who would ruin the reputation of the sport.

'I think the drug problem in athletics is symptomatic of a society where the end justifies the means, where the crime isn't doing it but getting caught. People always want to take short-cuts—you only have to look at politics or business—and I am not surprised when I see athletes doing exactly the same kind of thing. I understand the temptations because there is a lot of money and fame to be had at the top.'

The 400 metres hurdles' final was not the end of Kriss's Olympic career. He still had the 4 x 400 metres relay to run, as had been the case the year before at the World Championships. Few people expected the British team to repeat their masterful tactical win against the Americans, nor did they do so. The US team recognized their earlier complacency and this time approached the race diligently. They ran to their full potential and did not take winning for granted. Kriss and the relay team came third and Kriss returned home with two bronze medals, the only British athlete to have won medals in two events.

Once the Games were over Kriss began to think seriously of retirement. He announced his retirement from international championships and talked of his final season in 1993 being more a tour to say goodbye than one filled with ambition. He therefore decided to spend one more year in training before taking any firm decisions on the direction his future life would take. He fully realized that he would be unlikely to run at his peak in 1993 and there were no more summits to aim for which would stretch him mentally and physically to his limits, but he wanted to be able to run in front of the British crowds again, to thank them for their support in the past. He also wanted to enjoy a season in which he could use his drawing power as a star to earn a cushion of money which would sustain him while he readjusted to a new way of life. Kriss saw the track and field season of 1993 as a kind of benefit season. He was, however, well aware of the dangers of trying to stay at the top after his 'sell by date' and, shortly after winning his two Olympic bronze medals, he reflected on the subject of retirement.

'I have seen too many great British athletes go on too long. When you see people who have won medals and set world records, producing performances they would have laughed at in their prime, it saddens me. Some have gone on a year or two longer than they should have done and have not done themselves justice. I am determined not to make the same mistake.'

In 1993 Kriss did not make those mistakes, but his last season as a full-time athlete did not go as smoothly as he might have wished.

'I went to California as usual to train, but I did not train properly and was not as dedicated as I had been. I came back to Britain earlier than usual and found that I was working on other things besides my running.'

Kriss approached the new season as an athlete who had retired from international competition, but he wished to compete in his farewell year in a good enough condition to race on the Grand Prix circuit without cheating the spectators with a sub-international performance. However, his plans had to be revised when his replacements in the Great Britain squad were failing to meet the true international standard. Frank Dick of the British Amateur Athletics Federation asked Kriss to represent his country once more at the European Cup, to enable the team to maximize points in the 400 metres hurdles event. Kriss agreed and, after some additional preparation, came a respectable fourth.

While the B.A.A.F. was happy to call on Kriss to do his bit for the national team, B.A.A.F official Andy Norman appeared to Kriss to be less than willing to allow him full access to the Grand Prix circuit for his planned track farewell season.

'I was finding it easier to be accepted abroad at the going rate for an athlete of my standing than I was at home,' Kriss commented. When he was asked again to represent his country in the 400 metres hurdles in the World Cup he decided not to respond to this second appeal. Though the newspapers talked of a possible 'come-back', behind the scenes Kriss was not entirely happy with the invitation.

Quoted in the *Daily Mail* of 26 July 1993 he said, 'What bothers me is the idea that my country needs me. It is not Britain but the same organisation that has told me that it can't help me do a farewell tour of British meetings this summer.

'The patriotism bit is bogus. All I wanted of the British Amateur Athletics Federation is to run in front of my home crowd one last time against reasonable opposition . . . when I was at the very top everybody wanted to be my friend. Once you settle for less, they think that they can have a kick at you.'

Kriss felt that as the current European champion and the only double medal winner from the Barcelona Olympics—and as a proven crowd-puller—he should be offered appearance fees to match his standing. However, Andy Norman, Kriss's old adversary in athletics administration, thought otherwise. It was a tricky situation for Kriss; he did not want to appear mean-spirited and greedy, yet he was determined not to be exploited.

Kriss's last appearance on a British track was at Sheffield towards the end of the 1993 season.

'It was the very big farewell but curiously it did not make such an impact on me as racing at Edinburgh at the beginning of July. It was the scene all those years ago of my emergence into the international athletics reckoning. As I came out into the centre of the ground there was a huge cheer. I had a lump in my throat because then I realized this truly was my final year and the enormity of my decision to retire. I raced and came in first in a time of 50.45 with the Americans second and third. As with every race that season it was my opportunity to say cheerio.

'At Sheffield I enjoyed myself playing the clown and went out onto the track dressed in my slippers and dressing gown. I was making a statement to the crowd that from now on I was going to be an armchair athlete and be watching with them as a spectator.'

Eighteen months later Kriss has given up training and, although still lithe and fit, has lost his athletic edge. Although it was his joke at Sheffield that he would become a spectator, he has not attended an athletics meeting since he last raced. He misses the camaraderie of the track and the physical pleasure of training, but does not regret giving up the hard work involved in staying at the top. He still stays in touch with friends such as Roger Black, but these days seldom talks 'deep athletics' with him.

It took Kriss about a year after retiring to do any running at all. In 1993 he had carried on training for about five weeks after his last appearance but became very depressed with his results because his heart was not in it. It was still habit for him to time every run and write down his results, and the times became more and more disappointing. Fortunately by the time he started gentle training again at the end of 1994 he had broken the habit of keeping meticulous records, and now he runs twice a week and enjoys training for training's sake. He is not short of exercise as his Doberman (called Dillinger after Kriss's first dog) requires regular hard walking.

Kriss has no plans to find a young promising athlete and coach him or her to the top; he is too busy with his other commitments although it is possible that if one of his daughters should show promise he might become involved in planning and developing her career.

'I still compete at schools that I visit and sometimes race the kids but nowadays I have to be careful. One time I raced a little kid 20 metres and he took me to the wire. I knew then that I had lost it as an athlete. I am an elderly man as far as athletics is concerned. I haven't got the muscle definition in my legs that I once had. It is a direct result of not doing the work. I know I cannot do 400 metres hurdles now under 50 seconds, I am not the number one in Europe, I am not the number one in the country, and probably not even number one in Hampshire.'

There could be no turning back. In September 1993 Mike Whittingham arranged a dinner in Kriss's honour at the Park Lane Hotel in Piccadilly. He was presented with a silver salver 'in recognition of his outstanding contribution to British athletics: 1983–1993'.

As Kriss's life as an athlete wound down, his career as a public personality gathered momentum. For a while there was some overlap as when, in November 1991, Kriss was appointed the national promotions officer of the Duke of Edinburgh's Award scheme. For nearly forty years the awards have aimed at providing challenging and rewarding leisure-time activities for young people between the ages of fourteen and twenty-five. The scheme leaders describe how the award is designed to give opportunities for personal achievement, community and social involvement, adventure and the discovery of new talents and interests. Awards are granted at three levels, bronze, silver and gold. Although many schools promote the scheme strongly, taking part is voluntary and the awards aim not so much at rewarding excellence but in measuring and rewarding improvement and achievement so that all young people, including those with special needs, can participate fully.

Kriss's work with the scheme was profiled by Tim Bouquet in December 1993 in the *Reader's Digest*. He described Kriss at work motivating school children in Northern Ireland.

'Bombs in Northern Ireland are not usually followed by gales of laughter but today, 36 hours after an IRA blast in the border town of Strabane, pupils from four local schools can no longer contain their mirth. Within 30 seconds of Olympic athlete Kriss Akabusi's arrival, striding the assembly hall parquet with all the spring that powered him to a host of medals, he lets loose that seismic laugh. It gurgles deep inside, erupts all over his face and conquers his young audience ... Kriss spends three months a year travelling the UK, meeting award-winners and urging other youngsters, especially in inner cities, to join a scheme that in 37 years and 52 countries has helped more than two million 14- to 25-year-olds. They learn leadership, self-discipline and perseverance through community service, physical education, mastering new skills, and expeditions.

' "At first I thought it was only for young, white middle-class people—and I'm none of these—but when I saw the range of things they were doing, I jumped at the chance to help," says Kriss.

'For award director Michael Hobbs, Kriss was the perfect choice as role model. "As well as his blazing integrity and his ideals, he has an ability to enthuse young people and talk to them in a language they understand. It's a very rare combination."

'This meeting in Strabane is remarkable. For the first time pupils from all the town's secondary schools are to work together on Duke of Edinburgh's Award projects, regardless of the sectarian divide. "Having Kriss is brilliant. He is clearly not from either side. He's on their side," explains local organizer Ronnie Russell, the catalyst who has spent years paving the way for today.

'Wherever he goes on this two-day visit to a fractured province, Kriss's enthusiasm never flags. He makes every group of youngsters feel that he has come all this way just to meet them. The language is "pump it up", "let's get busy", 'nice one" and "goooood value", as he wends his way through schools, sports centres, youth clubs, probation centres and young offenders' institutions.

'At the Belfast Activity Centre Kriss captivates 200 school students with an animated thesis on team work: "Don't write off someone as a wally, because you might just need to rely on each other . . .

' "The only way you can really leave your mark is by investing in young people."

'His investment is paying off. On a visit to Hydebank young offenders' centre in Belfast—where there are hopes of using the scheme to rehabilitate criminals—he met 21-year-old Mark Kennedy, serving 30 months for armed robbery. Mark's been in trouble since he was 15 but now Kriss has inspired him to break free of crime. "When I get out of here I want to go straight," says Mark. "He showed me how to do it." '

As a public figure Kriss Akabusi is now better recognized than he was during most of his career on track. He even has a racehorse named after him! Kriss is a hero and role model to thousands of children who see him on television, on such programmes as 'Record Breakers', and then who can scarcely believe their good luck when he turns up at their school.

He was therefore an obvious potential victim for one of Noel Edmonds' 'Gotcha' practical jokes on the BBC 1 programme 'Noel's House Party'. Edmonds' elaborate hoax involved Kriss being invited, or so he thought, to be a guest presenter on a BBC 2 travel programme. He was invited to go on a Personal Development Weekend, a course for people leading over-stressed lives, at a Gloucestershire country house.

'He was supposed to go through all the experiences of one of their weekends in a couple of hours,' Guy Freeman, Noel's assistant producer explained. 'This included a body-cleansing movement class involving aerobics, Tai Chi and just about anything else they could think of.

'The leader of the group became more and more dodgy as his interview went on. It was funny because Kriss thought he'd seen through him and had found these people out—he thought he was on to a real scoop.'

When the penny dropped that it was he who was being had, Kriss 'laughed like a hyena,' Guy Freeman recalls, 'and kept saying, "You guys are good!" '

His good humour and pulling power as a personality resulted in an invitation in 1994 to appear on stage in a Christmas pantomime, following in the footsteps of Frank Bruno, Ian Botham and other sports personalities who have been lured, temporarily at least, into the theatre. He co-starred in *Dick Whittington* at Southampton with other well-known faces from television including Lesley Joseph from the sitcom 'Birds of a Feather', Windsor Davies and the television detective Bergerac, actor John Nettles. Kriss was cast as a baddie, a pirate who, in the true spirit of pantomime, came on stage to be booed. It was a strange experience for Kriss who from the very youngest age has thrived on popularity.

'I was King Rat's henchman. It was a bit part but it helped put bums on seats. I loved doing it, I would go on stage and at first there would be rapturous applause and cheers. But I didn't particularly enjoy playing the role. As the show went on I could hear the slow clapping and the booing. I realised how important it is to me to be appreciated by people. In this part I found that what I had done in fifteen years was destroyed in fifteen minutes. In that time everyone was booing me and that took a lot of getting used to. I didn't like it even though it was all make-believe. It offended my spirit, but I got used to it in the end.'

The success of the pantomime was such that should Kriss decide to pursue the option a lucrative annual pantomime contract could become a regular feature of his working year. But some of his friends, especially his Christian friends, might feel that pantomime is too frivolous a pursuit for Kriss. He is well aware that his life today does not have the direction it had when he was training for the track. There are many demands on his time and his support, and in the world of 'being a personality' there are many temptations to take the easy, lucrative options. Kriss now needs to plan a career carefully so that he is both being fulfilled himself and is also fulfilling his obligations to the community to which he owes so much.

With his formal work for the Duke of Edinburgh Award Scheme now over, Kriss's regular commitment is to the BBC 'Record Breakers' programme. He worked with the all-round entertainer and popular presenter Roy Castle before Roy died of cancer, and Kriss today describes Roy as having been his personal tutor. Roy would tell him to slow down and how to conserve his energy; towards the end of Roy's life Kriss's admiration for the consummate professional grew more and more.

'As presenter of the programme now I haven't taken over from Roy; no one can do that. The programme has a formula and I have had to fit my personality to that. It's not the same as Roy Castle's unique brand of all-singing, all-dancing, all-acting enthusiasm. He could play all those musical instruments. I can't. So now Cheryl and I don't do the great big theatrical stuff in the studios but we go out and about and package the show in our style.'

In the course of doing this Kriss meets some strangely dedicated people. There are custard pie throwers and experts at flipping beer mats. Some of the record breakers pursue inordinately obscure interests quite obsessionally. Kriss sometimes wonders about whether there are limits to the legitimate development of talent.

'Many of the activities I see are a complete waste of time, but they provide pleasure to people and when their particular interest is done well it gives them prestige.'

Working on 'Record Breakers' has given Kriss cause to ponder about his own future and how he should properly direct his talents off the track. He is not alone, however, when it comes to reviewing the purpose and direction of his life. For as well as discussing ideas with Monika he meets on a regular basis with a group of friends who advise him in an informal but valuable way.

Every month Stuart Weir from 'Christians in Sport', Nick Pollard from Solent Christian Trust, Martin Hughes, medical doctor and church elder, Steve McIntyre, home group leader, and Paul Finn, Kriss's Southampton pastor, meet together with Kriss to hear him report back on his life and share with them any concerns.

The meeting will last for perhaps an hour and a half and Kriss shares his ideas for the coming months and reviews his past work and achievement, in order to try and give his life shape and to discern the purpose behind events.

'I have no ultimate clear goal, but what I understand is that I will be working in television and the media for some time. If you were to put me on the spot I would say that this would be my life for the next fifteen years, being a celebrity possibly with my own show as time goes on.

'After that I do not know how my life might develop, although I would expect there to be a change and I would enter a new epoch. It might be politics or I may move on to some real calling in life which I will not know until then.

'I cannot imagine myself being a party politician as I am too much of an individualist, perhaps self-centred, to toe the party line. Neither am I very good at compromising. But in fifteen years' time I can imagine myself using the discipline I learnt in the army, using the fame I derived from athletics and the experience of interacting with, encouraging and even manipulating people I have acquired through the media to start out on a fourth career. It must be reputable service under God, as my work is a way I can worship God.

'I look at myself and my life in general, and at my character in particular, and see myself as a diamond. I am many-sided and if you shine a shaft of light through any side you'll see a different aspect of me and so no one else can see who I am. Some see the outlandish extrovert; Monika will often see the introvert. I am an optimist but I am also a pessimist. I can be very trusting, sometimes to the point of being foolish and on other occasions I can be so suspicious of people that I take that to the point of folly.

'When I was in athletics it gave me a goal, but even then it was only part of my life. Even then there were many sides to me. Before becoming a Christian I was the guy who was committing adultery and at the same time the guy who was a family man. Later when I was on the track, the furious single-minded competitor was also the man quietly praying in church.

'I now have security as a celebrity even though I am not working towards long-term goals. I am booked up for many months ahead but it is not the same as when I was training. Then I knew years ahead of time, that at precisely half past five on 5 August in a particular year I would be at the start of the race that would bring to fruition everything I'd been working for.

'In television if you mess something up you can do a retake. If it's live on stage you can laugh it off and there's always tomorrow. In athletics when the starter says 'on your marks', there's no getting it wrong. Two hundred million people are watching you. It is your only chance and a very public one.

'Today in this part of my life I am responsible to no one but myself and God.'

Not responsible to anyone else, perhaps, but Kriss as a public figure is accountable. He is now recognized wherever he goes, not just in his own locality, and people he has never met greet him as a long-lost friend. Normally he is very pleased to sign autographs and give words of encouragement to aspiring athletes, but there are times when he is craving peace and solitude, and has to draw on his patience and experience to preserve a façade of bonhomie.

'Everywhere I go I am public property. I have no privacy. Sports journalists were keen to write encouragingly about my sport. They were on my side. News and feature journalists want stories and new angles, whether they are flattering to me or not. Often these stories involve the family, and that is hard on them. These journalists want the gossip. It seems it is almost a crime in their eyes to become a personality. They see you as a target to be knocked off a pedestal. Now I have to be careful with journalists. Usually I'm happy to chat, now I have to be wary and ask myself, how might they be setting me up?

'Everyone wants a bit of the action. The hardest thing is saying no to the many charities who want a bit of my time. There just isn't enough time. I have to say no and it's very hard. And the charities have to get the message that I mean no, and yet I don't want to offend. Some charities do feel offended and some charities do attempt to apply pressure, they may appeal to your sense of pity or the sense that it is a good cause, or the sense that you are a Christian, and it may take two or three letters to explain that I really cannot divide my time between so many people. Some Christian organizations may say something like, "God has told me you are the one to do this job", or a secular organisation may say, "if you don't do it the guests will be disappointed."'

It is perhaps because of his early life and his feelings of abandonment as a child that Kriss is well aware of the many people in recent years who have reached the top in sport but once that career was over have gone downhill from there on. He knows of big football stars, who once had fame and glory and wealth, who now eke out a living on the dole. So, aware of the fickle nature of fame, Kriss has made sure that he is financially secure and that even if he never appeared on television again he would have enough money set aside for him and his family to live modestly but securely for the rest of their lives.

'I have seen husbands lose their jobs and go home and not be able to feed the kids. That is frightening. I look at Ashanti and

Shakira and they want for nothing. I would fear not being able to put bread on the table.'

Kriss receives many offers to invest his money in tempting projects which promise big rewards. He, however, sees the risks involved, not the profits.

'There are not so many dangers in being a rich man as there are dangers in making money your God. The danger to the soul is when money and material possessions come before God, the real risk comes when you give so much time, trouble and effort to building up wealth and a career that you forget God and he has no part in your life. I work very hard, but I understand that God is my God.'

The zestful newly-acquired Christianity which once threatened to divide Kriss from Monika has matured over the years. Through his formalized studies in California and his own personal devotions and reading Kriss has developed a broader, tolerant faith. It is still biblically based but Kriss now reads his Bible in a different way. It is no longer the amazing and exciting 'new' discovery he once found it to be. Nevertheless, he says, 'the Bible is just as important. I read the Bible every day. I have developed a taste for the Bible which is just as strong but I am now selective about which passages I want to read and when I want to read them.' He is now able to use the Bible as a resource when grappling with a particular deep issue.

'Monika and I have some really interesting discussions. She will often bring up a Christian topic. We are now halfway through our lives. We have known each other over fifteen years. And when we met her Dad was the same age as we are now. Monika's mother has died and her grandmother has died and death is real to Monika. It doesn't scare her but she knows that life is not for ever and I think that she has been asking spiritual questions, even though she hasn't arrived at any firm answers.

'Shakira calls herself a Christian. She is seven and she asks to go to church on Sunday. She loves the singing and has romantic ideas. I have no doubt that she is a spiritual person. She constantly asks spiritual questions and wants to know, "Where do I come from?" "If God didn't make the earth who did? Who made that person?' She's quite a philosopher. Whether she's a Christian I don't know, but she will be a person in tune with her spirit and her soul.

'Ashanti is more down to earth like her mother. The other day she asked if I had a Bible that she could read and understand so that she could decide things for herself. There are things I do in my life to encourage my children to think. We pray at table. We pray at night and they hear me talk about God on the radio. Ashanti understands that somewhere down the line she has got to make a decision.'

Kriss now sees it as part of his calling as a declared Christian to share his beliefs, not just with his own children, but with all the children that he meets in schools and youth clubs up and down the country.

'I don't just say you've all got to join up. I try and suggest that if their only aims in life are to get jobs, do well and acquire possessions then they are destined for disappointment. Whatever you do you can never get to the top, even when you get to the summit of your ambitions there is nothing there—it is all ephemeral. If you think that owning a big car is the ultimate goal, I tell the children that it's just headaches. Even being a gold medallist brings headaches and what God has given to me in life is the antidote to that disappointment.'

Kriss Akabusi's future now appears secure. His status as a celebrity is firm. Though not an ultra-wealthy man, he has achieved financial security, so important to him after his early years of insecurity. Kriss, however, will not stagnate or rest on his laurels. He will continue with his quest for knowledge and maintain his study of philosophy and theology, maybe through a formal academic route, maybe by pursuing his own interests guided by friends and his spiritual adviser. It will be fascinating to watch his continuing development as a Christian, and how his current life as a high-profile personality who makes no secret of his faith will evolve. Any fears that he might have had about the public spotlight turning away from him to favour younger stars have proved groundless. Kriss is destined to have far more than his fifteen minutes of fame.

He maintains a strong rapport with young people and has developed an excellent way of encouraging youngsters to achieve to the best of their varied abilities. In return Kriss is constantly amazed by the sparkle and innovation of the up-and-coming generation.

Through his faith and with the experience of years, he no longer has the insecurities he once had. He has grown away from being the boy from the children's home or the junior soldier needing to be one of the lads. Once his greatest aspiration was to have the flashiest of cars; now he no longer needs the trappings of status in order to enjoy the dignity of being himself.

At the end of his hurdles final at Tokyo, Kriss was asked by a television interviewer about his victory, and the sentiments expressed can surely be adapted to include not just his feelings about winning a medal at the World Championships, but also his feelings about his achievements in life. Typically, after the race, he did not keep the glory to himself. He took the chance of a live appearance on worldwide television interview to thank those who had helped him achieve what he had achieved. He thanked his two coaches, Mike Smith and Mike Whittingham. He thanked his family for their understanding and patience during his last weeks of preparation. And then, with the infectious Kriss Akabusi smile on his face, added a special word of gratitude to 'my God upstairs, who looks after me too'.

The Authors' Acknowledgments

When Ted Harrison approached me regarding transcribing my life story I really wondered whether there was anything worth telling. After all I have only just passed the halfway stage of an expected life span of three score years and ten, and my only claim to fame is that I can negotiate obstacles at a rapid speed of knots. In any one bookshop there may be a plethora of biographies ranging over the full spectrum of human interest. What would make mine any different from the others? Having decided to go ahead I did not want it to be a plain sportsman's journal with a few altercations thrown in. If the story was going to be told it would be told in its entirety.

In any attempt to reconstruct one's past there inevitably will exist the feeling that more could have been said, or things better expressed in a different manner. Like most people I have preconceived ideas of who I am and how I project myself in the world around me. When you open up your life to the microscopic eye of a journalist and allow your friends, past and present, to paint your picture, you had better be prepared for a few dents to the ego and personal pride.

The real difficulty, however, is for those with whom one has been closely associated. They may not be prepared for the things that are to follow. Old wounds may be re-opened and things that were done in the dark may be cast before the light. To anyone mentioned in the biography who feels personally wounded I sympathize and would say there is no malice intended. Just an attempt to tell the truth from my perspective. To all the people great and small with whom I have been acquainted, I am deeply indebted because it is my personal philosophy that they have been the stones on which this axe has been ground. I would not be the person I am had I not had the experiences I have been through and, for better or for worse, I would not change my life even if I was able to. I believe that in life God gives each and every one of us a series of parameters within which exist a permeation of choices. On each door is a label that says 'your choice', however, when you go back through the door the label on the back says 'God's choice'. Now I can't get into the theological implications of this right now, but it does raise the question, 'what choices has God been making in your life?'

My sincere hope is that this book will help people by showing that those who have achieved and are so often the envy of Mr Average are in fact real people with real problems.

I would like to take this opportunity to thank Ted Harrison for his time and dedication in compiling and writing up all this information. I would also like to thank Lion Publishing for having the courage to accept the manuscript and put it forth on the market. My pride of place goes to Monika: thank you for being God's gift of a companion, a 'helper' fit for me.

KRISS AKABUSI

It cannot be easy for anyone, however used to the public spotlight, to have a book written about them. Difficult, searching and sometimes painful questions have to be asked by the author, if an honest and fair word portrait is to be produced. I cannot therefore thank Kriss and Monika enough for their friendship and willingness to talk openly about themselves. I am also grateful to all Kriss's friends whose memories and impressions I have used. I am grateful, too, to Kriss's mother and father. I have been mindful of the tensions they have been under and I hope they feel that while I have been honest in writing about them as they relate to Kriss, I have also been sympathetic. And my special thanks go to Kriss's brother Riba for his courage in recounting to me some particularly painful but revealing memories.

TED HARRISON

Index

More life stories from Lion Publishing:

CLIFF RICHARD: THE BIOGRAPHY

Steve Turner

The revealing biography of one of the world's top entertainers.
Rock journalist Steve Turner interviewed nearly 200 people
closely involved in Cliff's life and career and enjoyed unparalleled
access to Cliff and his management.

'A pacy and frequently racy read. This sympathetic, sagacious
and highly enjoyable book tells you everything you ever wanted to
know about Cliff. Turner's Cliff Richard is refreshingly human,
though not without his faults'—*The Sunday Telegraph*

'An unbeatable Cliff reference book which gets well below the
surface. Turner paints a subtly shaded portrait of one of Britain's
most famous Christians.'—'*Q*' *Magazine*

ISBN 0 7459 2789 0

KING OF THE CON MEN

Doug Hartman with Roger Day

Shady black-market deals in wartime Berlin gave Doug Hartman a taste for crime. It was a taste that became an irresistible part of his life for over forty years.

Doug's bank frauds—which frequently landed him in prison—were major enough to force a complete change in the system of cheque clearance in the UK in 1992. But during one stay in prison, his life altered dramatically.

This king of the con men recently appeared on the Easter edition of BBC Television's 'Songs of Praise'. His wife, who has re-married him, was by his side.

Here their moving story of forgiveness and hope is told in full.

ISBN 0 7459 3123 5

DOROTHY L. SAYERS: A CARELESS RAGE FOR LIFE

David Coomes

Known to millions as the creator of Lord Peter Wimsey and the bestselling author of a dozen detective novels, Dorothy Leigh Sayers was in reality a complex woman—moved, she said, by 'a careless rage for life'. It is this complex Sayers, brilliant student, controversial apologist, witty, bawdy, intolerant of fools—the woman 'terrified of emotion'—who is revealed in this new biography which draws extensively on the thousands of letters Sayers wrote.

'The book crackles with wit and vigor ... One of the greatest letter-writers of all time is finally revealed in this new biography ... Coomes is a biographer who serves his subject properly, who relishes Sayers' wit and responds to her faith.'—
Dr Nancy M. Tischler, Professor of English and Humanities

ISBN 0 7459 2241 4

A SEASON IN ST PETERSBURG

Jenny Robertson

To its many visitors St Petersburg is a romantic city, a glittering world of theatre and ballet, Baroque churches and the fairy-tale palaces of the Russian tsars. But to live there is to discover a city in which people and buildings alike are falling apart in the chaos of turmoil and change. Jenny Robertson and her husband have lived there since 1991 and have seen the real St Petersburg.

'Mrs Robertson has certainly captured the flavour and tenor of a city which has sampled freedom but can't cope ... the eye for personal detail, and the skilful portrayal of others, gives the book richness which is obviously missing in St Petersburg ... She portrays the struggle and pain many go through simply to survive: but also the joys and excitements of ordinary, everyday things.'— *The Oxford Times*

ISBN 0 7459 3047 6

GOOD OLD GEORGE
The life of George Lansbury

Bob Holman

George Lansbury led the Labour Party in the crisis years of the early 1930s. Throughout that time, he campaigned with passionate sincerity for a just society.

He was a working man, and he spoke his message of social justice in words that ordinary people could understand. He sought practical ways to relieve poverty. To the end of his days, he lived modestly in the East End of London.

His sincerity and commitment to the cause of social justice have made him what A.J.P. Taylor has described as 'the most loveable figure in modern politics'. But Lansbury himself would probably have appreciated more the chants of children whenever he appeared at schools or playgrounds: 'Good old George'.

Bob Holman's biography sheds new light not only on his political career and socialist commitment, but also on the sincere Christian faith that inspired and maintained him.

ISBN 0 7459 1574 4